£25.00

special £12.50

B234

RAILWAYS AND THE ECONOMIC DEVELOPMENT OF WESTERN EUROPE, 1830–1914

St Antony's/Macmillan Series

General editor: Archie Brown, Fellow of St Antony's College, Oxford

Archie Brown and Michael Kaser (editors) SOVIET POLICY FOR THE 1980s
S. B. Burman CHIEFDOM POLITICS AND ALIEN LAW
Wilhelm Deist THE *WEHRMACHT* AND GERMAN REARMAMENT
Ricardo Ffrench-Davis and Ernesto Tironi (editors) LATIN AMERICA AND THE NEW INTERNATIONAL ECONOMIC ORDER
Bohdan Harasymiw POLITICAL ELITE RECRUITMENT IN THE USSR
Richard Holt SPORT AND SOCIETY IN MODERN FRANCE
Albert Hourani EUROPE AND THE MIDDLE EAST
THE EMERGENCE OF THE MODERN MIDDLE EAST
Paul Kennedy and Anthony Nicholls (editors) NATIONALIST AND RACIALIST MOVEMENTS IN BRITAIN AND GERMANY BEFORE 1914
Richard Kindersley (editor) IN SEARCH OF EUROCOMMUNISM
Gisela C. Lebzelter POLITICAL ANTI-SEMITISM IN ENGLAND, 1918–1939
C. A. MacDonald THE UNITED STATES, BRITAIN AND APPEASE-MENT, 1936–1939
Patrick O'Brien (editor) RAILWAYS AND THE ECONOMIC DEVELOPMENT OF WESTERN EUROPE, 1830–1914
Roger Owen (editor) STUDIES IN THE ECONOMIC AND SOCIAL HISTORY OF PALESTINE IN THE NINETEENTH AND TWENTIETH CENTURIES
Irena Powell WRITERS AND SOCIETY IN MODERN JAPAN
T. H. Rigby and Ferenc Fehér (editors) POLITICAL LEGITIMATION IN COMMUNIST STATES
Marilyn Rueschemeyer PROFESSIONAL WORK AND MARRIAGE
A. J. R. Russell-Wood THE BLACK MAN IN SLAVERY AND FREEDOM IN COLONIAL BRAZIL
Lewis Siegelbaum THE POLITICS OF INDUSTRIAL MOBILIZATION IN RUSSIA, 1914–17
David Stafford BRITAIN AND EUROPEAN RESISTANCE, 1940–1945
Nancy Stepan THE IDEA OF RACE IN SCIENCE
Guido di Tella ARGENTINA UNDER PERÓN, 1973–76
Rosemary Thorp and Laurence Whitehead (editors) INFLATION AND STABILISATION IN LATIN AMERICA
Rudolf L. Tőkés (editor) OPPOSITION IN EASTERN EUROPE

Railways and the Economic Development of Western Europe, 1830–1914

Edited by

Patrick O'Brien

Lecturer in Economic History and Faculty Fellow of St Antony's College, Oxford

in association with
St Antony's College, Oxford

First published 1983 by
THE MACMILLAN PRESS LTD
London and Basingstoke
Companies and representatives
throughout the world

ISBN 0 333 33000 5

Printed in Hong Kong

For Bob Fogel and Al Fishlow

Contents

List of Tables and Figures

TABLES

FIGURES

Acknowledgements

Preliminary versions of four of the papers included in this
volume (the introduction and the chapters on France, Germany
and Spain were read as seminar papers to the St Antony's
seminar in international economic history. We are pleased to
thank the Warden and Fellows of St Antony's for the
hospitality and financial assistance which made that seminar
possible. These same papers, together with a paper on Italy,
were delivered in December 1979 to an international conference
on the history of European railways organised in Madrid by
RENFE (Spanish railways), the Faculty of Economic Sciences of
the University of Madrid and the Institute for the Study of
Transport and Communications, Madrid. Their authors much
appreciated the occasion afforded by their Spanish hosts to
expound and discuss their research before a distinguished body
of scholars in the field of transport economics and the
history of railways.

Kind permission to republish G. Hawke and J. Higgins,
'Transport and Social Overhead Capital in the British
Industrial Revolution' was given by the editors, R. Floud and
D. McCloskey, of *The Economic History of Britain since 1700*,
vol. 1, and by Cambridge University Press, the publishers of
that volume.

Finally, all the authors appreciate the opportunity to
publish a collection on the history of Europe's railways which
they hope will prove useful and illuminating for students of
economics, history and economic history under the auspices of
the St Antony's/Macmillan series. They wish to convey their
warm appreciation for all the efforts made to bring their
scholarship into print by Tim Farmiloe of Macmillan and Archie
Brown and Michael Kaser at St Antony's, and Mrs Elizabeth
Stevens for typing a difficult manuscript into final copy.

Patrick O'Brien

Notes on the Contributors

PATRICK O'BRIEN is University Lecturer in Economic History
at Oxford and Faculty Fellow of St Antony's College, Oxford.
His published books include *The Revolution in Egypt's
Economic System* (London, 1966), *The New Economic History of
Railways* (London, 1977), *Economic Growth in Britain and
France* (with C. Keyder) (London, 1978) and an edited collec-
tion of papers with Rainer Fremdling, *European Productivity
in the 19th and 20th Centuries* (Stuttgart, 1982).

FRANÇOIS CARON is Professor of Economic History at the Uni-
versity of Paris, Sorbonne. His published books include
*Histoire de l'exploitation d'un grand reseau: la compagnie
chemin de fer du Nord des origins a la nationalisation*
(Paris, 1973) and *An Economic History of Modern France* (New
York, 1979).

STEFANO FENOALTEA is Associate Professor of Economics, Duke
University. His study of *Italian Industrial Production,
1861-1913: A Statistical Reconstruction* is forthcoming
(Cambridge).

RAINER FREMDLING is Associate Professor of Economic History
at the Free University of Berlin. His publications include
Eisenbahnen und deutsches Wirtschaftswachstum, 1840-79
(Dortmund, 1975) and he has edited two books, *Industriali-
zation and Space* (with Richard Tilly) (Stuttgart, 1981) and
European Productivity in the 19th and 20th Centuries (with
Patrick O'Brien) (Stuttgart, 1982).

ANTONIO GOMEZ-MENDOZA is a Lecturer in Economic History at
the University of Madrid and a Research Fellow of the Bank
of Spain. His doctoral thesis *Railways and Spanish Economic
Growth in the late 19th Century* (D.Phil., Oxford, 1981) will
be published in 1983.

GARY HAWKE is Professor of Economic History at Victoria University of Wellington, New Zealand. His publications include *Railways and Economic Growth in England and Wales, 1840-70* (Oxford, 1970), *Economics for Historians* (Cambridge, 1980) and *Between Government and Banks: A History of the Reserve Bank of New Zealand* (Wellington, 1973).

JIM HIGGINS is a Senior Lecturer in the Department of Economic History at Victoria University of Wellington, New Zealand. He is the editor (with Sidney Pollard) of *Aspects of Capital Investment in Great Britain, 1750-1850* (London, 1971).

MICHEL LAFFUT is an Assistant Professor at the University of Liège. His research, *Les Chemins de fer Belge, 1835-1913* will be published as vol. VIII of *Histoire quantitative et développement de la Belgique au XIXème siècle.*

GIANNI TONIOLO is Professor of Economic History at the University of Venice. His published books include *L'Economia dell' Italia facista* (Rome, 1980) and two edited collections of papers, *L'Economia italiana nel periodo facista* (Bologna, 1976) (with Pierluigi Ciocca) and *Industria e banca nella grande crisi, 1929-34* (Milan, 1978).

1 Transport and Economic Development in Europe, 1789–1914

PATRICK O'BRIEN

1. THE GROWTH OF THE ECONOMY AND THE DEVELOPMENT OF TRANSPORT

European economic growth, which accelerated in the second half of the eighteenth century, was accompanied by an expansion in the supply of transportation. Demand for transport services increased when industrialists and farmers purchased their inputs from a resource base which widened in space and as they sold a growing proportion of their output on markets at an ever greater distance from their enterprises. As commodity output went up, the share marketed increased even more rapidly because improvements in transport made it possible to sell further afield and because specialisation (a major impetus to economic growth between 1789 and 1914) led to more trade between firms, farms and industries. In the traditional economy of early modern Europe production tended to occur within integrated forms of enterprise geographically concentrated in well defined regions. But over the nineteenth century the co-ordination of production came to be achieved through organised commodity and input markets serviced by extended and increasingly efficient transport and distribution networks. Adam Smith's twin processes of market penetration and specialisation implied increased demands for transport.

At the same time a series of innovations raised the efficiency of Europe's transport systems which lowered the cost of inputs used by farmers and manufacturers and the prices of their outputs. Such innovations, which were diffused gradually throughout the continent, included: surfaced roads, improved water and railed ways, the embodiment of new materials such as iron, and later steel, in the capital stock of national transport sectors and above all, the replacement of wind, water, animal and man power by steam power. These innovations, chronicled by historians of transport, provided producers with speed and continuity of delivery, and lowered the costs of transporting almost all goods across time and space. They were particularly important for commodities heavy or bulky in relation to value –

1

transport-intensive goods such as coal, mineral ores,
building materials, grain and metal goods. The effects of
innovations within the transport sector appeared as changes
in price differentials between commodities sectors and
regions of the European economy. Such 'forward linkages'
operated upon the structure of relative prices and fostered
regional specialisation and trade. The concomitant effects
on the allocation of resources, labour migration, urban
development and rates of capital formation were complex and,
for some economies, profound.

Furthermore, the new and expanded transport networks made
direct demands for the products of several industries which
supplied the companies, responsible for the carriage of
goods and people by rail and water, with their iron, steel,
coal, construction materials and engineering products. To
appreciate the force of these connections (or 'backward
linkages') economic historians have measured the share of
total output delivered by particular industries to the
transport sector, and have attempted to analyse the degree
to which the pressures of such demand promoted economies of
scale and generated more rapid diffusion of technical progress
in supplying industries.

Accelerated rates of capital formation which took place in
transport sectors throughout Europe in the nineteenth century
also gave rise to a range of externalities, or spinoffs,
which are not captured either in the declining real price for
transport services or changes in the structure of relative
prices. For example, railways (but also canals) trained
labour - engineers, foremen and managers - whose skills
(initially acquired in transportation) contributed to the
development of other industries. First canals and later
railways made voracious demands for capital over relatively
short periods of time which prompted the expansion and
improvement of financial intermediaries for the mobilisation
of domestic and foreign savings. Once established such
institutions continued to meet the needs of other sectors of
the economy. By tapping and mobilising new sources of
finance the railways pushed up average rates of saving and
investment over the long run. And in some countries where
the construction of railways occurred in a contracyclical
manner, the timing of their expenditures on capital goods
reduced instability which presumably encouraged more
investment and a greater willingness to assume risks
throughout the economy.

Economic historians must do more than simply point out the
range of interconnections between transport and economic
growth. By looking (as this book does) at the history of
transport across several nations they can compare output for

the whole transport sector country by country for bench-mark
years from the late eighteenth century through to 1914. That
output should be broken down into intermediate output (ton-
kilometres of freight per capita) and final output
(passenger kilometres per head of the population) for major
European economies. The latter is not only an index of how
rapidly the idea of travel diffused among Europeans but it
is a useful indicator of labour mobility (1). Personal travel
(kilometres per passenger) grew more rapidly than services to
producers, and a rising percentage of receipts from the
provision of the entire range of transport services emanated
from the sale of this 'new good' (2). For example, in France
it rose from under 10 per cent of transport revenues in the
1830s to over 30 per cent by the end of the century (3).
Almost the whole of the addition to passenger output came
from railways and the railway systems of Europe consistently
derived more than half of total receipts from the purchase of
travel for business and pleasure. They supplied a novel, safe,
comfortable and speedy service for which there was no real
alternative before the development of the internal combustion
engine. Demand for travel seems to have been both price and
income elastic. Even the Dutch, who had enjoyed the most
efficient mode of passenger transportation by water in Europe,
switched to rail as soon as that facility became
available (4).

Levels of intermediate output also provide historians with
a useful index of market penetration in different economies
which also cross checks on levels of commodity output across
Europe. There is a fairly close correlation between the
growth of commodity output and the increased volume of goods
handled by the transport sector, and it may be possible to
estimate a range of coefficients to link the two series. For
countries which lack adequate statistics on movements in
output, cautious and qualified inferences might be drawn
about possible rates of growth from transportation data, if
that happens to be available. French, British and Belgium
data indicate that freight output expanded at more than
double the rate for commodity output as a whole between 1830
and 1913 (5). For other countries (such as Germany and Spain)
less favourably endowed with roads and waterways in the
early nineteenth century, the growth of freight transported
was probably even more elastic with respect to output (6).

Two kinds of influence should be distinguished when we try
to explain why the share of transportation to gross domestic
product more than doubled in most European countries over the
nineteenth century. First the income effects are reasonably
clear and the high income elasticity of demand for travel has
already been mentioned. Furthermore, rising incomes in

particular regions and countries had for centuries generated
demand for more varied consumption and stimulated international and interregional trade. Foreign and internal
commerce expanded much faster than output as the diversified
produce of remote countries and regions entered the
consciousness and consumption patterns of new social groups.
Studies of diet, dress and taste by historians suggest that
the nineteenth century was a century when European families
found spice and variety by incorporating the products of
alien cultures and remote regions into their traditional
consumption patterns. In this process the demand curve for
transport and distribution shifted to the right.

Two sorts of price effects also stimulated demand for
transport. First, as improvements in economic efficiency
depressed the prices of final outputs to consumers and the
costs of inputs to producers, markets widened. Furthermore,
regional specialisation, based initially upon natural and
increasingly upon uneven rates of capital formation and
technical innovation widened the gaps in productivity and
altered price differentials between the regions of Europe.
Lags in the diffusion of technology, the accumulation of
capital and organisational improvements between countries
and regions generated greater demands for transport. New
techniques reduced costs of production for several
commodities such as iron, coal, building materials and grain,
which could then afford to carry the transportation mark-ups
involved in marketing goods, heavy or bulky in relation to
their retail or final sales prices.

Secondly, technical progress within the transport sector
also widened the market and stimulated additional demand for
freight and passenger services. Although indices of changes
in total factor productivity have been constructed for
British, French and German railways, almost no econometric
research of a similar kind has been undertaken for transport
along European waterways and roads (7). But it is certainly
evident that real costs per passenger kilometre and per ton-
kilometre of transport services fell sharply with the
diffusion of railways and steam locomotives. British and
French data testify to the considerable reductions in price
per kilometre, which the railways offered to travellers. For
example, in nineteenth-century France it was two to three
times more expensive for passengers to travel by road than
by rail (8). And in the 1860s a British Royal Commission
compared first-class coaching at two shillings per mile with
first-class rail fares of between two and three pence a
mile (9). When and where trucks drawn by steam-powered
locomotives competed with carriages and carts pulled along
roads by horses, oxen and mules, railways offered producers

a far cheaper service per ton-kilometre of freight carried.
Thus between 1855 and 1913 it was three to four times more
expensive for French firms to send merchandise by road (10).
As early as 1850 on average it cost nine centimes a ton-
kilometre to despatch freight by road in Belgium compared to
five centimes by rail (11). And in the 1860s, coal was
carried by British railways at about one twentieth of the
cost by road (12).

Whenever the new technology competed with waterborne
transport the decline in costs per ton-kilometre of freight
carried was, however, much less obvious, particularly where
steam-powered boats competed with locomotives by carrying
heavy and bulky commodities along inland and coastal waterways (13). In France, Belgium and Italy (but not in England)
costs per ton-kilometre were lower by boat (14). Railways
competed with waterways by offering producers a speedier and
more reliable service but at a comparable or even higher
tariff per ton kilometre. If speed was necessary (for example
in the carriage of perishable produce) this service could be
described as indispensable. Furthermore, the diffusion of
railways compelled carriers who used waterways to lower
their prices in order to compete; and by eroding the rents
or monopolistic profits of carriers by water (and road) the
railways made a further contribution towards extending the
market and promoting economic growth.

The precise impact of the rise in total factor
productivity in transport can only be properly assessed when
it becomes possible to compare movements in the prices of
transport services with trends in wholesale prices. More
price indices are required to measure how far the relative
price of transport declined between 1789-1914. The evidence
for Britain, France and Germany suggests that this decrease
was really significant (15). A significant decline implies
that the increase in total factor productivity in the
European transportation sectors was sufficient not merely to
meet rising demands for its services from other sectors of
the economy, at constant real prices, but made an
'autonomous' contribution to economic growth. Here lies the
difference between transport operating to complement
productivity growth achieved by industry and agriculture,
and transport acting as a leading sector in the process of
widening markets and altering the structure of relative
prices for commodity output and inputs. The degree to which
such an autonomous contribution occurred would be reflected
in a fall in the average share of the transport margin in the
selling prices of goods and services marketed throughout the
continent. Such effects would vary from commodity to
commodity, region to region, and sector to sector. They would

depend on the share of transport embodied in the market price
(and would thus be more significant for transport intensive
commodities). The effects also depended upon the price
elasticity of demand for particular goods. For example,
although the transport margin embodied in the retail prices
of flour and sugar is similar, a fairly small cut in sugar
prices could perhaps widen the market far more than a
comparable cut in the price of flour.

Although prices fell, studies on the pricing policies
pursued by enterprises concerned with transport by road, rail
and water, reveals how the monopolistic nature of the
industry and government intervention (in many cases more
concerned with public revenue than consumer welfare) operated
to hold the prices charged by transport companies at levels
which were suboptimal for the overall growth of the economy.
For example, Fenoaltea's analysis for Italy reveals how the
high tariffs charged by Italian railways constrained
specialisation and the extension of the market while the more
efficient French and German companies set their prices closer
to marginal cost and were not burdened by onerous obligations
to transfer a high percentage of their operating revenues to
the state (16). But in other countries, including Britain,
Belgium and the United States, actual and incipient
competition from waterborne transport probably kept railway
tariffs closer to competitive norms (17).

To conclude: transportation grew more rapidly than national
output because demand for travel was income and price elastic
and because the sector was called upon to carry a rising
proportion of commodity output across greater and greater
distances. For example, in France in the 1830s the average
lead or distance travelled by freight from the point of
production was 50-60 kilometres by road. By 1905-13 this
average had risen to 190 kilometres by rail (18). Technical
progress with rising factor productivity occurred in all
forms of transport: in surfacing roads, improving inland
waterways, in laying down railed ways, but above all in the
application of steam power to carriers by rail and water.

Over the nineteenth century the growth of European output
was not constrained as it had been in past centuries by
increasing costs of transportation. On the contrary,
extensions to and improvements in the transportation networks
in most European countries made a positive and autonomous
contribution to national rates of growth. Without the
revolution in transport which raised its productivity a
greater volume of scarce resources would have been diverted
into that sector in order to cope with the rising demand for
freight services (and for travel) between 1789 and 1914. If
European economies had been confronted with rising real costs

of transport, trade and specialisation would have been
constrained and the overall growth of output would have been
slower. If, in turn, historians could answer the question how
much slower, then they would be in a position to measure the
contribution to the growth rate made by improvements in the
efficiency of transport networks. Interconnections between
transport and other sectors of the economy can be specified,
but historians are still a long way from 'measuring' the
contribution of transport to economic growth between 1789 and
1914. They have not and perhaps cannot quantify the decline
in the rate of growth of gross national product which would
have occurred if total factor productivity in transportation
had remained constant over time.

2.   THE SIGNIFICANCE OF RAILWAYS: SOCIAL SAVINGS

New economic historians have, however, attempted to measure
something more restricted, namely the impact of the diffusion
of railways on economic growth. In focusing upon railways
they selected the core element in the transport revolution of
the nineteenth century. Although technical change occurred
throughout the transportation sector and steam power was also
utilised by waterborne carriers, the construction of networks
of lines across Europe rising from nearly 3000 kilometres of
track in 1840 to 362 000 kilometres by 1913 placed railway
companies in a position to provide nearly all the additional
passenger kilometres sold to consumers of travel between 1840
and 1910 (19).
    They also met the demand for an extremely high proportion
of the extra ton-kilometres supplied for the transportation
of freight around Europe over the nineteenth century. For
example, French statistics show that while output of roads,
canals and coastal shipping remained roughly constant between
1830 and 1914 the ton-kilometres of transport services
supplied by railway companies expanded to a point where they
supplied nearly 70 per cent of total freight transportation
in 1914 (20). No doubt statistics for other economies would
also reveal the dominance of railways in the expansion of
internal transportation over the nineteenth century. Thus in
Belgium, railways moved from a position where they supplied
7 per cent of freight transportation in 1845-6 to where they
provided 77 per cent in 1908-13 (21). Although railways
clearly met most of the additional demand for transport
which emerged after 1840 it cannot be assumed that railways
alone possessed the techniques and capacity to obviate a
potential 'transport bottleneck' to the growth of output over
the nineteenth century. But can their contribution be

measured or quantified?

One well-known approach to answering this question is to estimate social savings from railways some decades after national networks had been in full and efficient operation. This approach postulates that the importance of railways to any economy could be measured as the *costs* of coping without them over one year.

Table 1.1: *European railway development (territory and population in relation to kilometres of lines)*

	1860	1880	1900	1910
UK	44	66	69	69
Belgium	30	60	88	102
France	18	44	77	87
Germany	21	54	70	75
Sweden	3	32	61	76
Switzerland	28	63	79	88
Russia	1	10	21	24
Spain	6	23	40	58
Italy	6	23	38	38

Source: P. Bairoch, 'Niveaux developpement economique de 1810 a 1910', *Annales, ESC,* December 1965.

The method envisages a counterfactual situation in which a given national network is closed down for twelve months but producers continue to despatch exactly the same volume of freight to the same destinations as before by using roads and waterways. But, in order to maintain a constant level of transportation when denied access to railways, farmers and industrialists would clearly incur extra costs because:

(a)   freight despatched by road and water had to pay higher tariffs per ton-kilometre;
(b)   their goods would usually move along more circuitous and longer routes;
(c)   the time taken between despatch and delivery would lengthen;
(d)   transportation by wagons and boats was more risky, more subject to delay and loss than transportation by rail.

Assuming that the extra costs of sending commodities by water and road (instead of by rail - the preferred and

cheaper method) could be estimated, new economic historians
have ostensibly measured social savings which they define as
equal to the *extra* or marginal benefit derived by a society
from the normal operation of its railway system (22).

Estimates of social savings on ceteris paribus assumptions,
first formulated for the United States, have now been
manufactured for several European countries (including
Tsarist Russia) and the statistics expressed as a ratio of
Gross National Product are set out in Table 1.2.

Of course there are formidable problems connected with the
quality of the data deployed to estimate social savings and
a major theoretical controversy has arisen around the extent
to which historical records of prices charged by road
hauliers, inland waterways and railways provide adequate
proxies for the 'real' or opportunity costs of the resources
employed by transportation networks of Europe and America (23).
Formidable index number problems inherent in the concept are
also still unresolved. For example, what are the implications
of assuming that enterprises would continue to despatch the
same volume of freight with and without railways? If the cost
differences between railways and other modes of transport are
large and the derived demand for transport is price elastic
the volume of freight transported is not independent from the
introduction of railways (24).

Finally social savings estimates are sensitive to the
assumptions made about the real opportunity costs of the
resources 'released' to the economy from the transport sector
through the operation of railways. If the rise in labour
productivity simply adds to the volume of unemployment or to
emigration (pace Italy) then the gains to the national
economy are reduced (25). For Spain the availability of
seasonally underemployed agricultural workers reduced the
social savings from railways from 11.8 per cent to a feasible
7.5 per cent of GNP (26). Debate over the new economic
history of railways continues and has been reviewed and
summarised elsewhere (27). Let us presume that the available
estimates of social savings provide rough outer-bound
measures of the percentage falls in gross national products
which might have followed from the closure of railways
during the years specified in Table 1.2. It then becomes
instructive to analyse the variations in social savings
attributed to railways across countries and over time.

With all their theoretical and empirical imperfections,
estimates of social savings do enable historians to dispose
of claims that railways were 'vital' or 'indispensable' for
economic progress, because they show that (apart from Spain
and Mexico) closure of a fully operational railways network
would have led to a fall of less than one tenth of national

Table 1.2: *Estimates of social savings on freight transported by railways*

	Date	SS expressed as a share of GNP (%)	
England and Wales	1865	4.1	(a)
England and Wales	1890	11.0	(a)
USA	1859	3.7	(b)
USA	1890	8.9	(c)
Russia	1907	4.6	(d)
France	1872	5.8	(e)
Germany	1890s	5.0	(f)
Spain	1878	11.8	(g)
Spain	1912	18.5	(g)
Belgium	1865	2.5	(h)
Belgium	1912	4.5	(h)
Mexico	1910	25-39	(i)

Note: These estimates all based on the ceteris paribus assumption are comparable.

Sources:

(a) G. R. Hawke, *Railways and Economic Growth in England and Wales, 1840-70* (Oxford, 1970) p. 196. The 1890 estimate has been calculated from the data presented on p. 89 and an estimate for the National Income of England and Wales for 1890 based upon the assumptions specified on p. 196.
(b) Calculated from A. Fishlow, *American Railroads and the Transformation of the Ante-Bellum Economy* (Harvard, 1965) pp. 37 and 52.
(c) This is Fogel's unadjusted estimate based on ceteris paribus assumptions and calculated from data in R. Fogel, *Railroads and American Economic Growth* (Baltimore, 1964) chapters 2 and 3.
(d) J. Metzer, 'Railroads in Tsarist Russia: Direct Gains and Implications', *Explorations in Economic History,* 13 (1976) p. 90.
(e) See p. 44.
(f) See p. 139.
(g) See p. 154.
(h) See p. 221.

Table 1.2 - *Continued*

(i)   J. H. Coatsworth, 'Indispensable Railroads in a Backward
      Economy: The Case of Mexico', *Journal of Economic
      History* XXXIX (1979) p. 952, This estimate is expressed
      as a share of GDP.

outputs. Nevertheless a fall of 10 per cent of GNP (or even
5 per cent (for that matter) is still a very large magnitude.
Railways were clearly important (and in the Spanish case very
important) for the growth and maintenance of commodity
production at observed levels. Just how important can only be
assessed by comparing the social savings achieved by railways
with the social savings for other major nineteenth-century
innovations, such as steel, power looms, canals, chemicals,
etc.
      The increase over time in the benefits derived from
railways (the rise in the ratio of social savings to national
income) reflects the continuous improvement in the efficiency
of railways which occurred through the steady diffusion of
better techniques in railway engineering, the replacement of
iron by steel rails and in business organisation (28). Thus
freight rates on German railways declined over the nineteenth
century to one quarter of their level for 1845 (29). In
Belgium the rates per ton-kilometre declined from 10.8
centimes in 1845 to 3.6 centimes in 1913 and in France they
fell by 50 per cent (over the same decades) (30). Improvements
in productivity helped railways to hold their own against
competition from waterborne transport which also became more
efficient over the nineteenth century and which (in those
countries well endowed with rivers or coastal shipping lanes)
enjoyed advantages in the form of lower track costs per ton-
kilometre carried. Over longer distances railways competed by
offering producers speed and regularity of delivery. For
large countries like Russia, the Austro-Hungarian Empire and
the United States railways did not provide a much cheaper
service than waterways per ton mile carried over long and
comparable routes, and the social savings on that account
could be fairly small, even negligible. Thus where trunk
lines were constructed to compete with waterways over long
distances, and the track accommodated to existing locations
and patterns of internal trade, the initial gains to the
economy would be positive but not dramatic. Belgium, France
and Germany continued to build canals during the second half
of the nineteenth century (31). Furthermore, it is difficult
to speculate ('counterfactually') how waterborne transport
might have developed without railways. It is not unreasonable

to assume (pace Fogel) that without railways the efficiency of waterborne and road transport would have improved more rapidly than it did with competition from railways.

As time went on gains increased because railway companies expanded their lines outside and beyond the networks of trade already serviced by waterways. And they helped to create more trade and production in new locations. Social savings really went up when railways captured an ever increasing share of freight carried along roads over medium distances. The differential in average costs per ton-kilometre between railways and roads was already considerable in the 1840s and that differential widened over time because productivity in road transport failed to go up very much over the next seven decades (32). Although road networks expanded at a high rate technical progress in that subsector of transportation was minimal before the internal combustion engine provided a substitute for animal and man power used for cartage. More-over, the opportunity costs of the principal inputs used to carry goods by roads (labour, animals and animal feed) rose with the development of agriculture and industry (33). For example, 32 per cent to 43 per cent of the hectares devoted to the cultivation of bread grains would have been required to cope with the extra demand for animal feedstuffs generated by the hypothetical shutdown of Spanish railways in 1878 (34). Thus the 'savings' in resources which emanated from the shift of freight from roads to railways was far greater than from the reallocation of merchandise from boats to trains and it increased over time. Considerations of this kind explain the relatively low ratios of social savings to national income for 1859 in the United States, 1865 in England and 1907 in Russia (see Table 1.2). Three or four decades later when the output of the transport sector had increased the ratio nearly trebled in Britain and America and the same tendency was certainly more pronounced in Russia because estimates for 1907 relate to the early stages of development. Between 1907-39 ton-kilometres supplied by rail multiplied four times to account for 82 per cent of Soviet transportation output. In 1907 84 per cent of freight services supplied by Russian railways could have been provided by waterways and that ceased to be true when transportation output expanded very rapidly over subsequent decades (35).

Similar observations follow from comparisons of social savings across countries. Thus the higher the percentage of freight taken off the roads and onto railway networks the greater the gains to an economy from its investment in railways. Countries badly endowed with navigable rivers, afflicted with a terrain hostile to the construction of

canals, and with poor natural facilities and opportunities
for coastal trade gained most from their investment in
railways. Railways alleviated the adverse economic effects
on internal trade of an unfavourable natural endowment. Thus
over the long run Mexico, Spain, Russia, certain regions of
France, the Upper Po valley in Italy and Germany obtained
higher returns from the diffusion of railways than Britain,
the rest of Italy, Holland, Belgium or the United States.
The significance of this point can be measured by the
percentage of freight which would be diverted from rail to
water in the counterfactual case of a shutdown of the
railway network. For example, during hypothetical closure of
Spanish railways in 1878 coastal shipping and inland waterways supplied only 10 per cent of the ton-kilometres
required to maintain a constant level of transportation; in
France (1872) waterborne carriers provided 30 per cent (and
in Britain (1865) they took about half of the traffic).
Italian trunk lines were unprofitable because of the
availability of coastal shipping (36).

To a more limited extent the relative significance of
railways for different economies can also be discerned in
terms of their effects on the levels of stocks held by farms
and industrial firms before the construction of national
networks. Railways supplied producers with transport which
was faster, safer and far more immune to seasonal and
geographical obstruction than roads or waterways. In the
middle of the nineteenth century a barge took no less than
86 days to carry a load of coal from Mons to Paris and to
return to its mooring (37). Where and when transport by road
and water was both slow and irregular, firms could partially
insure production against costly interruptions to inputs and
sales by holding higher inventories of raw materials,
finished goods and work in progress. Railways obviated the
need to invest in stocks, and thereby enabled producers to
convert circulating into fixed investment. This saving could
be particularly important for economies like Spain and Russia
where traditional transport of goods by road and water was
highly seasonal (38). Nearly a quarter of the social savings
achieved by Russian railways in 1907 came from a reduction
in the cost of inventories (39). In Britain with its
temperate climate, gentle terrain and specialised road and
water-borne services, the gains from additional speed and
regularity supplied by railways was less than 4 per cent of
the social savings for 1865 (40).

To sum up: it appears that the traditional inefficiency
and rather limited technical progress achieved in transportation by road made railways important in countries badly
endowed with waterways. Over long and medium hauls road

transport utilised more capital labour and other inputs per
ton-kilometres than the two alternative modes of production,
although road transport continued to dominate short distance
transportation, particularly within cities it lost freight
(first to waterways and then increasingly to railways on
long and passenger hauls) (41).

3. RAILWAYS AND LONG-RUN GROWTH

Nowhere in Europe did railways make the difference between
development and stagnation and economic historians are still
a long way from measuring their contribution to the growth
rates of particular economies. Although the social savings
methodology represents a big step forward, static equilibrium
analysis cannot deal effectively with the dynamic effects of
railways over time. For such influences the relevant counterfactual is not the shutdown for one year (used with
illuminating effect by Fishlow, Hawke, Metzer, Caron and
Gomez) but a hypothetical refusal by a national government to
establish a railway network at any time between 1830 and 1914.
In this context and with the aid of general equilibrium models,
the entire range of influences exercised by railways on
savings and investment, location patterns, markets, the
product mix, scale, technical progress and innovation, labour
training, government policy, urbanisation, international
flows of capital and labour, etc. could in theory be
quantified. But even if models could be designed to capture
the complex interconnections of railways to economic growth
through time, empirically the task of quantification seems
impossible - a point exemplified by the recent debate between
Fogel and Williamson (42). Historians can, however, write
more or less rigorously about the impact of railways on
economic growth. They can also quantify some of the more
important backward and forward linkages.

For example, several economic historians have analysed and
measured the 'feedbacks' derived from the establishment and
extension of railways. The great bulk of investment
expenditures feedback to the construction industry. For
example, between 1861-95 Italy's engineering and metalmaking
industries absorbed only a tiny percentage of railway
investment (43). For industry as a whole, even at peak
levels of demand, railways absorbed far too low a percentage
of total output to qualify as a 'leading sector' in the
growing process. Industry normally delivered well over 90
per cent of its output to other producers and consumers.

Deliveries to railways did, however, exercise an important
influence on the development of particular industries -

including iron and steel, coal, bricks, timber and
engineering (see Table 1.3). Of course the relative
significance of railway demand hinges entirely on the level
of disaggregation used to define an industry. Thus for Italy:
'the growth in railway related production seems to have
represented significant growth for the machinery and metalmaking industries but relatively unimpressive growth for the
entire metalworking group' (44).

Even for industries strongly stimulated by the establishment and maintenance of a railway system, the significance
of 'feedback effects' was never extraordinary. Backward
linkages were, moreover, concentrated over particular cycles
of production, when a large proportion of the increment to
output was delivered to railways. Thus demand for iron and
steel, engineering products and other manufactured
commodities could be important for the growth of a small
range of industries over fairly short periods of time in the
nineteenth century when the boost from the establishment of
large-scale extensions to a national network pushed
production up onto a higher plateau. Thereafter normal demand
for replacement and extensions to the network and its stock
of equipment accounted for a tiny proportion of the annual
additions to industrial output.

During these boosts to total demand, firms and industries
supplying railways might realise economies of scale and
introduce improved technology more rapidly. Railway
expenditures could even accelerate technical progress,
particularly in metals and engineering. Historians have
traced such influences on the South Wales iron industry; on
the development of locomotive production and bar iron in
Germany; on the steel industry in France and the United
States, and upon specific sectors of the engineering
industry in Belgium, Russia and Germany (45). Feedbacks to
steel production stand out as significant for the expansion
of capacity and the diffusion of technology in France,
Germany, United States and Italy (in the late nineteenth
century) (46).

Of course the impact of backward linkages varied from
country to country and their importance for industrial
development depended primarily upon the extent to which
demand for capital goods required to establish the main
network and its rolling stock was directed towards imported
inputs and equipment. At the outset almost every country
except Britain and Belgium laid down imported rails and
hauled freight with foreign locomotives. But in some
countries the process of import substitution quickly re-
directed demand towards domestic industry. In others the
lags, for a variety of reasons, were long, and the

Table 1.3: *Percentages of Output delivered to railways*

	Pig Iron (%)	Steel (%)	Coal (%)	Bricks (%)	Wood (%)	Transport Equipment (%)
USA	5–21 (1840–60)	50–87 (1867–80)	2–20 (1840–90)	–	3–10 (1840–60)	25 (1859)
England & Wales	5–13 (1835–69)	–	2–14 (1865)	30 (1840s)	–	–
Spain	6.0 (1890–1914)	8.5 (1890–1914)	18–29 (1865–1914)	–	–	–
Germany	22–37 (1840–59)	–	3 (1860s)	–	–	–
France	–	12–18[a] (1845–85)	–	13–18[b] (1845–85)	1 (1875–84)	–
Italy	–	12–13[c] (1861–1913)	–	16–23[d] (1861–1913)	–	5–11[e] (1861–1913)
Belgium	6 (1860–1913)	–	–	4–10 (1865–1913)	–	–

Note: Iron and Steel output delivered has been defined as a net flow of output.
(a) iron and steel; (b) building materials; (c) all ferrous metals;
(d) construction materials; (e) engineering products.

Source: See Table 1.2, O'Brien, *New Economic History of Railways* (1977) ch.5, pp. 38–9, 60–72, 123–32, 157–63, 209–14.

establishment of the initial networks exercised almost no
impact upon local metallurgy, coal and engineering but
contributed to the continued development of British, French
and Belgium export industries. For example Spain, Italy and
Tsarist Russia are all examples of countries where, until
late in the nineteenth century, foreign suppliers derived the
most of the benefits from orders for their rails and rolling
stock (47). While in France and Germany rapid and decisive
moves towards import substitution - initially in the rolling
mill sector of the iron industry and in the construction of
locomotives, but then followed by the shift into the
manufacture of coke-smelted pig iron - imparted a significant
stimulus to domestic metallurgy and to the transition from
charcoal to coke-smelted pig iron (48).

Why did Tsarist Russia, Italy and Spain not take full
advantage of 'potential linkages' to industrialisation,
advantages which had been demonstrated during the construction
of railways in other countries? One possible explanation is
that their governments failed to impose tariffs on cheaper
foreign rails and rolling stock, either because their
statesmen were ideologically blinkered in favour of free
trade or because the foreign capitalists and companies, who
provided a large share of the finance required for the
establishment of rail networks in Spain, Italy and Russia,
insisted on directing the order for rails and equipment
overseas (49). While such explanations are not without point,
they seem to rest too heavily on the lack of foresight
exhibited by statesmen and the bias of foreign investors
towards their own national industries. At the time the
decision presented itself as a problem of how quickly local
capacity in metallurgy and engineering could be expanded to
cope with a 'bunched' and cyclical demand for rails,
locomotives, rolling stock and other manufactured inputs
required by the railways. In Germany, France and Belgium the
metallurgical and engineering industries had attained levels
of development and efficiency from where import substitution
could proceed smoothly. In other words, the fairly rapid
reallocation of demand towards local suppliers which occurred
in these economies did not lead to bottlenecks, intolerable
delays and prohibitive costs for the establishment of railway
networks (50). Furthermore (in contrast to Spain, Italy and
Russia) these economies seem far less dependent on foreign
capital to provide the finance required for investment in
social overhead capital. Spain, Italy and Russia were short
on domestic venture capital. Their levels of production trade
and income rendered that investment a more expensive and
riskier proposition. Their relatively 'difficult' terrains
increased the ratio of capital to output in transportation.

Their existing plant and manpower in metallurgical and engineering industries compared unfavourably with France, Germany and Belgium. Only a handful of engineers worked in Russia in the 1860s (51). At the onset of railway construction in 1856 Spain possessed sufficient capacity to produce only 15 000 tons of iron compared with a demand for rails over the next five years of around 30 000 tons per annum. And Italy emerged from the Risorgimento with very limited capacity to produce pig and wrought iron (52).

In short, the preconditions for the kind of successful import substitution which occurred in Germany, France and Belgium were not present everywhere even in Western Europe and in some states the imposition of tariffs on imported railway equipment would surely have led to costly delays in construction and the emergence of a railway network saddled with considerable capital charges and compelled to charge high prices for freight and passenger services. Thus by implication the criticism of Cavour, Kankrin, Bunge, Luxan and other European statesmen for their failure to utilise protective tariffs to take advantage of opportunities for backward linkages is an argument for a railway system heavily subsidised by governments. The unexplored premise of that view is that the long-term social gains generated specifically by railway demand for the products of the metallurgical and engineering industries would more than compensate for the delays, higher costs and increased taxes necessitated by constructing and maintaining national railways networks with domestic rather than foreign rails, rolling stock and other equipment. Part of the costs of protection afforded to iron and steel would (as the Italian example shows) be borne by industries utilising metals, particularly engineering and shipbuilding (53).

For Spain, Italy, Russia and other parts of Eastern Europe the counterfactual scenario of tariffs, import substitution and railway construction combining to promote rates of industrial growth at far higher levels than those achieved with free trade seems altogether improbable, and the examples of France, Belgium and Germany are not relevant for countries with limited capacities in engineering and metallurgy at mid century.

Railways influenced the volume of capital formation as well as variations in rates of investment. For example, net investment in railways dominated investment in the Tewerbe, or modern sector of the German economy from 1851-79 (54). But to assess their influence on the long-term growth of particular economies historians need to specify a model which exposes interconnections between railway investment and other relevant variables in a closed and open economic system. Such

models are, however, easier to adapt from economic theory
than to use to quantify the influence of railway expenditure (55). Several historians have, however, analysed the
extent to which investment expenditures on railways operated
to impart greater stability to economies afflicted by
fluctuations in the level of economic activity. Apparently in
Britain and America such expenditures helped to induce booms
and to alleviate depressions (56). But for Italy Fenoaltea's
analysis 'suggests a mild boost to industry's cyclical
instability' while French investment in railway companies
also intensified the amplitude of cycles in the nineteenth
century (57). But in Germany railway investment fluctuated in
the approved contracyclical manner (58). The sequence of
expenditures on railway networks is likely to vary from
country to country and from period to period. No definite
conclusions can, however, be drawn from these correlations
until the connections between cycles of investment in
railways and of economic activity are analysed and elucidated
at the level of industries and even firms.

More important questions should be raised about connections
between opportunities to buy shares in railway companies and
the total volume of investible funds made available to an
economy. If we assume inflexible rates of domestic saving as
well as the availability of other projects competing for funds
with railways, their influence on the level of capital
formation will be seen as negligible. But if expenditures on
railways attracted foreign funds or new savings to finance the
networks, then it becomes possible to argue that railways
raised the overall rate of investment by some positive
percentage. Railroads apparently attracted both foreign
capital and immigrants into the United States (59). Although
sceptics maintain that capital migrates in search of profits
not railways, there can be no doubt that European investors,
banks and other financial institutions, weaned on the paper
securities of British and French railways, were geared towards
similar opportunities in Belgium, Italy, Spain and Russia (60).
While the voracious demands for capital made by railway
companies over short cycles of economic activity influenced
institutional developments in the capital markets of Britain
and France which not only mobilised funds but educated new
social groups in impersonal investment and increased
propensities to save (61). Debate on the precise importance
of effects of this kind is likely to remain inconclusive.

Finally, railways widened markets which promoted economies
of scale, encouraged the relocation of economic activity,
stimulated competition and increased trade and specialisation.
Williamson's important analysis of these 'forward linkages'
from railways to the economy of the Midwestern United States

demonstrates that they could be profound. Nothing like his general equilibrium model has been applied to the economic history of Western Europe (62). Prima facie it seems that for most parts of Europe broad patterns of interregional and international trade established before the advent of railways continued and the iron road carried forward the process of integrating local economies into national and international markets. Trade in the nineteenth century emanated basically from natural and traditional advantages. Comparative advantages of the kind stressed by Ricardo (and adumbrated by Heckshers and Ohlin) were becoming more important and railways reinforced tendencies towards industrial specialisation based upon favourable endowments of skilled labour, accessible supplies of capital and those 'temporary' gains which accrued to pioneers in new products and technology. Nevertheless the composition of commodities traded between the countries and regions of Europe did not alter profoundly between 1840 and 1914, when railways provided particular regions with greater opportunities to export products in which they enjoyed cost advantages (63).

For several economies (including Britain and Holland) well served by waterborne and road transport, relatively small gains flowed from the integration of national economies and from linking interior regions and natural resources to world markets. Even in Spain, the location of vineyards and mineral ore deposits near to the sea implied that railways were not a necessary condition for the rapid growth of wine and ore exports in the second half of the nineteenth century, although they did bring Spain's isolated agricultural regions into competition with each other (64). In Italy, despite the high hopes of post-unification governments, the trunk lines built before the 1880s did not promote a rapid expansion of inter-regional trade. Many regions remained too poor to trade, their capacity to absorb exports from other parts of Italy remained low and complementarity in production among Italian regions was not marked. Integration exacerbated dualism between North and South and encouraged imports (65). But rail links from the Upper Po Valley to the sea permitted the industrial triangle (Turin, Milan and Genoa) to develop (66).

For other economies the stimulus to production seems more marked. Thus Belgium's planners tried from the outset to build lines which would integrate the local economy into Western Europe (67). In Russia railroads increased regional specialisation and 'there was a major reorientation of resources towards those areas offering a higher level of productivity in the cultivation of rye and wheat'. Exports of Russian grain increased roughly four times between 1860-4 and 1875-9 and added about 4 per cent to national income (68).

Furthermore, they linked Donbas coking coal with Krivoi Rog
iron ore deposits and created a new heavy industry complex in
the Ukraine (69). Their forward linkage effects on the growth
of Germany's coal and metallurgical industries were profound
enough for Fremdling to label the railroad as 'the hero of
Germany's industrial revolution' (70). In France their advent
led (as Caron shows) to the spread of wine cultivation in
Languedoc, and stock raising in the Charente (71).

Railways carried forward the reduction in transportation
costs initiated by waterborne carriers and thereby widened
markets, stimulated competition and provided access to natural
resources and more efficient locations for productive activity.
Their capacity to bring about reductions in costs per ton-
kilometre were maximised in those parts of Europe where access
to productive resources was prohibitively expensive by
waterways and roads and where they successfully appropriated
freight over medium hauls from road transportation. Only in
special cases, such as the trade in meat or perishable farm
produce, were railways a necessary condition for the extension
of the market. Access to markets was, for most products,
available by road and in many places by water.

Clearly it will not be possible to quantify the manifold
effects of railways on Europe's regional and international
trade. And associated with the spread of railways, there also
occurred geographical shifts by enterprises within well-
defined economic regions and such gains from the relocation
of economic activity could, in aggregate, exceed the gains
from longer distance trade. But they seem difficult to detect
and impossible to measure, except as a by-product of business
or industrial history. But railways invariably lowered freight
costs per ton-kilometre and the cuts in transport margins were
passed on in the form of lower prices. Such reductions seem to
have been particularly important for fuels, construction
materials and agricultural surpluses - meat and wine. Thus
railways exercised their most profound effects on long-run
growth by altering the structure of relative prices and the
terms of trade between regions and sectors of the European
economy. They appear to have had greater effects on primary
production - agriculture and mining - than upon manufacturing
industry. But their dynamic effects on capital formation,
technical progress and the reallocation of resources which
flowed from the reduction in transport mark-ups have not been
measured. Nevertheless, Williamson's central question: what
would have happened to economic development if price
differentials had remained at their pre-railway levels, is the
kind of counterfactual approach which will appeal to a
traditional historiography which sees railways as a pervasive
and extremely important element in the economic growth of

Western Europe from 1840-1914.

Not all regions benefited equally from railways. As always the gains depended on the elasticities of demand and supply or the capacity of a given economy to take advantage of the opportunities to trade afforded by railways. If consumers resident in a particular region responded to falling prices by importing heavily from another region, a substantial gain would occur in consumer surplus and their welfare. If a region's capacity to supply was elastic because resources were underemployed in the pre-rail situation or because inputs could be augmented at low cost, production could expand rapidly in response to the diffusion of cheaper transport. Unfortunately there were many parts of Europe (particularly in southern and eastern Europe) whose people remained too poor to take advantage of the opportunities for cheaper and more variegated consumption provided by railways. Their capacity to respond to the widening of markets continued to be restrained by unfavourable resource endowments and rising marginal costs of production.

For these regions the gains from railways before 1914 were positive but more limited than the gains which accrued to North Western Europe and the United States. For some parts of Europe (Southern Italy, Castille, Hungary and Romania) the benefits from trade creation may have been offset by the losses from trade diversion to other regions. Their workers had no option but to migrate in search of higher incomes (72).

Perhaps the contrasting economic histories of Germany and Spain from 1850-1914 will illustrate how railways could carry forward but not propel rapid industrialisation. In Germany the railroad linked backwards and forward to agriculture and to a multiplicity of industries (already in the process of sustained economic growth), while Spain lacked several pre-conditions for an accelerated rate of economic change. Spanish agricultural productivity was lower; its industrial base (particularly its metallurgical and engineering sectors) was less developed; regional specialisation seems less marked; and the complementary networks of roads and waterways were not in place. Spanish railways did shift the Spanish economy closer to its production possibility boundary, but their effects were less profound than they were in Germany (73). Thus in countries like Spain, Italy, the Austro-Hungarian Empire, Tsarist Russia and other parts of Eastern Europe railways accomplished a great deal by 1914. But despite all the euphoria which accompanied its introduction and the hopes placed on its supposed potential for both political and economic integration, the iron road was never a panacea for development.

NOTES AND REFERENCES

I would like to thank Stefano Fenoaltea for helpful comments on this chapter.

1. Relevant data is contained in B. Mitchell, *European Historical Statistics* (London, 1975) section G.
2. A. de Fouille, *La transformation des moyens de transports* (Paris, 1880) pp. 141-7 and L. G. McPherson, *Transportation in Europe* (London, 1910) pp. 69-78.
3. J. C. Toutain, *Les Transports en France* (Paris, 1967) p. 286.
4. J. De Vries, *Barges and Capitalism, Passenger Transportation in the Dutch Economy* (Wageningen, 1978) p. 236.
5. See pp. 34, 214-15 and Toutain, *Les Transports en France,* p. 298.
6. See pp. 121, 132, 152.
7. See pp. 40-2, 132-3; G. Hawke, *Railways and Economic Growth in England and Wales* (Oxford, 1970) Ch. XI; F.Caron, 'Recherches sur le Capital Des Voies de Communication en France au XIXe Siècle' in *Colloques Internationaux du CNRS,* no. 540, *L'Industrialization en Europe au XIXe Siècle* (Lyon, 1970) pp. 256-61; R. Fremdling, *Eisenbahnen und Deutsches Wirtschaftswachstum, 1840-1879* (Dortmund, 1975) pp. 35-51.
8. Toutain, *Les Transports en France,* p. 277.
9. Hawke, *Railways and Economic Growth,* p. 44.
10. Toutain, *Les Transports en France,* pp. 277-9.
11. See pp. 215 and 220.
12. Hawke, *Railways and Economic Growth,* pp. 179-80.
13. De Vries, *Barges and Capitalism,* pp. 245-8 and 359-61.
14. See pp. 42-5. 95-6 and 220; Toutain, *Les Transports en France,* pp. 277-8 and Hawke, *Railways and Economic Growth,* pp. 85-6, 173, 187-8.
15. Toutain, *Les Transports en France,* p. 283; and Fremdling, *Eisenbahnen und Deutsches Wirtschaftswachtum,* pp. 57-60.
16. See pp. 82-6.
17. L. Girard, 'Transport' in M. Postan and H. J. Habakkuk (eds), *Cambridge Economic History of Europe,* vol. VI, part 11 (Cambridge, 1966) and H. Parris, *Government and the Railways in Nineteenth Century Britain* (London, 1965).
18. Toutain, *Les Transports en France,* p. 244.
19. P. Bairoch, *Commerce extérieur et developpment économique de l'Europe au XIXe Siècle* (Paris, 1976) p. 32.
20. Toutain, *Les Transports en France,* p. 248.
21. See p. 221.

22. P. K. O'Brien, *The New Economic History of Railways* (London, 1977) chs. 2 and 3 and see pp. 184-8.
23. R. Fogel, 'Notes on the Social Savings Controversy', *Journal of Economic History*, XXXIX (1979) pp. 13-38.
24. J. G. Williamson, *Late Nineteenth Century American Development: A General Equilibrium History* (Cambridge, 1974) pp. 184-7.
25. See pp. 229, 232-3.
26. See pp. 154-7.
27. O'Brien, *New Economic History of Railways*, Fogel, 'Notes', and T. R. Gourvish, *Railways and the British Economy, 1830-1914* (London, 1980).
28. Hawke, *Railways and Economic Growth*, ch. XI; A. Fishlow, 'Productivity and Technological Change in the Railroad Sector' in National Bureau of Economic Research, *Studies in Income and Wealth*, 30 (New York, 1965) pp. 583-646; Fremdling, *Eisenbahnen und Deutsches Wirtschaftswachstum*, pp. 35-101; Caron, 'Recherches sur le Capital des Voies', pp. 237-61, and see pp. 34-5 and 40-2.
29. Fremdling, *Eisenbahnen und Deutsches Wirtschaftswachstum*, pp. 18-19 and 57.
30. Toutain, *Les Transports en France*, p. 278 and see p. 216.
31. R. Price, *The Economic Modernization of France, 1750-1880* (London, 1975) p. 16; Toutain, *Les Transports en France*, (New York, 1979) pp. 68-9, see pp. 139, 218 and 221.
32. See pp. 217-20. In France, the differential was roughly 2.4:1 in 1845-54 and widened to 4.6:1, 1905-13 – see Toutain, *Les Transports en France*, p. 279.
33. P. S. Bagwell, *The Transport Revolution from 1770* (London, 1974) pp. 145-9 and F. M. L. Thompson, 'Nineteenth Century Horse Sense' in *Economic History Review*, XXIX (1976) p. 78.
34. See pp. 152-4.
35. Unpublished paper delivered by A. Aslund to St Antony's Seminar in International Economic History, 1978 and Metzer, 'Railroads in Tsarist Russia', pp. 88-96.
36. See pp. 93-4.
37. See p. 220.
38. See pp. 150, 155-6.
39. Metzer, 'Railroads in Tsarist Russia', pp. 95-6.
40. See p. 191.
41. In France in 1830 80 per cent of the receipts for transport of merchandise accrued in the road system:by 1895-1904 the proportion had fallen to 41 per cent – see Toutain, *Les Transports en France*, p. 286; De Vries, *Barges and Capitalism*, pp. 223-30, and Fogel, 'Notes on the Social Savings Controversy', pp. 49-51 and see pp. 216-21.
42. Fogel, 'Notes on the Social Savings Controversy'; J. G. Williamson, 'Greasing the Wheels of Sputtering Export

42. *Continued*
    Engines: Midwestern Grains and American Growth', *Explorations in Economic History*, 17 (1980) pp. 211-12 and see
    S. Fenoaltea, 'Railroads and Italian Industrial Growth,
    1861-1913', *Exploration in Economic History*, IX (1972).
43. See pp. 60-72.
44. See p. 72.
45. Hawke, *Railways and Economic Growth*, pp. 215-30; Caron,
    'Recherches sur le Capital Des Voies'. pp. 239-47, see
    pp. 45, 123-32, 212-13; J. N. Westwood, *A History of
    Russian Railways* (London, 1964) pp. 91-8 and R. Fremdling,
    'Railroads and German Economic Growth: A Leading Sector
    Analysis', *Journal of Economic History*, XXXVII (1977)
    pp. 587-8.
46. F. Caron, 'French Railroad Investment, 1850-1914' in
    R. Cameron (ed), *Essays in French Economic History*
    (Homewood, 1970) pp. 315-40; R. Fogel, 'Railroads as an
    Analogy to the Space Effort', in P. Temin (ed), *New
    Economic History* (London, 1973) pp. 238-42; Fenoaltea,
    'Railroads and Italian Industrial Growth', p. 336 but
    see his amended estimates, pp. 64-5. R. Tilly, 'Capital
    Formation in Germany in the Nineteenth Century' in
    P. Mathias and M. Postan (eds), *The Cambridge Economic
    History of Europe*, vol. VII (Cambridge, 1978) pp. 414-18.
47. See pp. 67, 158-9; V. K. Yatsunsky, 'The Industrial
    Revolution in Russia', in W. Blackwell (ed), *Russian
    Economic Development* (New York, 1974) p. 127, and J. Nadal,
    'Spain, 1830-1914', in C. Cipolla (ed), *The Fontana
    Economic History of Europe*, vol. 4(2) (London, 1973)
    pp. 596-9.
48. See pp. 39, 123, 127, 130 and F. Crouzet, 'Essor declin
    et Renaissance de l'industrie Française des locomotives,
    1838-1914', *Revue d'Histoire Economique et Sociale*, 55
    (1977), pp. 121-52.
49. Nadal, 'Spain', pp. 596-9 and 551-2; F. J. Coppa, 'The
    Italian Tariff and the Conflict Between Agriculture and
    Industry. The Commercial Policy of Liberal Italy, 1860-
    1922', *Journal of Economic History*, XXIV (1964) pp. 742-6;
    L. Cafagna, 'The Industrial Revolution in Italy, 1830-1914',
    in C. Cipolla (ed), *Fontana Economic History of Europe*,
    vol. 4(1) (London, 1973) pp. 286-92; M. Falkus, *The Indus-
    trialization of Russia, 1700-1914* (London, 1972) pp. 56-7.
50. Crouzet, 'Essor declin et renaissance', pp. 121-52; Caron,
    Economic History of Modern France, pp. 155-9 and see pp.
    123-30 and 209-12.
51. O. Crisp, 'Labour and Industrialization in Russia', in
    P. Mathias and M. Postan (eds), *Cambridge Economic History
    of Europe*, vol. VII(2) (Cambridge, 1978).

52. See p. 64 and B. Mitchell, 'Statistical Appendix, T.4 to C. Cipolla (ed), *Fontana Economic History of Europe*, vol. 4(2) (London, 1973).
53. See p. 57.
54. See pp. 123–4.
55. Fenoaltea, 'Railroads and Italian Industry Growth', and see p. 72 and Williamson, *Late Nineteenth Century American Development*, ch. 9.
56. Hawke, *Railways and Economic Growth*, p. 376 and Fishlow, pp. 103–16.
57. See pp. 34–5 and Fenoaltea, 'Railroads and Italian Industrial Growth', pp. 338–9.
58. See p. 123 and Fremdling, *Eisenbahnen und Deutsches Wirtschaftswachstum*, pp. 151–8.
59. Williamson, 'Greasing the Wheels', pp. 203–9; Fishlow, pp. 117–18 and pp. 302–3.
60. See pp. 164 and 205 and Fenoaltea, 'Railroads and Italian Industrial Growth', p. 327, and O. Crisp, *Studies in the Russian Economy Before 1914* (London, 1976) chs. 7 and 8.
61. See pp. 28–9 and M. C. Reed, *Investment in Railways in Britain, 1820–40* (London, 1975) and G. R. Hawke and M. C. Reed, 'Railway Capital in the United Kingdom in the Nineteenth Century', *Economic History Review*, XXII (1969) pp. 269–86.
62. But see R. Dumke, 'The Political Economy of German Unification: Tariffs Trade and Politics in the Zollverein Era' (unpublished PhD, University of Wisconsin, 1976).
63. Bairoch, *Commerce extérieur*, pp. 81–7.
64. See pp. 165–66.
65. V. Zamagni, 'Railways Building and Market Integration in Post Unification Italy', unpublished paper delivered to RENFE Conference on *Railways and Market Integration* (Madrid, 1980).
66. See pp. 95–6.
67. See p.206.
68. J. Metzer, 'Railroad Development and Market Integration: The Case of Tsarist Russia', *Journal of Economic History*, XXXIV (1974) pp. 529–49 and W. Kelly, 'Railroad Development and Market Integration in Tsarist Russia: Evidence on Oil Products and Grain', *Journal of Economic History*, XXXVI (1976) pp. 908–16.
69. C. White, 'The Concept of Social Savings in Theory and Practice', *Economic History Review*, XXIX (1976) pp. 88–9.
70. See p. 137.
71. See pp. 45–6.
72. Zamagni, 'Railways Building and Market Integration', and

72. *Continued*
V. Zamagni, *Industrializzazione Esquilibri Regionali in Italia* (1978), chs. 2 and 5.
73. See pp. 148–9, 164–6.

2 France

FRANÇOIS CARON

This chapter will consider interconnections between railways
and economic growth in France: first, relations between railways and the formation of a market for investible funds;
second, connections between railway investment and cycles in
economic growth; third, railway demand and industrial
development; fourth, the evolution of productivity on the
railway network and finally social savings and the widening
of the market.

1.   RAILWAYS AND THE FORMATION OF A CAPITAL MARKET

Did the demands of railways for capital promote the formation
of a stock market? To answer this question, it will be necessary to analyse how railway building was financed.
  During the first stages of construction the situation in
France was very different from England, where commercial and
industrial capital generated funds for railway development.
Thus the Stockton and Darlington and Manchester and Liverpool
lines were promoted by local businessmen who wished to develop
markets for their products and to break the monopoly exercised
by canals. Although there are comparable examples of manufacturers and traders promoting lines (e.g. Lyon–Saint Etienne
line and first Alsatian railways) these examples are rare and
rather unimportant.
  In France, where costs of construction per track kilometre
were higher than Britain, industrial capital played a less
important role and the state was more careful to maintain its
control over the new transport system which was considered to
be an integral part of the public domain. As the Chairman of
the Committee on railways, 1842, observed: 'our fortunes are
moderate, our external trade doesn't represent for us the
admirable resources of Great Britain, which has provided her
with internal improvements', but he warned, 'the financial
resources of the state aren't without limit' (1). Furthermore
the engineers at 'Ponts et Chaussées', who formulated and
implemented policy in the public works sector, were
absolutely opposed to the idea of private ownership of rail-

ways. But in 1838 Parliament voted against a project that
provided for the construction by the state of trunk lines
emanating from Paris. Thus there was only one solution - the
concession and the system of concessions, already used for
small lines before 1838, became general.

Before 1847 the state auctioned a concession to operate a
given line to the contractor who offered to bring the railway
into operation in the shortest period of time. The contractors
frequently formed a syndicate and shared the capital of the
company amongst themselves. For example, Compagnie du Chemin
de Fer du Nord was founded as a result of an agreement, concluded in July 1845, between Rothschilds, Barings, Hottinguer,
Laffitte, Blount and other Parisian bankers. In the 1840s and
1850s only the great Parisian banking houses had the financial
resources to bid for concessions. Under the July Monarchy the
engineers at Ponts et Chaussées reduced the duration of concessions as far as they could. During the 1840s 4000 kilometres
of track were the subject of concessions and the average
duration of a concession was 46 years. While the fall of Louis
Philippe was not considered as a catastrophe by the bankers
they had to wait until 1852 to obtain an extension of the concessionary period to 99 years.

During the 1850s 'les six grands commandements industriels',
were formed (2). The conventions of 1856 and 1859 allowed them
'space and time' to build new lines, in exchange for a
monopoly of a given region of France (3). Thus the state con-
ceded 'new lines' to the companies of Nord, Est, Ouest, Paris-
Orleans, PLM and Midi and guaranteed the interest payable on
the bonds they issued to finance new lines. During the 1860s
the monopolies were fought by new companies who seized the
opportunities afforded by the law of 1865 on local lines. But
the big companies defended themselves and in the 1870s many
local companies failed or were bought out by the big companies.
The new convention of 1883 ended the lack of order created by
a system of lines built not only by small local companies but
by the state, which began to build lines after 1879 under the
Freycinet Plan. From 1883 all lines were integrated into the
six 'big networks'. But between the Western and the 'Paris-
Orleans' territories the state created a new network 'L'Etat'.
All private railway companies in France enjoyed the 'garantie
d'interet' on their shares and bonds. Although once a pres-
cribed level of profits had been distributed to shareholders
the residual was shared with the state.

This complex legal history explains why French railways were
financed mainly by bonds. In England 25 per cent of railway
capital in 1880 consisted of bonds but in France the comparable percentage was 80 per cent. The companies issued bonds
and shares in denominations small enough to be bought by small

investors. They even sold the bonds at stations and reached a
large public of small savers. Their securities were
absolutely safe because of the 'garantie d'interet' by the
state and the main lines paid high returns. Railway
securities became 'des placements de pére de famille' and
immediately took an important place in the portfolios of most
savers. Small investors became accustomed to buying assets
other than government securities and in this process railways
made a bridge between rents and industrial equities. The
weight of railway assets in the wealth of France is easily
illustrated. For example in 1898 the nominal value of railway
shares came to 38 per cent of the total nominal share capital
of all Societes par actions while railway bonds amounted to
72 per cent of the nominal value of all bonds issued by these
joint stock companies (4). In 1900 the shares of the major
networks amounted to 37 per cent of the nominal capital and
42 per cent of the 'valeur boursière' (market value) of all
shares quoted on the Paris Stock Exchange (5). But by 1913
these proportions had fallen to 23 per cent and 18 per cent
respectively. Bonds issued by the big companies came to 44
per cent of all bonds issued on the French market between 1892
and 1900 and 35 per cent between 1901-13 (6).

Finally, in the portfolios of Bordeaux investors which were
studied by Guillaume in 1911, 20 per cent of their assets took
the form of railway securities (6.5 per cent in shares and
13.5 per cent in bonds) (7). Rente amounted to 18 per cent.
Unfortunately comparisons cannot be made with the structure
and market for paper assets in the pre-railway era. But there
can be no doubt that the massive issues of railway securities
over the second half of the nineteenth century (which peaked
in the 1890s) dominated and widened the market for paper
securities in France right up to 1900.

2.   RAILWAY INVESTMENT AND CYCLES IN ECONOMIC GROWTH

To explore this problem the first step is to delineate cycles
of capital formation in railways. Tables 2.1 and 2.2 and
Figure 2.1 have been constructed from statistics published by
the Ministry of Public Works and by the major companies.
Indices of investment have been constructed from figures in
current values, deflated to constant values by a price index
for capital goods purchased by railways. The index refers to
gross investment and is the sum of new and maintenance expenditures on trunk and local lines. The base and reference years
are 1908-12.

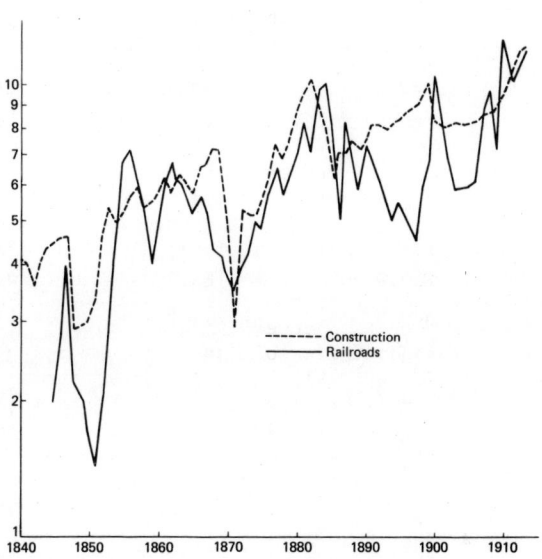

Source: F. Caron, 'Investment Strategy in France', in
H. Daems and H. Van der Wee (eds), *The Rise of
Managerial Capitalism* (Leuven, 1974).

Figure 2.1: *Indices of gross capital formation*

Table 2.1: *Investment expenditures on French railways*

	(Millions current francs average per year)		Index number in constant prices (100 = 1908–12)
	Gross investment	Net investment	
1845–49	163.0	155.3	26.1
1850–54	180.8	161.8	27.9
1855–59	406.4	354.9	58.6
1860–64	396.7	321.7	59.9
1865–69	317.8	225.7	49.6
1870–74	290.9	183.2	41.2
1875–79	380.8	224.9	59.1
1880–84	578.1	396.0	85.7
1885–89	423.2	275.3	70.1
1890–94	401.1	241.0	61.6
1895–99	375.7	200.0	55.3
1900–04	531.9	342.0	75.6
1905–09	562.0	341.0	75.9
1909–13	693.7	476.6	112.6

Sources: Caron, 'Investment Strategy in France'. The deflator can be found in the archives of La Compagnie du Chemin de Fer du Nord and is referred to in F. Caron, *Histoire de l'exploitation d'un grand reseau: la compagnie du Chemin de Fer du Nord des origines a la nationalisation* (Paris, 1973) pp. 99, 305–6.

Table 2.2: *Indices of investment in railways*

	1	2		1	2		1	2
1828		23	1860	47.3	365	1890	73.6	349
1829		0	1861	59.5	671	1891	67.5	887
1830		15	1862	68.6	981	1892	61.5	716
1831		0	1863	64.6	946	1893	55.9	427
1832		21	1864	60.1	1010	1894	49.8	663
1833		23						
1834		67	1865	52.7	515	1895	54.1	88
1835		0	1866	57.3	950	1896	49.5	554
1836		0	1867	53.0	1177	1897	45.2	250
1837		19	1868	42.8	535	1898	59.9	282
1838		15	1869	42.2	713	1899	68.2	353
1839		65						
1840		187	1870	38.1	502	1900	103.1	268
1841		138	1871	35.1	-219	1901	84.9	227
1842		27	1872	40.3	566	1902	67.6	623
1843		229	1873	42.1	731	1903	64.2	104
1844		2	1874	50.7	550	1904	58.6	257
1845	20.5	52	1875	48.1	677	1905	60.3	232
1846	27.8	439	1876	57.4	554	1906	61.5	185
1847	40.2	510	1877	67.3	680	1907	89.0	
1848	22.4	388	1878	58.2	1163	1908	97.6	
1849	20.0	639	1879	64.4	617	1909	71.4	
1850	16.4	151	1880	75.7	871	1910	125.9	
1851	14.6	544	1881	82.3	1462	1911	102.3	
1852	21.2	324	1882	70.9	1065	1912	102.2	
1853	40.3	190	1883	98.9	835	1913	120.2	
1854	47.2	629	1884	100.9	1346			
1855	68.4	886	1885	83.5	1090			
1856	71.8	664	1886	50.7	749			
1857	62.4	1221	1887	83.6	530			
1858	50.1	1261	1888	74.2	882			
1859	40.7	393	1889	58.7	549			

Notes: 1 is the index number of gross investment in constant prices referred to in the text and cited under Figure 2.1. 2 is the length of track in kilometres opened each year (main lines only).

Sources: See Figure 2.1 and Ministère des Travaux Publiques, Statistiques des Chemins de Fer.

Two long swings can obviously be demarcated. The period 1840-84 witnessed a remarkable but irregular increase in investment. Peaks occurred in 1847, 1856 (and 1862) and in 1884. The annual rate of growth was 6.6 per cent between the two first peaks, and 1.3 per cent between the following peaks and 2.5 per cent from 1847 to 1884. The increase in railway investment is a major part of the rise in social overhead capital during this period and the same increase in capital formation occurred in building and for the infrastructure in general. After the 1880s railway investment declined but rose steadily again after 1906. Peaks emerged in 1884, 1900 and 1913 (see Table 2.2).

The observed long-term evolution is due to two factors: first came the opening of new lines followed by a secondary round of expenditures generated by the growth of traffic along existing lines and including the expenditures for engines, rolling stock and stations. The kilometres of track opened each year between 1854-67 amounted to an annual average of 833 kilometres. During the 1840s and 1850s new trunk lines were highly profitable but after 1860 the additional lines were secondary lines and not so profitable because they served less rich and populous districts. From 1868-79 the railway network expanded at a rate of 587 km per annum. From 1880-5 the rate jumped to 1128 km during the Freycinet Plan, when railway investment was financed by government loans. But the financial crisis of 1882 forced the state to reduce the number of kilometres of track laid down year by year. From 1886 to 1892 the annual average fell to 666 km and from 1893 to 1906 to 322 km.

The average annual rate of growth of traffic was about 4 per cent between 1851 and 1913. This growth was rather regular with one slowdown between 1882 and 1904. Thus from 1867 to 1882 the average rate of growth was 3.94 per cent. From 1882 to 1902 it fell to 3.17 per cent, but it rose to 4.33 per cent from 1905 to 1913. The slowdown of traffic coincided with a deceleration of capital expenditures on railways, while the period before the First World War (1906-13) witnessed an acceleration both of traffic and the growth of investment. Traffic flows appear to have exercised a disproportionate effect on investment and a slight slowdown of traffic led almost to a stagnation of capital expenditure on railways.

Furthermore, technical progress explains the decline of expenditures on rolling stock, engines and stations during periods when traffic continued to grow. Technical progress was capital saving. For instance the principal virtue of steel for the railway companies was to prolong the durability of rails. Managers of the 'Compagnie du Chemin de Fer du Nord' defined their organisation as 'système d'exploitation intensive'. Their goals were to reduce investment expenditures by intensive utilisation of plant, equipment and labour. During the 1870s several innovations were perfected (steel rails, electrical signals, lighting, gravity shunting operations, continuous brakes) which were capital saving and reduced capital-output ratios during the following decades. From the early 1880s French railways suffered from excess capacity due to the high level of investment during the 1870s and at the beginning of the 1880s, and the capital saving innovations embodied in this spate of capital formation. The figures presented in Table 2.3 for the Compagnie du Chemin de Fer du Nord illustrate these short cycles in railway investment very well.

The figures in Table 2.3 are, in fact, incremental capital output ratios expressed in current francs. They exhibit a decline until the beginning of the first decade of the twentieth century, with an upswing during the years 1899-1903. But in spite of the rise in receipts after 1905 they again increased in 1909-13. The policy of economising capital was very efficient up to this time and became less efficient thereafter because it had proceeded too far and depreciated capital had to be replaced.

Figure 2.1 shows that France (like the United States) experienced a 'transport building cycle' with peaks in 1847, 1856, 1862, 1884, 1900 and 1913 and troughs in 1851, 1869, 1897 and 1904 (see Figure 2.1 and Table 2.2) (8). Each of these cycles was the outcome of a complex historical process. From 1851-69 the cycle was dominated by the building of new main lines and a first group of secondary lines (the 'new lines' of the 1859 convention). The 1869-97 period was dominated by the construction of the lines of the Freycinet Plan (1879-84) and by the rise of supplementary expenditure on the old lines generated by the growth of traffic. The third cycle is much shorter. It is dominated by a boom in the construction of secondary lines and tramways around 1900 and by a rise in supplementary expenditures while the rapid increase of investment between 1907-13 is due to an exceptional increase in traffic, in connection with the industrial boom of these years.

Fluctuations of investment by railway companies contributed to the amplitude of business cycles in the nineteenth century, particularly to the depression of 1847-52 and the boom of 1879-83. These fluctuations were closely connected with the rhythm of railway construction, changes in the profitability of operating different lines, the intensity of traffic flows and the policies of government. Managers of railway companies were often accused of placing their orders in ways which followed the business cycle. In the first decade of the twentieth century, government officials recommended that railway companies regularised their investment expenditures in order to reduce the intensity of the building cycle. But the companies were reluctant to comply because implicitly this policy compelled them to fore-

Table 2.3: *Supplementary investment expenditures per million of incremental receipts for Compagnie du Chemin de Fer du Nord (in millions of francs at current prices)*

	Net investment expenditures					
	1884-8	1889-90	1894-9	1899-1903	1904-8	1909-13
Supplementary works	6.580	2.298	1.670	3.074	1.856	1.677
Engines and rolling stock	5.971	1.996	1.447	3.168	1.856	2.426
Total expenditures including new lines	24.876	5.903	4.354	6.912	3.846	4.493
Gross investment (net investment plus maintenance expenditures)						
Including new lines	53.768	12.877	10.361	15.604	9.031	8.226
Excluding new lines	41.490	11.224	9.126	14.917	8.129	7.820

Note: Investment expenditures in current prices were divided by receipts in current prices and averaged over 5-year intervals.

Source: **Caron,** *Histoire de l'exploitation d'un grand reseau,* pp. 343-4.

cast their orders over the medium run and to reveal their
needs in advance to their suppliers.

Two conclusions: during the period 1840-84 the engine of
growth in France (and in Germany) seems to be the investment
in the 'secteurs de base', and specifically in railways and
building; railways played a primary role in both the long-
and short-term cycles in the French economy. Gross investment
expenditures by railways (mainly on tracks and rails)
amounted to 10 per cent of gross domestic capital formation
in France between 1845-54 to 14.4 per cent between 1855-64;
to 11 per cent, 1865-74; and 15 per cent from 1875-84.
Investment in infrastructure (including railways) averaged
about 70 per cent of gross domestic capital formation. But
from 1885-1913 the shares of both infrastructure and railways
in capital formation declined to 56 per cent and 11 per cent
respectively.

3. <u>RAILWAY DEMAND AND INDUSTRIAL DEVELOPMENT</u>

The third connection between railways and economic growth is
involved with railway purchases of industrial commodities and
the influence of such 'feedbacks' on technical progress.
During the years 1830-80, total expenditure on public works
for the entire transport sector (railways, canals, roads,
ports) represented between 6 per cent and 9 per cent of the
Markovitch estimates for the value of industrial and artisanal
output, and railway expenditures came to between 3 per cent
and 5 per cent. But as Table 2.4 shows, the value of railway
orders represented higher proportions of the product of
particular industries (e.g. 12 per cent to 18 per cent of iron
and steel output) and their importance peaked during the years
1855-64. We must also point out that railways were more important than any other single customer. They were reliable buyers
and placed orders for several years ahead. Thus from the 1860s
onwards more and more contracts were concluded for periods of
five years. Even if these 'long term' orders did not represent
a very high percentage of the factory output they imparted an
element of stability to several industries.

Furthermore, railway orders challenged traditional production techniques. Railway companies were not only particular
customers but they imposed stringent conditions on the firms
they dealt with. Examples are numerous: the perfecting of iron
processes in the 1840s and 1850s, the diffusion of the
Bessemer process in the 1860s and the Gilchrist-Thomas process
in the 1870s were direct consequences of pressure exerted by
the railways on their suppliers. The need for more durable and
stronger metals for rails was behind improvements in

Table 2.4: *The value of public works expenditures (for transport) compared to total industrial product*

	Railways + roads + canals + ports (gross expenditures) (%)	Railway gross expenditures (%)	Railway net expenditures (%)
1835–44	4.3	0.56	0.54
1845–54	6.0	2.71	2.52
1855–64	8.1	5.50	4.80
1865–74	6.0	3.85	2.86
1875–84	9.2	5.27	3.72

Notes: Gross investment = total investment.
Net investment = gross minus maintenance and replacement expenditures.

Table 2.5: *Railway orders compared to total production for selected industries*

	1845–54 (%)	1855–64 (%)	1865–74 (%)	1875–84 (%)
Iron and steel	13.1	18.3	11.7	13.6
Transformation of metals	5.5	7.6	4.1	5.3
Building materials	18.0	15.8	14.8	12.7
Wood	0.9	0.7	0.6	1.0
Building and public works	3.5	5.1	3.3	4.9

Notes: The percentages in Tables 2.4 and 2.5 are expenditures by railways (estimated from data in the archives of Ministère des Travaux Publiques (F.14)) divided by the value of production as estimated by T. J. Markovitch, L'industrie Française de 1789 à 1964', *Cahiers de l'ISEA*, serie AF, no. 6 (1967).

Sources: See Table 2.4.

techniques introduced into the iron and steel industry.
According to the 'Statistiques de l'industrie Minerale' 'rails
constitute a major part (83 per cent in 1879) of output
produced by the new processes' (9). In 1854 Ernest Gouin,
president of the 'Societe des Batignolles' (founded in 1846 in
order to construct locomotives) described the techniques used
to assemble metal bridges that his company had recently
developed. 'Assembly', he observed 'presents no difficulty nor
uncertainty. Parts fit and holes correspond to each other
without any need for adjustment; the result presents such a
rigidity that mathematical predictions are entirely
realised' (10). This technique was the direct outcome of
orders for 5000 tons of iron bridges for the southern network
and that same technique permitted the company to build bridges
throughout the world. Later the company used this technique to
build ships.

Finally, railway companies played a prominent role in
promoting the use of electricity between the 'First' and the
'Second' Industrial Revolutions. Inventions characteristic of
the 'Second' Industrial Revolution (steel, electricity, continuous brakes) are responses to technical problems engendered
by the application of techniques to sectors such as transport
in earlier phases of industrialisation. Innovations resulting
from railways cannot be described (as Fogel suggests) as
'restricted devices'.

Railway companies systematically promoted competition among
firms supplying them with equipment, raw materials and other
inputs. They actively discouraged collusion among their suppliers and if there was but a single supplier, they attempted
to encourage the formation of a rival enterprise. In this
nineteenth-century 'buyers' market' they successfully forced
prices down, but it may also be the case that their purchasing
strategy prevented firms from attaining optimal scale.

While railway construction from 1840-80 did not turn the
French industrial society upside down, it certainly nurtured
several new sectors of industry, made possible some new innovations and reduced the cost of capital formation. But we
must not forget that 40 per cent of total expenditures by
railways up until 1886 were orders for the output of
traditional industries such as building and public works;
although the measured impact of feedbacks to industry may
appear limited, their long-run influence on technological
progress was certainly not unimportant (11). In several
industries the challenge of railways led to technological
change.

4. THE EVOLUTION OF PRODUCTIVITY

Total factor productivity (labour plus capital plus fuel) of
the railways increased at an annual average rate of 2.06 per
cent between 1851-73; the most rapid growth occurred before
1855 (see Figure 2.2). The main reasons for this improvement
can be found in the full utilisation of capacity. During this
initial period, in which large sections of the French system
were established, traffic surged and the movement in the
index of total factor productivity reflects, as Hawke noticed
for England, 'the delay between capital investment and the
full utilization of the resulting asset' (12). The same
effect can be observed also for labour. Innovation and technical progress exercised only a moderate influence on
productivity, because (apart from locomotives) railway
technology remained somewhat basic and the operation of the
system continued to be rather labour intensive. The network
was not well adapted to the speed and power of locomotives.
Iron rails were not strong enough to bear heavier trains;
signals were manual and brakes were not able to stop heavy
trains over short distances. The loading of trains was not
adjusted to the traffic system and accidents and congestion
of lines became more and more frequent. In brief there was a
disequilibrium or imbalance in the evolution of different
sectors of railway technology.

The years 1874-86 are marked by a decline in productivity
and coincide with the inauguration of secondary lines. The
efficiency of these lines depended on the effective utilisation of a work force which could not be reduced easily.
Moreover the imbalance between different sectors of the
operating system between 1851-73 led to serious difficulties
and stimulated a series of remarkable innovations: steel
rails, two axle traction, compound locomotives, electric
signals, continuous brakes. Their diffusion, which was
accompanied by a spate of improvements at the operating stage,
continued right up to 1914. But the essential mutation
occurred from 1874-86.

The diffusion of these innovations explains the subsequent
growth of productivity at an annual average rate of 1.85 per
cent from 1887-1914. This emanated from a slower increase of
labour input between 1883 and 1904, and the growth of capital
input was also less rapid than the growth of output, despite
the fact that the new techniques permitted a large replacement of labour by capital. Furthermore, a large part of these
capital expenditures were concentrated on the construction of
secondary lines and some of these lines were underutilised.
The annual average growth of labour productivity reached

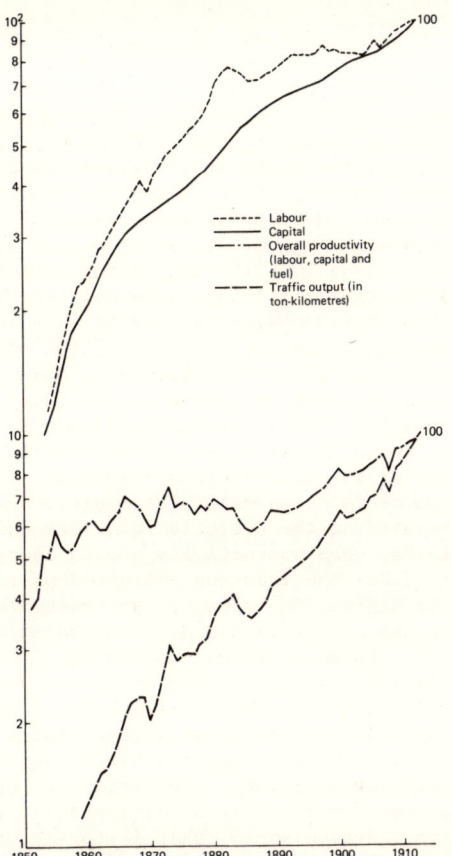

Source: Author's calculations in F. Caron, 'Recherches sur le capital des voies de communication en France', CNRS Colloques Internationaux, L'industrialisation en Europe au XIXème siècle (Paris, 1972).

Note: The index of overall productivity is the ratio, index of traffic output: index of total factor input (capital - labour - fuel). Each input was weighted by its share to total cost.

Figure 2.2: *Productivity indices*

2.75 per cent between 1886 and 1904, that of capital 1.4 per
cent. But after 1904 both inputs increased at rates closer to
the rate of growth of output which was a disquieting sign for
French railways.

For the Compagnie du Chemin de Fer du Nord, costs fell
rapidly until 1867, thanks to the 'utilisation effect' (see
Figure 2.3). They went up after 1856 until the end of 1870s
and then dropped continuously between the 1880s and 1905 in
response to technical innovation and a decline in the price
of supplies. From 1908 to 1913 costs rose again because the
increase in productivity did not compensate for increases in
wages and prices. Railway workers refused to go on working
intensively and the strike of 1910 (the first major strike
in French railway history) reflected their change of attitude.
'The organisation', wrote the director of state control in
1911, was like a fine steel spring in the mechanism. A moment
came when the limits of electricity had been surpassed. As the
equilibrium was disturbed, the mechanism disrupted' (13).

The evolution of rates (average costs per ton-kilometre)
was closely related to the evolution of costs and productivity.
Thus in the 1870s, when productivity growth decreased, rates
remained steady. But the long-run evolution of railway rates
is difficult to explain in terms of the evolution of costs
simply because the companies did not command accurate data on
operating costs. Students of the problem should distinguish
between the company policy, government policy and the pressure
of circumstances. The companies followed the prescriptions of
Jules Dupuit and fixed rates to maximise returns (14). This
implied a plurality of rates adapted to the different marginal
utilities of railway users. But the state soon prevented
companies from pushing a policy of differential rates too far.
And the 'traites particuliers', that is to say, the contracts
made with one consignor for a guaranteed dispatch of goods,
were forbidden in the 1860s. Nevertheless, in contrast to
Britain, the French companies created a plurality of 'tarifs
speciaux' in order to adapt rates to the diversity of demand
while the government brought pressure on companies to bring
about greater uniformity and cuts in charges per ton-kilometre.

5. THE DIRECT AND INDIRECT IMPACT OF RAILWAYS

In 1884 Albert Sartaux (Ingenieur des Ponts et Chaussées and
future Managing Director of Compagnie du Chemin de Fer du
Nord) marvelled that 'les chemins de fer ont donné une valeur
à des choses qui n'en avaient pas, ont crée la richesse
mobiliere, presque inconnue il y a quarante ans; ils ont doublé
la richesse publique; ils ont rendu à tous la vie moins penible

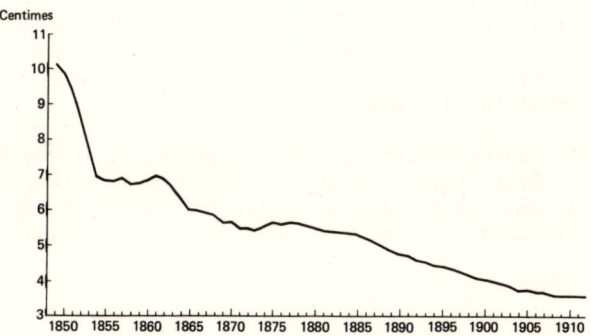

Source: F. Caron, *Histoire de l'exploitation d'un grand reseau* (Paris, 1973) p.588.

Figure 2.3: *Costs of freight per ton-kilometre charged by Compagnie du Chemin de Fer du Nord, 1849-1912 (three year averages).*

et l'ont allongée; ils ont empêché le retour des
disettes' (15). It will be instructive to juxtapose his
eulogy against a calculation of the social savings from
railways.

Social savings which compare the cost of sending freight by
rail with the hypothetical cost of despatching it by alternative forms of transportation were calculated by French
engineers preparing the Freycinet Plan in the 1870s. For 1872
my provisional calculation is as follows:

(a) *for passengers:* the number of passenger kilometres supplied was 4.27 billions; the percentage of third-class
kilometres can be estimated as 60 per cent of the total. The
costs of travel by alternative modes of transport might be:

```
  2.54 billions x 12 centimes per
                    kilometre   = 304.8 million francs

+ 1.73 billions x 15 centimes per
                    kilometre   = 294.1 million francs
  ----                            -----
  4.27 billions                   598.3 million francs

- Passenger receipts              227   million francs
                                  -----
           Social savings = 371.9 million francs,
                                  roughly 1.67 per
                                  cent of national
                                  income.
```

(b) *for goods:* railways supplied 7.58 billion ton-kilometres
of output and received 531 million francs in payment. The
percentage of lines in competition with canals was about 30
per cent, that is to say 2.27 billion ton-kilometres.
Hypothetical 'non-rail' costs were:

```
  for canals: 2.27 x 2.4 centimes per ton-
                          kilometre    =   54.48 million francs

  for roads:  5.31 x 30  centimes per ton-
                          kilometre    = 1593.00 million francs
                                         -------
                                       = 1647.48 million francs

                                       -  531.00 million francs
                                         -------
           Social savings              = 1316.48 or 5.8 per cent
                                                  of national
                                                  income.
```

   Social savings on freight and passenger traffic were about
7 per cent of national income for 1872. Railways also made
possible the transformation of quantities of circulating
capital into fixed capital, through a reduction in the cost of
inventories which are not included in my preliminary estimates
of social savings. In addition, railways widened the market for
passengers and goods. For example the rate for passenger travel
around 1840 (before the advent of railways) was between 11 and
16 centimes per kilometre. With the advent of railways it fell
to 7 centimes in the 1840s, 4.7 centimes in 1883 and to 3.4
centimes in 1913. In the early 1890s popular travel became
widespread. Sharp reductions in the costs of freight (see
Figure 2.3) occurred in the initial phases of operation.
Express transport by road cost 40 or 45 centimes per ton-
kilometre before the 1840s and the normal transport rate was
between 23 and 28 centimes. By the end of the 1870s normal
transport by rail came to a mere 6 centimes and the decline
continued from the 1880s to 1908 when the ton-kilometre rate by
rail was about 4 centimes.
   It is necessary to distinguish several stages in order to
analyse the economic effects made possible by these sharp
reductions in the costs of moving freight around France.
Before the advent of railways the cost of transport was so
high that it precluded certain kinds of production in given
regions and areas of the country. The stage which followed the
opening of new lines and the sharp decline in freight rates
witnessed new patterns of localisation. In a book published in
1867 Jacqmin (Director of Compagnie du Chemin de Fer de l'Est)
described how the railway 'had eliminated a factor of social
unrest which existed in a large number of villages in France,
and which may still exist in a few cantons: I mean the total
lack of work (16). The relocation of productive activity came
about in three ways: a fall in the costs of intermediate
products in line with the decrease in the transport costs
(especially for bulky goods such as coal and iron); the decline
of the prices of final products for the same reason and which
gave it access to new markets; and finally production costs
went down with the adoption of new techniques and economies of
scale due to the widening of markets. Each of these effects
can be illustrated for both agricultural and industrial
products. The development of Languedoc vineyards, stock raising
in Thierache and Charentes, fishing off Boulogne, coal, sugar,
oil, iron and steel in the north and east of France and
mechanical and food processing industries in and around Paris
were developed through the enlargement of old plants and the
foundation of new enterprises. During this second stage of
development (that is to say in the 1840s and 1850s – and for
some regions and some products, the 1860s) the new networks and

patterns of location did not damage the traditional activities
of other regions. The beneficial effects of trade creation
were so strong that the competition between different centres
of production did not really matter because new markets (such
as Paris) opened up by railways were large and dynamic.

But little by little from the 1860s the continued decrease
in freight rates and the more general widening of markets had
more deleterious effects on some regions of France. When the
market became national, old fairs (such as Arras for wheat)
declined. Some regions experienced 'de-industrialisation' as
railways carried cheaper substitutes throughout France. Before
the 1860s French growth proceeded smoothly and was dualist in
character in the sense that during these decades labour-
intensive industries using traditional techniques and capital-
intensive industries using new technologies grew in a symbiotic
relationship. After the 1860s growth was unequal and favoured
regions able to develop capital-intensive industries. But this
'confrontation' between producers was a factor in the growth
of the nation because it promoted the development and location
of production processes at points of optimal location.
Consequently it made possible the very rapid decreases of
prices which were experienced in the last quarter of the
nineteenth century. It explains the rise of urban standards of
living over this period, which then fed back to and made
possible a further acceleration of growth. In brief, it was
through the reallocation of resources that railways (like free
trade) had beneficial effects on growth.

6. CONCLUSIONS

To sum up: first I argued that railways assisted the growth of
the French economy by widening and improving the market for
capital. Next I observed that long-term growth was accompanied
by cycles and fluctuations in the level of economic activity
and that investment in railways raised the rate of investment
but accentuated economic fluctuations over the second half of
the nineteenth century.

Thirdly, there can be no doubt that the gains from the growin
productivity of railways were transmitted to other sectors of
the economy in the form of lower prices. The French system of
concessions (as defined by the law of 1883) prompted the
companies to lower rates rather than share their profits with
the state. Lower prices widened markets and stimulated industrial development. In this process some regions of France
benefited more than others because they possessed the comparative advantages to exploit the opportunities offered by
railways.

Finally, while the social savings on French railways were at a level which compares with their direct impact upon other European economies (except Spain), they seemed to be a more important stimulus to the industrialisation of France than they were in England. This stimulus was particularly important through feedback effects to iron and steel and building materials in the period 1855-74. But the spinoffs to innovation and competition and the forward linkages through the widening of markets were even more significant.

NOTES AND REFERENCES

1. A. Picard, *Les chemins de fer français*, vol. 1 (Paris, 1884) p. 252.
2. L. Girard, *La politique des travaux publiques sous le second Empire* (Paris, 1952) p. 181.
3. Ibid., p. 185.
4. Calculated from figures in 'Les sociétés françaises d'après leur objet', *Bulletin de statistique et de legislation comparée, 5ème année* (1901) pp. 160-99.
5. J. Denuc, 'Dividendes, valeur boursière et taux de capitalisation', *Bulletin de la statistique générale de la France* (1933) pp. 696-767.
6. F. Marnata, *La bourse et le financement des investissements* (Paris, 1973) pp. 61-6.
7. P. Guillaume, 'Les fortunes bordelaises', in A. Daumard, *Les fortunes françaises au XIXème siècle* (Paris, 1973) p. 521.
8. W. Isard, 'The Transport Building Cycle', *Review of Economics and Statistics* (1942).
9. Ministère des Travaux Publiques, *Statistique de l'industrie minérale,* Année 1879 (Paris, 1881) p. 56.
10. Archives de la société des Batignolles. Archives nationales (89 AQ, 151 Mi), Assemblée des commanditaires de janvier 1855.
11. F. Caron, 'Recherches sur le capital des voies de communication en France', CNRS Colloques Internationaux, 'L'industrialisation en Europe au XIXème siècle' (Paris, 1972) p. 243.
12. G. R. Hawke, *Railways and Economic Growth in England and Wales, 1840-1870* (Oxford, 1970), pp. 306-7.
13. Documents Parlementaires (Senat, 1911) no. 148, p. 9.
14. J. Dupuit, 'De l'influence des péages sur l'utilité des voies de communication', *Annales des Ponts et Chaussees,* Memoires et Documents, serie 2, vol. 17 (1849).
15. A. Sartiaux, 'Les chemins de fer'. Conference faite à Lille le 24 janvier 1884 (Lille, 1884) p.10.

16.   F. Jacqmin, *De l'exploitation des chemins de fer,* vol. 2
      (Paris, 1868) p. 247.

3 Italy

STEFANO FENOALTEA

1. INTRODUCTION

This survey examines the contribution of the railway to the
modernisation of the nineteenth-century Italian economy, with
particular attention to industrial growth.

The growth of Italy's railways was heavily influenced by
political events. Only the first regional networks, notably
in Tuscany and Piedmont, were built in the 1840s and 1850s.
The achievement of political unity in 1861 led to a first
railway boom, mainly in the construction of national trunk
lines. The transfer of parliamentary power from the Right to
the Left led to a sharp increase in public spending and a
second railway boom, mainly in the construction of secondary
lines, in the 1880s and early 1890s. A third railway boom,
mainly in reconstruction and improvement, followed the railways' nationalisation in 1905.

Industrial production, in turn, appears to have grown slowly
in the 1860s and 1870s, and relatively rapidly in the 1880s.
The 1890s were marked by recession and recovery, and the early
1900s by a second decade of rapid growth. That experience has
been interpreted as a sequence of stages of growth induced by
the loosening of supply-side constraints on industrial production; but the evidence suggests that the supply side was
generally permissive, as resources flowed readily into and out
of Italy, and that the primary source of the fluctuations in
industrial production was a cycle in the demand for durables.

An examination of the railways' consumption of industrial
products suggests that the market for modern industry created
by the mature railway system was altogether more significant
than that created by railway expansion. One reason is the shift
in the composition of railway investment: initial construction
was mostly a matter of traditional pick-and-shovel work, while
rails and rolling stock absorbed a far greater share of the
subsequent expenditure for reconstruction and improvement. The
other reason is the growth of railway maintenance, especially
of rolling stock. On a value-added basis, the maintenance of
these vehicles was as important as their initial fabrication;
and, unlike the latter, it was quite immune from foreign

competition.

The direct impact of railway investment on the composition of production thus appears to have been small, and to industry's advantage only from about 1900. The indirect impact may have been more significant, since railway investment could induce international resource flows and thus alter even the level of aggregate production. Preliminary explorations with a very simple model suggest that railway investment may have somewhat amplified the cycle in industrial production; more significantly it may have induced the tariffs on semi-finished metal that locked the domestic engineering industry into the small and fluctuating domestic market. These induced effects cannot be established empirically, however, without far more information than is currently available.

As a provider of transportation, the railway appears to have improved the Upper Po Valley's access to the sea, but to have done relatively little to unify the domestic market. This limited impact seems due not only to the relatively high operating costs induced primarily by the rugged terrain, but also to implicit taxes that kept railway rates well above marginal costs. The state thus discouraged the utilisation of the railway network even as it encouraged its extension; while this policy was certainly curious, the constraints on public revenues, the military value of the railways, and the electoral advantages of public works projects all suggest that it may not have been as irrational as it seems.

The net benefits provided by the railways may be assessed by comparing the capital costs incurred by their construction to the producers' and consumers' surplus generated by their use. Sample estimates for the entire network suggest that the benefits of the entire system were at most just equal to its costs. Disaggregated estimates suggest that the major Po Valley lines yielded significant net benefits, while the other major lines incurred significant net costs. The large system of minor lines also incurred net costs, but on a much reduced scale, as a majority at least of these lines appear to have paid for themselves. The large-scale construction of minor lines undertaken by the Left in the 1880s and 1890s thus appears altogether less wasteful, and that of peninsular trunk lines undertaken by the Right in the 1860s and 1870s altogether less useful, than is commonly thought. The most useful lines were those in northern Italy, largely built before the achievement of national unity; and since internal waterways were available from the Lombard lakes to the Adriatic, the most conspicuous net beneficiaries from the construction of those lines were no doubt Piedmont and the neighbouring Ligurian ports.

2. THE GROWTH OF THE RAILWAYS

Italy's railways experienced four main periods of development
before the First World War (1). The first period, from the
opening of the first rail line on Italian soil (Naples-
Portici) in 1839 up to the creation of the Kingdom of Italy
in 1861, saw the establishment of the first local systems. A
mere 500 kilometres were built in the 1840s, including the
early lines around Naples (some 50 kilometres linking royal
residences and military camps), the major Tuscan valley lines
(some 200 kilometres linking Leghorn, Pisa, Siena and
Florence), a good part of the line from Milan to Venice (some
200 kilometres along the northern edge of the Po Valley), and
the first Piedmontese line (some 50 kilometres from Turin to
Asti). A further 1500 kilometres, most of them in northern
Italy, were added through 1860. The Piedmontese network
quickly became the largest in Italy, with 800 kilometres in a
grid linking the major centres of the Upper Po Valley to each
other and to the sea at Genoa. The line from Milan to Venice
was completed in 1857, and subsequently extended to reach
Piedmont in the west, Tyrol in the north and Illyria in the
east, for a total of approximately 600 kilometres. The
Neapolitan and Tuscan systems were extended to some 100 and
300 kilometres, respectively; and in the late 1850s the first
railways appeared in Latium (some 100 kilometres, most of
them from Rome to the sea at Civitavecchia) and in Emilia-
Romagna (some 100 kilometres along the southern edge of the
Po Valley from Piedmont through Parma to Bologna). By the end
of 1860, then, Italy possessed some 2000 kilometres of rail
lines. This was a relatively paltry figure on the Western
European scale, placing Italy well behind Great Britain,
France and Germany, and roughly on a par with Spain (Table 3.1,
cols 1-3); but even this limited mileage was enough to link
Italy's major inland cities, and the future 'industrial
triangle', to the sea.

The second period, from 1861 to 1880, saw the establishment
of a national network. The strategic value of peninsular trunk
lines to the new national state produced a sharp acceleration
in the pace of construction: 4000 kilometres of line were
added in the 1860s, trebling the existing network, and a
further 2500 kilometres were added in the 1870s. The railhead
at Bologna shot forward to and along the Adriatic coast, on
relatively easy ground entirely within the Kingdom; Ancona
was reached in 1861 and Lecce, at the tip of the boot's heel,
in 1866. The further extension of this line along the Ionian
coast was altogether slower, and the entire route to Reggio
Calabria, at the tip of the boot's toe, was not completed

Table 3.1: *Railway development in Western Europe, 1860 and 1913*

| | (1) | 1860 | | 1913 | |
| | | (2) | (3) | (4) | (5) |
	Area (a) (000 sq km)	Population (a) (000,000)	Railways (a) (000 km)	Population (000,000)	Railways (000 km)
Italy	287	25	2	35	18
Great Britain	228	23	15	42	33
France	536	35	9	39	41
Germany	541	37	12	68	64
Spain	504	16	2	20	15

(a) within the borders of 1913.

Source: See the Appendix to this chapter.

until 1875. The central valley route that provided the initial
links between the existing local systems was also quickly
established: Rome and Naples were joined in 1863, Bologna and
Florence in 1864, and Florence and Rome in 1866. The west coast
line branched out of the Tuscan network, growing south to reach
Civitavecchia and Rome in 1867, and north, through the more
difficult Riviera, to reach Genoa and the French border in 1874.
With the further addition of the first Sicilian and Sardinian
lines (from the early 1860s and early 1870s, respectively), and
of a succession of transpeninsular routes (from Rome to the
Adriatic in 1866, from Naples to the Adriatic in 1870, from
Naples to the Ionian in 1880), the Italian trunk system was, by
1880, virtually complete.

The third period, from 1881 to 1895, saw a renewal of very
rapid growth: 6500 kilometres were added in fifteen years,
increasing the total network by over 75 per cent. This expansion
was part of the vast programme of public spending introduced by
the Left shortly after it came to power in 1876; while it
included the southern extension of the west coast trunk route
along the poor and rugged coast from Naples to Reggio Calabria,
its principal focus was the construction of a large number of
minor lines, of essentially local interest.

In the fourth period, from 1896 to 1913, the growth of the
railway network reverted to the slow pace of its early years:
only 2500 kilometres were added in nearly twenty years, for a
total system, on the eve of the First World War, of about 17500
kilometres. On the Western European scale, this total left
Italy much where it had been fifty years earlier: still well
behind Great Britain, France and Germany, and roughly on a par
with Spain (Table 3.1, cols 1, 4-5).

Administratively, Italy's early railways were built and
operated by a relatively large number of concessionaires.
Numerous minor lines were to survive as independent entities;
but the main network underwent three major reorganisations. In
1865, it was entrusted to five regional groups: the Alta Italia,
operating north of Pisa-Florence-Bologna; the Romane,
operating the west coast and valley routes between Florence and
Naples; the Meridionali, operating the Adriatic coast line
south of Bologna and across Southern Italy to Naples; the
Calabro-Sicule (taken over by the Meridionali in 1873) operating
in the lower South; and the Sarde, operating in Sardinia. In
1885, the operation of the main network, by then largely in
public ownership, was entrusted to four companies, including
two major systems on the continent (the Rete Mediterranea in
the west and the Rete Adriatica in the east) and two minor
systems on the islands (the Sicule and the Sarde). In 1905,
finally, the operations of the main network was taken over by
the Ferrovie dello Stato. The latter inherited a system that

had been badly run down in the expectation of that takeover;
as they rebuilt and replaced their track and rolling stock,
they gave rise to a reconstruction boom comparable in
intensity to the construction booms of the 1860s and 1880s.
Italy thus experienced three major waves of railway investment:
two in new construction, induced by political change (the
achievement of national unity, the parliamentary triumph of
the Left); and one in reconstruction, induced by administrative change (the shift from private to public operation).

3. THE GROWTH OF INDUSTRY

In general, it would appear, Italy's industry grew slowly in
the 1860s and 1870s, and rather faster in the 1880s; it fell
back and then recovered in the 1890s, grew rapidly in the first
decade of the present century, and slowed again in the last few
years before the war. The limits and intensities of the growth
spurts differ from index to index (Table 3.2): Gerschenkron's
1955 index (col 1) indicates growth at 5 per cent per annum
from 1881 (its initial year) to 1887, and 7 per cent per annum
from 1896 to 1907; Istat's 1957 index (col 2) indicates growth
at 3 per cent per annum from 1880 to 1887, and 6 per cent per
annum from 1898 to 1908; and my own 1967 revision and extension
of the Gerschenkron index (col 3) indicates growth at 8 per
cent per annum from 1879 to 1887, and 11 per cent per annum
from 1902 to 1908. The specific differences between the Istat
index and the others are hard to trace, since the description
of the calculations underlying that index are very sketchy; the
differences between the Gerschenkron index and my own are
traceable in part to a revision of the underlying series (which
tends to raise the growth rate in the 1880s, and reduce it
around the turn of the century), and in part to a different
weighting scheme (which increases, perhaps to excess, the
volatility of my index). But these differences in dates and
growth rates are ultimately a matter of detail, of little import
given the crude nature and limited scope of all three of these
indices. In the large, the three series agree on the existence
of an earlier, weaker growth spurt in the 1880s, and a later,
stronger one in the early 1900s (2).
    This rough consensus on the facts of Italy's industrial
growth has been accompanied by thorough disagreement as to their
interpretation. In the late 1950s and early 1960s, the most
vigorous polemic was that between Gerschenkron and Romeo (3).
They shared a certain amount of common ground: both understood
Italy's early industrial development as a sequence of stages,
with an 'industrial revolution' or 'big push' early in this
century; and both attributed the acceleration in trend growth
rates to an increase in the supply of industrial capital.

Table 3.2: *Indices of industrial production (1900=100)*

	(1) Gerschenkron (1955)	(2) Istat (1957)	(3) Fenoaltea (1967)
1861		57	37
1862		57	37
1863		57	37
1864		57	37
1865		62	36
1866		62	37
1867		59	39
1868		59	39
1869		65	40
1870		68	42
1871		62	42
1872		65	43
1873		70	45
1874		73	46
1875		73	47
1876		73	47
1877		73	48
1878		70	48
1879		70	48
1880		68	53
1881	54	76	57
1882	57	73	61
1883	64	76	65
1884	63	78	67
1885	65	81	72
1886	67	78	76
1887	73	84	88
1888	74	81	88
1889	72	81	86
1890	72	81	82
1891	67	76	73
1892	64	76	69
1893	70	76	72
1894	72	81	76
1895	73	84	78
1896	75	81	79
1897	78	84	82
1898	86	84	88

Continued

Table 3.2 - *Continued*

	(1) Gerschenkron (1955)	(2) Istat (1957)	(3) Fenoaltea (1967)
1899	92	89	97
1900	100	100	100
1901	104	97	101
1902	109	105	104
1903	114	108	113
1904	117	111	119
1905	126	116	133
1906	139	127	152
1907	152	141	172
1908	163	149	196
1909	168	149	203
1910	169	149	211
1911	174	151	218
1912	182	162	222
1913	184	159	220

Source: See the Appendix to this chapter.

Beyond that, however, their approaches and conclusions were very different. Romeo's interpretation, rooted in a sophisticated critique of the Gramsci thesis, portrayed Italy's development as a relatively ordered process favoured by public policy and largely conditioned by railway construction; Gerschenkron's interpretation, rooted in his model of prerequisite substitution, portrayed Italy's initial industrial growth as a false start, public policy as a brake on development, and railway construction as a missed opportunity.

The so-called Gramsci thesis is the view that Italy's capitalist development was stunted by the failure of the Risorgimento to encompass an agrarian revolution creating peasant properties out of large estates (on the French model, and not of course on the largely opposite English one) (4). To Romeo's mind, a Gramscian land reform would have sharply reduced the supply of savings, and thus the rate of accumulation, by dissipating the agricultural surplus as peasant consumption. As it was, the peasants were forced to save; and the governments of the 1860s and 1870s created the infrastructure necessary for economic growth by taxing the surplus collected by the landlords. From the 1880s, the nation's scarce savings could be, and were, invested in industry, which was then aided by government orders and tariff protection; the industrial spurt of that decade was the lineal antecedent of the subsequent more general one. In this inter-pretation, industrialisation followed railway construction, causally as well as chronologically: because industry required the cheap transportation the national railway network would provide; and because industry was starved of scarce capital while the national railway network was being built. The direct contribution of railway orders for industrial equipment in the 1880s and early 1900s is also recognised, but considered altogether secondary.

The Gerschenkron model of prerequisite substitution links the institutional matrix of accumulation to the relative backwardness of the economy when rapid industrialisation begins (5). In advanced areas (e.g. England), private factories take the lead; in moderately backward areas (e.g. Germany), industrial banks substitute for scarce individual capital and enterprise; and in very backward areas (e.g. Russia), the state substitutes even for the banks. In Italy, the intensive railway construction of the 1880s provided a fine opportunity for a 'big push' in conditions of considerable backwardness; but the government did not rise to the occasion. Tariff policy was particularly inept, as it protected metal-making a (low value-added industry) rather than engineering (a high value-added industry). The growth of those years thus led nowhere; and the 'big push' was delayed fifteen years, until the German-style industrial banks entered Italy (1895) and began to play the entrepreneurial, capital-accumulating role that neither individuals (because of Italy's general backward-ness) nor the government (because of public ineptness) had been able to play. When the 'big push' did occur, moreover, it was slowed by the inappropriate tariff structure and the fact that railway construction was, by then, largely an accomplished fact (though a minor positive role may be attributed to railway reconstruction after 1905). In this interpretation, the railway as provider of cheap transportation is almost invisible; it is dismissed also as an absorber of scarce savings (on the grounds that the Italian capital market was not unified, so that railways and industry did not compete), and survives only as a purchaser of industrial equipment, in a role that could have been major (in the 1880s), but was in fact minor.

By the late 1960s, stages-of-growth models were clearly falling from favour; and my own early work questioned their applicability to the Italian experience as well (6). Italy's major industries, it seems, fall into three basic groups. The first consists of old consumers' goods industries such as milling and textiles; these grew at a relatively steady pace throughout the relevant period, either in step with the domestic market (milling) or with a steadily improving position in the international market (textiles, where decreasing imports gave way to increasing exports). The second group consists of new industries such as electric power generation and sugar extraction. Power generation appeared in Italy in 1883, just months after the world's first plant opened in the United States, and grew lustily ever after; sugar extraction took off with the successful introduction of the sugar beet in the Lower Po Valley in the late 1890s, and conquered the domestic market in the space of a few years. The third group consists of durable goods industries such as engineering and metal-making. Their production movements account for the fluctuations of the aggregate index; and those movements appear to result from an elastic adjustment to the fluctuations in domestic demand, both when it boomed in the 1880s and 1900s and when it collapsed in the 1890s. Metalmaking also achieved some import-substituting growth, thanks largely to increases in tariff protection in 1878 and 1887; but that same tariff increased the materials costs of the engineering industry, and apparently prevented it from breaking out of the small and fluctuating domestic market into sustained export-led growth.

In the circumstances, there are a number of reasons *not* to interpret the acceleration of growth from the 1880s to the 1900s as progress from an inferior stage of growth to a superior one. The first is simply that the acceleration in the aggregate index stems primarily from the secularly declining weight of slow-growing traditional industries, and not from any broadly-based acceleration within individual sectors. The second is of course the essential similarity of the earlier and later growth periods, as both were led largely by the demand for durables. The first upswing was thus inherently as mature as the second; and, since the demand for durables is inherently cyclical, the second was inherently as fragile as the first (7). The third and strongest reason is that there was no apparent change in industry's patterns of behaviour. This is clearly true of the cyclical industries, since their production rose and fell in step with their market opportunities; and it is also true of the new industries, since their appearance is traceable to novel opportunities (created by agricultural and technological development) rather than to improved response to existing opportunities (8).

In particular, there is no evidence of a discontinuous improvement in response traceable either to the completion of the infrastructure or to the importation of German-style industrial banks. On the former point, the essential difficulty with Romeo's interpretation is that the infrastructure was not an indivisible investment that absorbed funds in the 1860s and 1870s, and provided transportation from the 1880s. Rather, it

was a highly divisible investment that yielded transportation
improvements incrementally, with a relatively short average
lag; and the level of investment in railways and other public
works was conspicuously higher in the 1880s and 1900s, when
industry was growing most rapidly, than in the 1860s and 1870s.
The virtual completion of the railway trunk system around 1880
was thus in no way a watershed. On the benefits side, the
supply of transportation expanded continuously as those lines
were built, and any acceleration after 1880 would owe more to
current investments than to long past ones; on the cost side,
the absorption of capital by the infrastructure displays not
a sharp decrease around 1880 but an increase (9).

On the latter point, the essential difficulty with
Gerschenkron's interpretation is a straightforward econometric
result: the growth of the German-style banks is simply not
correlated with a growth in the ability of domestic industry
to capture existing markets. This result is perfectly
compatible with the fact that these banks were heavily involved
with industry, and even with the presumption that they improved
its absolute performance (10). It does mean, however, that there
is no evidence that they improved its *relative* performance; no
evidence, that is to say, that they represented the solution
to a problem (the accumulation of capital in industry) that was
more severe in Italy than in more developed countries; no
evidence, in sum, that they were in any way more important to
Italy's industrial development than any other innovation that
was widely adopted, in banking or anywhere else.

In general, then, Italy's early industrial growth appears to
have been characterised not by a sequence of stages but by a
business cycle; not by supply-side bottlenecks and breakthroughs but by the interaction of a fluctuating demand side
and a permissive supply side. This apparent ease with which
domestic industry could attract the resources needed for
expansion seems explainable, in turn, by two sorts of
considerations. One is simply that domestic industry was a
relatively small part of the domestic economy; in the presence
of functioning resource markets, industry was accordingly
without much influence on resource prices. The second and more
significant argument, which overcomes the limitations of the
first, is that the entire Italian economy was a similarly
small part of a larger international economy, with similarly
functioning resource markets: domestic industry was
accordingly without much influence on the price even of
specialised industrial resources (and these are, of course,
the ones that matter). The lack of supply-side bottlenecks
and breakthroughs thus seems attributable, in the first
instance, to the readiness with which not only goods but
labour, capital, entrepreneurs, technology and institutions

could flow into and out of Italy. One recalls, in particular,
the familiar international flows of labour, so large that
nearly six million Italians were living abroad in 1911, so easy
that over one million of these were temporary migrants (11).
One recalls also the capital flows that not only covered the
widening trade deficits during the investment booms of the
1880s and 1900s, but allowed the lira to appreciate in the
process - strongly suggesting that the capital flows were
induced directly by the domestic demand for funds, and were
thus rather the cause of, than caused by, the deficits in the
balance of trade (12).

Two more general points deserve perhaps to be made explicit.
The first is that the reliance on foreign capital to finance
such major investment programmes as railway construction does
not indicate that shortages of domestic capital prevented
development, or that domestic suppliers of capital failed to
react rationally to investment opportunities. Rather, such
capital imports indicate only that international supply
curves are more elastic than domestic supply curves (which is
only to be expected, since a single country's new investment
needs are a far smaller part of current world investment than
of its own current investment), and that domestic consumption
can be stabilised by borrowing from outside (just as when an
individual borrows to buy a house). Analytically, such capital
imports are entirely compatible with ordinary market behaviour,
and do not imply any sort of market failure; empirically, they
were as significant in the United States as in 'backward' Italy
or Spain. The second point is that economists customarily
assume that factors of production are perfectly mobile within
'nations', and perfectly immobile between them. From this
perspective, the substantive point at issue here concerns the
relation between economic 'nations' and historically defined
political units; there is obviously no reason to assimilate
them to each other a priori (13).

4.   THE RAILWAYS' CONSUMPTION OF INDUSTRIAL PRODUCTS

The railways' consumption of the products of the construction,
engineering and metalmaking industries is illustrated by the
estimates in Tables 3.3-3.6 (14). The construction series
(Table 3.3, cols 1-4) and the rail consumption series
(Table 3.6, col 2) clearly reflect the major waves of
construction activity beginning in 1861, 1881 and 1906, as
well as the progressive shift from first construction to
improvement. The rolling-stock consumption series (Table 3.4,
col 2) is also markedly cyclical, but with a strong trend
reminiscent of that in construction for improvements (and

Table 3.3: *Construction value added in the construction and maintenance of rail- and tramway lines (million lire per annum at 1911 prices)*

	(1) First construction Railways	(2) First construction Tramways	(3) First construction Total	(4) Railway improvements	(5) Maintenance Railways	(6) Maintenance Tramways	(7) Maintenance Total	(8) Rail- and tramway total	(9) Construction industry total
1861–65	112		112		3		3	115	400
1866–70	66		66		5		5	71	350
1871–75	67		67	4	8		8	79	400
1876–80	48	5	53	11	11		11	75	400
1881–85	94	8	102	23	14	1	15	140	500
1886–90	88	4	92	21	19	1	20	133	550
1891–95	76	3	79	2	20	2	22	103	500
1896–00	13	9	22	5	23	2	25	52	400
1901–05	23	5	28	11	28	3	31	70	450
1906–10	25	6	31	35	35	3	38	104	600
1911–13	47	15	62	39	41	4	45	146	750

Source: See the Appendix to this chapter.

Table 3.4: Engineering value added in the manufacture and maintenance of rail- and tramway rolling stock: aggregate estimates (million lire per annum at 1911 prices)

	(1)	(2)	(3)	(4)	(5)	(6)	(7)	(8)	(9)	(10)	(11)	(12)
	Rail- and tramway rolling stock					Track acces- sories (c)	All machinery (a)			Fabricated metal and machinery (a)		
	Domestic produc- tion	Production plus imports	Main- tenance	Domestic total	Overall total (b)		Produc- tion	Main- tenance	Total	Produc- tion	Main- tenance	Total
1861-65	2.2	6.2	3.1	5.3	9.3	0.7	21	16	37	49	273	322
1866-70	2.0	5.2	5.1	7.1	10.3	0.6	22	21	43	50	283	333
1871-75	3.1	8.5	8.2	11.3	16.7	1.0	26	27	53	59	294	353
1876-80	1.7	3.7	10.7	12.4	14.4	1.4	31	33	64	70	305	375
1881-85	9.0	13.5	15.6	24.6	29.1	3.0	55	43	98	123	321	444
1886-90	15.4	23.2	20.5	35.9	43.7	2.7	79	53	132	174	336	510
1891-95	4.6	4.7	22.7	27.3	27.4	1.1	52	62	114	113	351	464
1896-1900	11.8	14.1	27.1	38.9	41.2	0.9	65	74	139	139	369	508
1901-05	19.8	26.0	34.6	54.4	60.6	1.3	83	93	176	176	394	570
1906-10	45.8	66.8	44.4	90.2	111.2	3.1	166	114	280	347	422	769
1911-13	53.5	56.6	54.6	108.1	111.2	4.0	200	135	335	412	446	858

(a) excludes shipbuilding and the production of wood road vehicles.
(b) domestic total plus imports.
(c) production plus imports.

Source: See the Appendix to this chapter.

Table 3.5: *Engineering value added in the manufacture and maintenance of railway rolling stock: composition (million lire per annum at 1911 prices)*

	(1)	(2)	(3)	(4)	(5)	(6)	(7)	(8)	(9)
	Domestic production			Production plus imports			Maintenance		
	Locomotives (a)	Passenger cars (b)	Freight cars (c)	Locomotives (a)	Passenger cars (b)	Freight cars (c)	Locomotives (a)	Passenger cars (b)	Freight cars (c)
1861–65	0.1	0.6	1.5	1.6	1.3	3.3	1.4	0.7	1.0
1866–70	0.2	0.5	1.3	1.3	0.9	3.0	2.3	1.1	1.7
1871–75	0.4	0.5	2.2	2.3	0.9	5.3	3.4	1.8	3.0
1876–80	0.1	0.5	1.1	1.2	0.7	1.8	4.4	2.3	4.0
1881–85	0.7	2.0	6.3	3.9	2.4	7.2	6.8	3.3	5.5
1886–90	1.8	3.3	10.3	4.9	3.9	14.4	9.3	4.3	6.9
1891–95	1.1	1.2	2.3	1.2	1.2	2.3	10.4	4.9	7.4
1896–1900	3.7	2.0	6.1	3.4 (d)	1.9 (d)	8.8	13.1	5.4	8.6
1901–05	5.4	3.9	10.5	6.2	5.4	14.4	17.8	6.5	10.3
1906–10	10.8	5.1	29.9	17.8	9.5	39.5	23.3	8.9	12.2
1911–13	12.5	7.1	33.9	14.4	7.7	34.5	28.6	11.5	14.5

(a) includes rail-cars.
(b) includes mail and cell cars.
(c) includes baggage cars and tenders.
(d) production minus exports.

Source: See the Appendix to this chapter.

Table 3.6: Metalmaking value added in the manufacture of rail, accessories and metal for railway rolling stock (million lire per annum at 1911 prices)

| | Rails (a) | | Accessories: | Rolling stock metal (a) | | | Total market for railway metal (a) | |
| | (1) | (2) | (3) | (4) | (5) | (6) | (7) | (8) |
	Domestic production plus imports	Production plus imports	production plus imports (a)	Maintenance consumption (b)	Total consumption (b)	Potential consumption (c)	Actual	Potential
1861–65		1.2	0.2	0.1	0.3	0.6	1.7	2.0
1866–70		1.0	0.2	0.3	0.5	0.8	1.7	2.0
1871–75		1.7	0.3	0.4	0.8	1.5	2.8	3.5
1876–80		2.4	0.4	0.6	0.8	1.0	3.6	3.8
1881–85		5.3	1.0	0.9	2.0	2.5	8.3	8.8
1886–90	3.0	4.7	0.8	1.2	3.0	4.0	8.5	9.5
1891–95	1.6	2.0	0.4	1.3	1.8	1.8	4.2	4.2
1896–1900	0.8	1.5	0.3	1.5	2.9	3.3	4.7	5.1
1901–05	1.4	2.2	0.4	2.0	4.3	5.0	6.9	7.6
1906–10	4.4	5.5	1.0	2.5	8.2	10.6	14.7	17.1
1911–13	6.9	7.0	1.3	3.1	9.6	10.0	17.9	18.3

Continued

Table 3.6 – *Continued*

	(9)	(10)	(11)	(12)
		Total domestic value added		
	Semi-finished ferrous metal	All ferrous metal	All metal	Semi-finished ferrous metal: ratio of output to consumption
1861–65	3.8	4.1	6.1	0.49
1866–70	3.3	3.6	5.9	0.42
1871–75	4.4	4.7	6.9	0.44
1876–80	6.8	7.0	9.7	0.54
1881–85	13.0	13.3	17.5	0.57
1886–90	24.4	24.5	31.6	0.64
1891–95	18.4	18.5	26.8	0.75
1896–1900	24.3	24.5	35.0	0.81
1901–05	30.0	32.2	45.4	0.79
1906–10	64.9	67.1	85.2	0.78
1911–13	86.5	90.9	112.7	0.83

(a) value added in the manufacture from pig or scrap; manufacture from iron ore would raise the rail figures by 30 per cent, the other metal figures by 20 per cent.
(b) value added in metal actually produced or imported as such.
(c) includes the metalmaking value-added content of imported rolling stock.

Source: See the Appendix to this chapter.

indeed related to it, since both are induced by growing
traffic). In addition, the high plateau in railway construction in 1881–95 appears here as a sharp peak in 1886–90. One
reason for this is that it takes much longer to build the
right of way than the rolling stock, so that the upsurge in
railway construction naturally preceded that in the production
of complementary rolling stock; another is the business
depression of the early 1890s, which allowed the rolling stock
needs of new lines to be met, at that time, largely by trans-
ferring otherwise underutilised vehicles from the existing
network. A third reason would appear to be the reorganisation
of the railway system, which had much the same effect in 1885
as in 1905: since the rolling stock was the responsibility of
the operating companies, purchases would tend to decline as
reorganisation drew closer, and surge in its immediate
aftermath (15).

A comparison of these time series to each other sheds light
on the internal composition of railway investment demand. As
it turns out, railway construction involved a great deal of
traditional construction activity to prepare the right of way
(especially in the difficult terrain that characterises much
of Italy); even allowing for track accessories and rolling
stock metal (Table 3.4, col 6, Table 3.6, col 3 and the
difference between cols 6 and 4), the consumption of metal
and machines was comparatively quite minor. In fact, such
goods account for a far more significant share of investment
for replacement and improvement than of investment for expansion: paradoxically, perhaps, a mature railway system buys
relatively more from heavy industry than a growing one.

To illustrate this point, the present time series may be
reduced to two sets of averages: one for 1861–95, when the
network was largely being established; and one for 1896–1913,
when the network, though still growing, was substantially
mature. Allowing for the other materials consumed by construction, engineering and metalmaking, one obtains an average
annual investment close to 180 million lire per annum (at
1911 prices) in both these periods. In 1861–95, however,
construction alone accounted for approximately 50 per cent
of that figure, and the quarrying and processing of
construction materials accounted for another 25 per cent
(60 per cent of it in quarrying); engineering and metalmaking
accounted for 8 per cent between them (75 per cent of it in
engineering), and the balance was taken up by mining and
natural resources (including some 2 per cent for land, up to
3 per cent for scrap iron, and 12–15 per cent for coal and
iron ore). In 1896–1913, the share of construction was
reduced to 33 per cent, and that of the quarrying and
processing of construction materials to 10 per cent;

engineering and metalmaking took 30 per cent between them
(80 per cent of it in engineering), and the balance was
again taken up by mining and natural resources (including
some 2 per cent for land, up to 10 per cent for scrap iron,
and 15-25 per cent for coal and iron ore) (16).

These patterns are reinforced if we consider the proportion of railway investment accruing to the domestic economy
rather than to imports. Construction, construction materials
and quarrying are all essentially shielded from foreign
competition; on the other hand, Italy imported a substantial
share of its rails and rolling stock, particularly before
the tariff increases of the late 1870s and especially the
late 1880s. Thus, in 1861-95, the domestic engineering and
metalmaking industries accounted for only 3-5 per cent of
railway investment (including 3-4 per cent in engineering
and 0-1 per cent in metalmaking), or approximately half of
the 8 per cent for domestic production and imports together;
in 1896-1913, the share of those domestic industries rose to
21-25 per cent (including 19-20 per cent in engineering and
2-5 per cent in metalmaking), or approximately three-fourths
of the 30 per cent for domestic production and imports
together (17).

An established railway network appears even more important
than its original construction, as far as the consumption of
industrial products is concerned, if its maintenance needs
are considered along with its investment needs. Maintenance
demand, though initially much smaller than investment demand,
grew over time to quite significant levels; and it was always
relatively strongly orientated towards engineering, and almost
entirely reserved to domestic industry. As a result, it
represented about half of domestic industrial value added to
railway order even at the peak of the post-nationalisation
re-equipment boom; and in the early decades, when most railway investment was for expansion and rails and rolling stock
were largely imported, it represented much the larger part
of it. The establishment of repair shops clearly emerges as
the early railways' most significant direct contribution to
domestic industry (18).

The estimate of railway maintenance demand for construction,
engineering and metalmaking are presented in Tables 3.3 (cols
5-7), 3.4 (col 3), and 3.6 (col 4). For these three
industries combined, maintenance demand averaged 25 million
lire (of value added at 1911 prices) per annum in 1861-95,
and nearly thrice that in 1896-1913; by way of comparison,
investment demand averaged 111 million lire per annum in
1861-95, and 104 million lire per annum in 1896-1913. In the
case of metalmaking, maintenance demand (the consumption of
metal in the maintenance of rolling stock; Table 3.6, col 4)

was relatively minor: an average value added of just 0.7
million lire (of which perhaps half was lost to imports)
per annum in 1861-95, and still only 2.2 million lire (of
which perhaps one fifth lost to imports) per annum in
1896-1913. But even these paltry figures represented a
significant share of the railway's relatively small
consumption of metal (cols 7 or 8): around 15 per cent in
1861-95, and 20 per cent in 1896-1913 (19). Maintenance
demand for construction (Table 3.3, col 7) was altogether
greater: an average value added of 12 million lire per annum
in 1861-95, and 34 million lire per annum in 1896-1913. In
relative terms, these equalled 12 per cent of total railway
demand for construction (col 8) in 1861-95, and 37 per cent
in 1896-1913. The maintenance demand for engineering
(Table 3.4, col 3), in turn, was marginally greater than
that for construction: an average value added of 12 million
lire per annum in 1861-95, and 39 million lire per annum in
1896-1913. In relative terms, however, maintenance demand
equalled 57 per cent of the railway's total demand for
machinery (col 5) in 1861-95, and 50 per cent of it in
1896-1913 (20). Allowing for the importation of new rolling
stock, which was particularly significant in the early
decades, one finds that the share of maintenance in the total
domestic rolling stock industry equalled a dominating 69 per
cent in 1861-95, and 55 per cent in 1896-1913. Moreover, the
disaggregated estimates of engineering production (Table 3.5)
indicate that maintenance was concentrated in the technolo-
gically most demanding type of vehicle (locomotives) whereas
purchases and production were concentrated in the technolo-
gically least demanding type (freight cars). From the
standpoint of industrial skills ('human capital'), even more
than from that of engineering value added in general, the
railways' maintenance needs appear to overshadow their demand
for new production.

    The importance of railway demand for the construction,
engineering and metalmaking industries can be assessed, within
broad limits, by comparing the railway-specific production
and consumption figures discussed above to the typically much
rougher industry totals presented within those same Tables
3.3-3.6.

    In the case of construction, first of all, railway demand
(Table 3.3, col 8) averaged some 23 per cent of the industry
total (col 10) in 1861-95, and 16 per cent in 1896-1913;
this reduction is the result of a 15 per cent decline in
average railway construction, and a 19 per cent increase in
average total construction. Finer comparisons are difficult,
pending the calculation of less imprecise figures for the
industry as a whole; for what the present estimates may be

worth, a comparison of the change in railway construction (col 8) to the corresponding change in total construction (col 9) suggests that the former represented about 90 per cent of the industry's (minor) decline from 1861-5 to 1866-70, about 40 per cent of its increase from 1876-80 to 1886-90, about 55 per cent of the subsequent decline to 1896-1900, and about 25 per cent of the subsequent increase to 1911-13. A comparison of the change in railway construction to the corresponding initial level of total construction suggests that railway construction by itself represented a 15 per cent increase in total construction from 1876-80 to 1886-90, and a 24 per cent increase in it from 1896-1900 to 1911-13; both of these are equivalent to an average growth rate of approximately 1.5 per cent per annum (21).

In the case of engineering, secondly, the possible comparisons are multiplied by the presence of imports on the one hand, and of a variety of possible 'industry totals' on the other (22). The selection of the level of aggregation is particularly critical, since the relative shares of machinery and fabricated metal were very different in railway-related activity on the one hand and in aggregate activity on the other; railway demand thus appears altogether more significant next to the machinery industry by itself than next to engineering as a whole. Some relevant estimates are collected in Table 3.7. From the first group of comparisons, one sees that railway-related production and maintenance activities accounted for roughly one quarter to one third of the machinery industry (col 3), but only one twentieth to one tenth of the entire engineering industry (col 7); and that these figures are not much increased if one adds imports to domestic production (cols 4 and 8). If one neglects maintenance and considers new production only, one obtains somewhat lower ratios to the machinery industry (especially in the early years), but somewhat higher ones to engineering as a whole (cols 1-2, 5-6) (23). From the second group of comparisons, one sees that the change in railway-related activity represented roughly one third to two fifths of the machinery industry's growth from 1876-80 to 1886-90, and again from 1891-5 to 1911-13, but closer to one fifth of the entire industry's growth at those times; the hypothetical inclusion of imports again results in only relatively small increases in these ratios, while the neglect of maintenance (which grew relatively rapidly in the case of rolling stock) would here reduce those ratios across the board (cols 1-8). From the third group of comparisons, one sees that over those two major periods of growth the growth of railway-related activity represented an annual growth of

about 3-4 per cent per annum for the machinery industry
(whether maintenance is included or not), but only 1-2 per
cent per annum for the engineering industry as a whole. A
peak rate of nearly 5 per cent per annum, for machinery
production alone, is achieved if imports are added to
domestic manufacture: far from negligible, to be sure, but
still quite small compared to the 20 per cent per annum
and more characteristic of leading sectors.

In the case of metalmaking, thirdly, a variety of
distinctions again multiply the possible comparisons; a
broad sample of these is collected in Table 3.8. The
distinction between industry totals here has only a
relatively minor impact: since the manufacture of semi-
finished ferrous metal typically accounted for close to two
thirds of all metalmaking, the shares of railway-related
production in the latter are generally a comparable
proportion of its share in the former (compare cols 1-2
and 3-4, 5-6 and 7-8) (24). The distinctions between rails
and other railway metal on the one hand, and between output
and imports on the other, are more significant. From the
first group of comparisons, one sees that rail production
was actually only a minor part of the total: about one
twentieth of semi-finished ferrous metals production,
against one sixth for all railway metal (cols 1 and 5).
The addition of imports to domestic production would have
had a major impact in the early decades, trebling the share
of rails and doubling that of all railway metal together
(cols 2 and 6). From the second group of comparisons, one
sees that the growth of railway metal represented about a
quarter of the growth of semi-finished ferrous metalmaking
from 1876-80 to 1886-90, and one fifth of it from 1891-5
to 1911-13; rails were the larger contributor to the earlier
growth, and other railway metal to the later one (cols 1 and
5). In this case, the addition of imports to domestic
production affects the figures only slightly (cols 2 and 6:
the contribution of rails is reduced because the proportion
of imports declined over the relevant periods, while that
of all railway metal is increased because the growing
imports of rolling stock resulted in an overall rise in
railway metal imports). From the third group of comparisons,
finally, one sees that the growth of railway metal production represented an annual growth of about 6 per cent per
annum in semi-finished ferrous metalmaking from 1876-80 to
1886-90, and 3 per cent per annum from 1891-5 to 1911-13
(col 5). Once again, rail production dominates the earlier
contribution, and other metal the later one (col 1); since
much of the early growth in rail production was import
substituting, its contribution would be sharply reduced by

Table 3.7: *Comparisons of railway-related and total production in engineering*

	(1)	(2)	(3)	(4)	(5)	(6)	(7)	(8)
	Machinery only				All engineering			
	Production		Total (a)		Production		Total (a)	
	Actual	Potential (b)	Actual	Potential (b)	Actual (c)	Potential (b)	Actual (c)	Potential (b)
1. Level to level								
1861–95	0.13	0.21	0.23	0.27	0.08	0.11	0.05	0.06
1896–13	0.25	0.30	0.31	0.34	0.13	0.16	0.11	0.11
2. Change to change								
1876–80 to 1886–90	0.29	0.36	0.35	0.40	0.14	0.19	0.18	0.22
1886–90 to 1891–95	0.40	0.53	0.47	0.63	0.20	0.29	0.22	0.33
1891–95 to 1911–13	0.33	0.34	0.37	0.37	0.17	0.18	0.20	0.22
3. Change to initial level, converted to annual percentage rates								
1876–80 to 1886–90	3.7	4.8	3.2	3.7	2.0	2.6	0.6	0.8
1886–90 to 1891–95	-2.9	-4.7	-1.3	-2.4	-1.9	-2.3	-0.4	-0.7
1891–95 to 1911–13	3.6	3.7	2.9	2.9	2.0	2.1	0.9	0.9

(a) production plus maintenance.
(b) calculated by adding rolling stock imports to domestic production.
(c) counts all track accessories as domestic production.

Source: See the Appendix to this chapter.

the addition of imports to domestic production (col 6).

In summary, the growth in railway-related production seems to have represented significant growth for the machinery and metalmaking industries, but relatively unimpressive growth for the entire metalworking group, both in the 1880s and the 1900s; and this conclusion is substantially unaffected by the hypothetical addition of imports to domestic production. In the 1880s, the heyday of railway construction, the railway's consumption of industrial goods was too restricted to have represented an opportunity for a 'big push', even with a totally protected engineering industry; in the 1900s, the railway's consumption of industrial goods was significantly higher than it had been twenty years earlier precisely because it represented the industry-oriented maintenance and replacement demand of a mature system, and not the construction-oriented demand of a rapidly growing one. In this sense at least, the fact that Italy's railway network was largely completed by the turn of the century can be taken to have strengthened, and not weakened, the industrial growth of the early 1900s.

5.   THE IMPACT OF RAILWAY INVESTMENT

The railway's direct purchases of domestic industrial products are of course only one element of the overall impact of current railway investment on domestic industrial production. A more comprehensive evaluation must gauge the net impact of that investment both on the composition of final demand, and on its level; the latter also matters here, in view of the access to international resource markets, and the resulting flexibility of resource employment levels, that apparently characterised the nineteenth-century Italian economy. The empirical difficulty is that these overall effects of railway investment can only be traced through a general equilibrium model of the entire relevant economic system, and the results one obtains are accordingly very sensitive to the identity, as well as to the structure, of the relationships one chooses to contemplate.

Some illustrative estimates, and an indication of at least some of the critical variables and relationships, have been obtained with the aid of a very simple (static, linear, six-equation) model adapted from Mundell's analysis of capital movements and stabilisation policy under fixed and flexible exchange rates (25). On the one hand, that model is extended to include railway investment and industrial production as explicit variables; on the other, it is simplified by assuming that Italy is too small a part of the international

Table 3.8: *Comparisons of railway-related and total production in metalmaking*

	(1)	(2)	(3)	(4)	(5)	(6)	(7)	(8)
	Rails only compared to:				All rail-related metal compared to:			
	Semi-finished ferrous metal		All metal		Semi-finished ferrous metal		All metal	
	Actual	Potential (a)	Actual	Potential	Actual (b)	Potential (c)	Actual (b)	Potential (c)
1. Level to level								
1861-95	0.06	0.21	0.04	0.15	0.16	0.35	0.12	0.27
1896-13	0.06	0.08	0.05	0.06	0.17	0.23	0.13	0.17
2. Change to change								
1876-80 to 1886-90	0.17	0.14	0.14	0.11	0.27	0.31	0.22	0.25
1886-90 to 1891-95	0.23	0.37	0.29	0.44	0.36	0.58	0.45	0.67
1891-95 to 1911-13	0.08	0.07	0.06	0.06	0.19	0.20	0.15	0.16
3. Change to initial level, converted to annual percentage rates								
1876-80 to 1886-90	3.7	2.3	2.7	1.8	5.5	4.6	4.1	3.7
1886-90 to 1891-95	-1.2	-2.2	-0.9	-1.7	-2.5	-4.0	-1.4	-3.2
1891-95 to 1911-13	1.3	1.2	1.0	0.9	2.8	2.9	2.1	2.2

(a) calculated by adding rail imports to domestic production.
(b) assumes that railway metal other than rail was produced and imported in the same ratio as all semi-finished ferrous metal.
(c) calculated by adding rail imports and estimated other railway metal imports to domestic production.

Source: See the Appendix to this chapter.

economy to affect international interest rates. The alternative characterisations of the exchange rate are instead
retained, since Italy went off the gold standard in 1866, and
the lira traded below par through the 1870s and again in the
1890s. The essential relationships contemplated by the adapted
model may be summarised under the following three headings.
First, value added in industrial production is related
directly to the value of railway investment, other investment
and other income (expenditure); the parameters of these
equations reflect the share of domestic manufactured goods in
these various types of expenditure. Second, aggregate
expenditure (income) is defined as the sum of consumption,
investment and the balance of trade (exports minus imports).
Consumption, non-railway investment and imports themselves
depend on aggregate expenditure; exports and imports also
depend on the exchange rate. Third, money demand is assumed
to vary with aggregate expenditure, and set equal to money
supply.

   With the lira at par, and the exchange thus pegged at the
gold-import point, the model behaves in a straightforward
Keynesian fashion. Railway investment has the usual multiplier
effects on aggregate income, and therefore a markedly positive
indirect effect on industrial production (which varies with
the induced income, and even more strongly with the induced
investment); the money supply varies passively, through specie
flows, to adapt to money demand. In this context, the results
depend critically on the assumptions concerning induced
investment, since the resulting multiplier (and therefore the
measured effect of the exogenous impulse) can grow without
limit. Railway investment can thus be made as important as
one wants (in terms of the measured proportion of income and
industrial production which is attributed to it), without for
all that ever becoming more important than a similar amount
of exogenous spending for anything else (since the same high
multiplier would apply there too) (26). With the lira below
par, and the exchange free to vary, the model behaves
altogether differently. The money supply is exogenously given,
and money-market equilibrium determines aggregate income.
Railway investment does not affect the level of aggregate
demand: it is offset by the deterioration in the balance of
trade, as the exchange rate appreciates in response to the
capital flows induced by the pressure of investment demand
on the domestic interest rate. Its effects on industrial
production are exhausted by its effects on the composition
of demand, and therefore depend in the first instance on the
difference between the domestic industrial content of
railway investment expenditure on the one hand and the
displaced (i.e. 'all other') expenditure on the other. The

critical assumption, of course, is here the constancy of the
income velocity; but it is worth noting that its essential
result is to undercut the expansionary real effects that are
otherwise obtained by allowing international factor movements.
In a word, the flexible-exchange-rate model mimics, through
its restrictions on demand, the behaviour of a classical
fixed-resource, full-employment model restricted on the supply
side. In both cases, aggregate production is fixed, and the
only impact of railway investment is on its composition (27).
As noted above, moreover, the domestic (and also total)
industrial content of railway investment was relatively high
in the case of replacement and improvement, but relatively
low in the case of original construction. Railway investment
thus plausibly altered the composition of production to
industry's advantage from the turn of the century or there-
abouts, but to industry's *dis*advantage in the preceding
decades.

With plausible parameters, the demand-expansion effect on
industry is considerably larger than the demand-composition
effect (the former is essentially a product of railway
investment, a Keynesian multiplier, and the share of industry
in ordinary expenditure, while the latter is essentially the
product of unmultiplied railway investment and the *difference*
between the share of industry in railway investment and in
ordinary expenditure). The measured effect on industrial
production of railway investment, considered as a pure
addition to exogenous spending, thus varies primarily with the
presence or absence of the demand-expansion effect, i.e.
with the state of the exchange. In 1866-80 and 1891-1900,
with a floating exchange rate, the measured effect is the
demand-composition effect alone; it is thus small and plausibly
negative (of the order of minus 1 per cent, with illustrative
parameter values). In 1861-5, 1881-90 and 1901-13, with a
pegged exchange, the measured impact is dominated by the
demand-expansion effect; it is thus positive and not
insignificant (of the order of plus 5 per cent with illustrative parameter values, and this despite a negative composition
effect in the 1860s and 1880s). The measured effects of
railway investment thus follow a cycle that is roughly
coincident with, but much stronger than, the cycle in railway
investment itself; but the cycle in the effects is
attributable to the changes in the exchange rate (and thus
the impact of a unit of exogenous spending) rather than to
the changes in the volume of railway investment.

If the model is expanded to include a public budget constraint, railway investment is plausibly assumed to have been
financed not by borrowing alone but by a combination of
borrowing, money creation, tax increases and reductions in

other public investment (28). With the addition of this
relationship, the state of the exchange becomes far less
significant: the expansion of demand with fixed exchange
rates is sharply limited by the offsetting increase in taxes
and reduction in other public investment; and the increase
in the money supply now allows demand to expand even with
flexible exchange rates. The plausible impact of railway
investment on industrial production thus becomes small but
positive even with flexible exchange rates (of the order of
plus 1 per cent, with illustrative parameter values), and
not much larger with fixed exchange rates (of the order of
plus 2 or 3 per cent). With this expanded model, the cycle
in the measured effect of railway investment is attributable,
in roughly comparable proportions, to the changes in the
exchange rate on the one hand and in the level and
composition of railway investment on the other.

In general, then, it would seem likely that the cycle in
railway investment somewhat amplified the largely synchronous
cycle in industrial production; but the size of its effect
can only be conjectured. Moreover, as one recalls, that cycle
in industrial production seems attributable not only to the
fluctuations in domestic demand for investment goods, but to
the failure of the domestic producers of those goods to break
out of the small and fluctuating domestic market into
sustained export-led growth. The cause of that failure appears
to be the tariff on iron and steel, which raised the costs of
the Italian engineering industry to internationally
uncompetitive levels; and one wonders to what extent the
tariff on iron and steel was not itself due to the lure of the
market for rails and other metal created by railway investment.
It is altogether possible that railway investment influenced
Italy's industrial growth primarily, and deleteriously, by
altering the balance of political power between the free-
traders and the protectionists. The actual effect of railway
investment on Italian industry cannot be measured, in sum,
until more is known about the mechanisms that determined
private and public spending, international resource flows, the
exchange rate, money supply and demand, and tariff policy; and
even this list is only partial and preliminary (29).

6.   THE IMPACT OF RAILWAY TRANSPORTATION

In a closed economy, cheaper transportation increases the
productivity of domestic resources: as it unifies the market,
it induces a reallocation of resources to exploit relative
advantages and economies of scale. In an open economy, cheaper
internal transportation further increases the productivity of

domestic resources, and normally increases their density as
well: as it breaks down the barriers between the interior and
world markets, it eliminates domestic resource and demand
constraints, and attracts those internationally mobile
brokering and processing activities that characterise the
commercial capitals and workshops of the world (30). In Italy,
the rail links from the Upper Po Valley to the sea may thus
have permitted the development of the 'industrial triangle'
between Turin, Milan and Genoa; but railway transportation
appears to have done little to unify the domestic market and
undermine the traditional patterns of production that
prevailed through most of the peninsula.

In 1911, for example, the railways loaded some 40 million
tons of goods. About 11 million tons were loaded at various
seaports (45 per cent of them in Genoa alone, and another 25
per cent in nearby Savona and in Venice); another 2 million
were imported by rail (all of them, of course, into northern
Italy); and only 27 million tons were loaded in the country's
interior (31). In that same year, ships unloaded some 22
million tons of goods, including 17 million tons arriving from
foreign ports and 5 million tons from domestic ones (32). With
imports by rail offsetting the likely share of domestic goods
in railway seaport loadings, the volume of imports loaded by
the railways may be estimated at 11 million tons, or about 55
per cent of total imports and 28 per cent of total railway
shipments. Domestic commodities accounted for the other 72 per
cent of railway shipments, or 29 million tons; and the latter
figure implies that average shipments by modern overland means,
per ton of domestic commodity production, were then just one
fifth of the level achieved with the cheap transportation of
our own day (33). Of the residual four-fifths, a large part
was no doubt moved by traditional means; and another large part
was no doubt not moved at all, as resources consumed in direct
production were substituted for relatively expensive
transportation.

An essentially similar picture emerges from the disaggregated
evidence in Table 3.9. Column 1 presents the tonnages of the
principal commodity groups shipped by the state railways in
1911. Since such rankings are heavily influenced by relative
degrees of disaggregation, and the table covers only 60 per
cent of total shipments, the present sample may seriously
underrepresent some significant groups of commodities; but it
is clear (and not at all surprising) that fuels, construction
materials and agricultural outputs and inputs by themselves
accounted for over half of total shipments by rail. Cols 2-4
provide a comparison to imports, exports and domestic
production. The railways seem heavily involved in the distribution of bulk imports: thus coal, most spectacularly, but

also cereal (1.3 million tons of which were loaded at the
seaports) phosphates and Thomas slag, raw cotton and probably
lumber (34). The collection of bulk exports is also discernible,
clearly in the case of sulphur, and more ambiguously in that of
building stone (marble) or citrus fruit. The volume of internal
shipments, in contrast, seems relatively limited. Of the goods
produced in large quantities, only high-grade construction
materials (lime and cement) and chemical fertiliser travelled
extensively by rail; significantly, these are industrial
products that are both relatively valuable (compared to other
bulk industrial goods) and sold to widely dispersed consumers
(construction,agriculture). Low-grade construction materials,
agricultural products and semi-finished industrial products
(metal) appear instead to have used the railways only a small
percentage of the time (particularly since the railway-shipment
categories often group commodities across successive stages of
production, while the present production figures refer to only
one such stage) (35). The limited shipments of semi-finished
industrial products no doubt reflect the spatial concentration
of industrial production in the 'industrial triangle', and
perhaps a relatively high degree of vertical integration; but
since industrial structures and location are themselves
influenced by transport costs, the observed configuration of
industry may well be, at least in part, an endogenous response
to expensive transportation. The limited shipments of agricultural and other bulk commodities point instead to a low volume
of interregional trade, and correspondingly, to the large-
scale survival of the traditional local economies based on an
exchange between the towns and their immediate surroundings.
The influence of expensive transportation was here no doubt
compounded by that of emigration, as the emigrants' remittances
allowed the South to pay for imported manufactures without
exporting more of its limited food supply. But emigration too
reflects in part the incidence of high transport costs: the
barriers between the interior and world markets helped make
the South a relatively high-cost location, with a tendency to
export labour services directly rather than as value added to
commodity exports. For similar reasons, the major cities of
the South were nearly all located on the seacoast; but the
relatively high cost of overland transport meant that coastal
locations were more cheaply reached - and, in the absence of
tariff barriers, often more cheaply supplied - from northern
Europe by sea than from northern Italy by rail (36).

The Italian railways' ability to unify the domestic market
thus seems to have been limited by the high price of their
services, and not, as the international comparisons of
network lengths in Table 3.1 might have suggested, by the

Table 3.9: *Principal railway shipments, international trade and comparable domestic production in 1911 (million tons)*

	(1) Shipments (a)	(2) Imports	(3) Exports	(4) Comparable production
1. lime and cement	1.7	0.0	0.0	2.6
2. lumber	1.7	1.5	0.0	1.1
3. building stone	1.3	0.0	0.4	13.9
4. bricks and tiles	1.2	0.1	0.1	7.8
5. sand	0.6	?	?	1.4
6. asphalt	0.1	0.0	0.0	0.2 (rock only)
Subtotal	6.8			
7. cereal and flour: wheat	1.8	1.5	0.1	5.1 (cereal only)
8. cereal and flour: other	1.8	0.6	0.1	4.0 (cereal only)
9. wine	0.9	0.0	0.1	4.8
10. animal feed, straw, etc.	0.5	?	?	23.4 (forage crops only)
11. sugar beet	0.5	?	?	1.6
12. animals	0.4	0.1	0.0	0.9 (slaughtered live weight only)
13. grapes and must	0.3	0.0	0.0	7.7 (grapes only)
14. citrus fruit	0.3	0.0	0.4	1.0
15. sugar, coffee, etc.	0.3	0.1	0.0	0.2 (crude sugar only)
Subtotal	6.7			

Continued

Table 3.9: *Continued*

	(1) Shipments (a)	(2) Imports	(3) Exports	(4) Comparable production
16. coal, lignite, charcoal	6.0	9.8	0.1	0.7 (mine products only)
17. firewood	0.3	0.1	0.0	2.5
Subtotal	6.3			
18. chemical fertiliser	0.7	0.0	0.0	1.0
19. phosphates, Thomas slag	0.4	0.6	0.0	0.0
20. natural fertiliser	0.4	0.0	0.0	?
Subtotal	1.5			
21. pig and scrap iron	0.4	0.6	0.0	0.7
22. ingot and semi-finished metal	0.3	0.2	0.0	1.1 (semi-finished metal only)
Subtotal	0.7			
23. yarn and cloth	0.2	0.0	0.1	0.3 (yarn only)
24. raw cotton	0.2	0.2	0.0	0.0
25. other textile fibres	0.1	0.1	0.1	0.1
Subtotal	0.5			

Continued

Table 3.9: *Continued*

	(1) Shipments (a)	(2) Imports	(3) Exports	(4) Comparable production
26. other chemicals	0.4	0.3	0.1	0.4 (final products only)
27. sulphur	0.4	0.0	0.4	0.4 (fused sulphur only)
28. mineral and vegetable oils	0.3	0.3	0.1	0.2 (petroleum and olive oil only)
29. paper	0.2	0.0	0.0	0.2
Total	23.8			

(a) on the state railways

Source: See the Appendix to this chapter.

comparatively small size of their network. This is clearly
brought out by the turn-of-the-century figures on the intensity of network use on the major Italian, French and German
systems: even allowing for the relative incidence of multiple
tracking, the Italian rail lines were relatively lightly used
(Table 3.10, rows 2-4). This restricted use of the railway
network, in turn, seems only partly justified by inescapably
high operating costs; much of it seems due to a public policy
that kept prices well above marginal costs.

Wages in Italy were rather lower than elsewhere; but this
advantage was more than offset by high energy prices, an
unfavourable terrain, diseconomies of small scale, and
probably unbalanced traffic flows as well. The high price of
imported coal made for expensive fuel, and also, though less
so, for expensive energy-intensive materials and activities
(metal parts, repairs and the like). The high incidence of
curves and gradients made for high fuel consumption, slow
speeds, light or often double-headed trains, and rapid
deterioration of the right of way. The low utilisation of
rail lines meant that administrative, surveillance and
station personnel costs were distributed over a small volume
of output; that frequencies could only be maintained by
accepting light average loads; and that the rail lines were
rationally equipped to relatively low standards, thus
constraining engine weights and power and effectively
compounding the limitations imposed by the terrain (37).
Chronological or directional imbalances in demand may have
been relatively severe, in view of the importance of bulk
imports and agricultural perishables in the Italian systems'
traffic (Table 3.9); and such imbalances would make for high
capacity costs per unit of output, whether load factors were
allowed to drop or kept high by pruning off-peak
capacity (38).

The comparative figures in Table 3.10 provide some evidence
of the impact of these various handicaps. Overall, current
costs per unit of output (row 21) were about two thirds
higher on the Italian systems than on the major French and
German ones. Load factors in both passenger and freight
operations (rows 6-7) were close to the averages of those
prevailing elsewhere (and not relatively high, as they
presumably would have been if the relatively high cost of
hauling empty cars had not been compounded by relatively
difficult demand conditions). Since freight load factors were
everywhere much higher than passenger load factors, however,
the low share of freight traffic on the Italian systems made
for low overall load factors (rows 5 and 8); and the latter
imply that the Italian systems' costs appear somewhat less
high per unit of capacity (row 22) than per unit of output.

Table 3.10: *Comparative statistics for the principal Italian, French and German railway systems in 1898*

	(1) RM (a)	(2) RA (b)	(3) Nord (c)	(4) PLM (d)	(5) VPH (e)
1. Kilometres of line track	6909	6277	6236	13178	41948
Traffic per kilometre of line track:					
2. thousand passenger kilometres	168	146	321	226	294
3. thousand freight ton-kilometres	178	173	496	406	531
4. thousand total traffic units (f)	346	319	817	631	826
5. Share of freight in total traffic	0.514	0.542	0.607	0.643	0.643
6. Load factor: in passenger operations	0.215	0.221	0.202	0.219	0.249
7. in freight operations	0.383	0.375	0.344	0.419	0.404
8. in all operations	0.278	0.284	0.270	0.316	0.331
9. Average loads: passengers per passenger train	57	49	63	59	93
10. freight tons per freight train	113	135	125	171	145
11. payload units (g) per train	79	75	92	105	121
12. payload units (g) per locomotive	57	52	75	83	?
Employment per million traffic units (f):					
13. in administration	0.8	1.0	0.3 (h)	0.4 (h)	0.5
14. in track surveillance and maintenance	6.6	8.3	2.0	2.2	2.7
15. in other activities (i)	12.9	10.8	6.2	6.4	6.8
16. total	20.3	20.1	8.5	9.0	10.0

Continued

Table 3.10: *Continued*

	(1) RM (a)	(2) RA (b)	(3) Nord (c)	(4) PLM (d)	(5) VPH (e)
17. Labour costs per employee (thousand lire)	1.32	1.23	1.59 (j)	1.59	1.50
Current costs actually incurred:					
lire per thousand traffic units (f):					
18. for labour	26.9	24.7	13.5 (k)	14.3	15.0
19. for fuel	5.8	5.1	1.6	2.6	3.1 (1)
20. other	8.9	9.8	6.8	6.8	8.1 (1)
21. total	41.6	39.6	21.9	23.7	26.2
22. lire per thousand capacity units (m)	11.6	11.3	5.9	7.5	8.7
23. lire per thousand actual weight units (n)	23.3	21.6	10.7	12.6	14.0
Current costs, calculated with Italian wages and material costs:					
24. lire per thousand traffic units (f)	41.6	39.6	28.4	28.6	32.1
25. lire per thousand capacity units (m)	11.6	11.3	7.7	9.1	10.6
26. lire per thousand actual weight units (n)	23.3	21.6	13.9	15.2	17.1
Operating revenues:					
27. lire per thousand passenger kilometres	45.7	45.4	33.9	42.4	33.6
28. lire per thousand freight ton-kilometres	68.2	69.2	47.9	54.4	46.2
29. Ratio of operating revenues to current costs	1.38	1.47	1.94	2.11	1.59

Continued

Notes:

Table 3.10: *Continued*

Notes: Continued

(c) Chemins de Fer du Nord
(d) Chemins de Fer de Paris à Lyon et à la Méditerranée
(e) Vereinigte Preussische und Hessische Staatseisenbahnen
(f) traffic units are unweighted sums of passenger kilometres and freight ton-kilometres
(g) payload units are unweighted sums of passengers and freight tons
(h) estimated on the basis of expenditure
(i) sales, operations and rolling stock maintenance
(j) assumed equal to that on the PLM
(k) based on estimated labour costs per employee
(l) assumes the same distribution of non-labour costs as on the PLM
(m) capacity units are unweighted sums of seat-kilometres and capacity ton-kilometres
(n) actual weight units are ton-kilometres computed with the actual weight of the passenger and freight cars and payloads

Source: See the Appendix to this chapter.

On the other hand, if one also allows for relative vehicle and payload weights, a unit of freight traffic represented a much higher gross weight actually hauled than a unit of passenger traffic; so the low share of freight on the Italian systems also means that their relative costs per unit of output understate their relative costs per ton-kilometre of gross weight actually hauled (row 23).

Most of the Italian systems' relative disadvantage seems traceable to unusually low labour productivities. Fuel costs (row 19), though often stressed in the literature, seem relatively unimportant: even if high coal prices and high fuel consumption made for fuel costs some three times higher than in France or Germany, the share of fuel in total costs was so low that its overall impact was clearly very minor (39). The prices and consumption levels of other non-labour items (row 20) may also have been relatively high in Italy, and their share of total costs was significantly larger than that of fuel; since their prices reflected Italy's relatively low wages as well as its high coal prices, however, the Italian systems' cost disadvantage in these items cannot have been more than a fraction of their disadvantage in fuel alone. Estimates of the French and German systems' costs on the basis of Italian-level fuel costs (calculated per ton-kilometre of gross weight actually .hauled), other non-labour costs (calculated with a generous two-thirds increase over their actual levels), and labour costs per employee thus leave more than half of the actual cost differences still to be explained (rows 24-6) (40). This large residual points to Italian staffing levels significantly higher, and correspondingly to labour productivities significantly lower, than can be accounted for by the relatively low ratio of wages to materials prices. The Italian systems' high employment levels and labour costs were thus not just the indirect result of high non-labour costs, but largely the direct result of a poor operating environment. The rugged terrain made for high maintenance needs, low (and unbalanced) traffic made for underutilised administrative, surveillance and station personnel, and both together made for light average loads per train and especially per locomotive; as a result, the output productivities of Italian railway workers were relatively low right across the board (rows 9-16).

The optimal utilisation of the railway network is in principle that which results from prices equal to marginal costs. Italy's unfavourable topography and natural resource endowment no doubt meant that marginal costs at any given level of utilisation were relatively high, and optimum utilisation rates relatively low. The utilisation rates that actually prevailed appear to have been well below the optimum,

however, since public policy kept prices well above marginal
costs. The state was both generically responsible for railway
fares (which were subject to public control), and specifically
responsible for claiming a 28 per cent share of the operating
revenues of the Rete Mediterranea and the Rete Adriatica (with
no corresponding contribution to their costs). This revenue-
sharing arrangement was equivalent to an excise tax on railway
fares at the rate of 39 per cent (the ratio of 28 per cent to
the residual 72 per cent); and it imposed a twofold constraint.
In the first place, since the companies had to be induced to
stay in business, the general fare level had to be high enough
to allow expected total revenues gross of tax to exceed
expected total costs by at least 39 per cent, or not much less
than the average actually observed (row 29); and since the
diseconomies of small scale meant that marginal costs were
below average costs, the average railway fare had to exceed
marginal costs by a correspondingly even greater
percentage (41). In the second place, since the companies had
to be induced to pursue sales at every relevant margin, *every*
railway rate and marginal revenue gross of tax had to exceed
the corresponding marginal cost by at least 39 per cent. The
rates faced by marginal traffic would be constrained by
average cost plus tax if the configuration of market demands
or legally imposed price ceilings prevented significant price
discrimination; they would instead be constrained by marginal
cost plus tax if inframarginal costs could be recovered by
above-average inframarginal rates, and marginal traffic
pursued by below-average marginal rates. A priori, all one
can say is that the revenue-sharing arrangement would make all
railway rates at least 39 per cent too high, with an even
greater excess in some or most (42).

The state seems constantly to have kept railway rates high
enough to yield, and let it capture, a significant operating
surplus. Its arrangements with the early regional groups had
made for operating revenues 60 per cent above current costs
in 1875; the state's share of marginal revenue was then
typically 50 per cent, implying railway rates and marginal
revenues equal to at least 200 per cent of marginal costs (43).
In 1911, the state railways' operating revenues were still
20 per cent above current costs; and most of the decline from
the roughly 40 per cent of 1898 seems attributable not to fare
reductions but to a sharp increase in costs following the
railways' nationalisation (44). At the same time, the state
constantly stimulated the construction of railways, either by
building them directly or by guaranteeing the builders a
subsidy per kilometre of line, and its annualised subsidy and
construction costs generously exceeded its annual income from
railway operations (45). On the face of it, this policy of

simultaneously encouraging the construction of railways and
discouraging their use was self-contradictory and absurd; but
a number of considerations warrant a more cautious judgement.

The taxation of railway traffic no doubt meant that the
network was inefficiently used, and therefore, in principle,
that total income was lower than it would otherwise have been.
In practice, however, the state surely faced a financial
constraint, and railway income was no doubt far more easily
taxed than the even greater income that would have accrued to
railway users had prices been set closer to marginal costs.
The inefficient use of the railway network cannot therefore
be condemned as wasteful without an appreciation of the
possibly greater inefficiencies that would have been produced
by increasing other public revenues or curtailing public
spending. Nor is it at all certain that the damage done by
the tax could have been reduced, at constant yield, by
altering its form. As noted above, a tax built into an operating contract in a context of economically or politically
constrained price discrimination would limit utilisation
through its effect on *average* cost, and its form was to that
extent a matter of indifference. In the case of concessions,
where the tax on revenue was in fact a progressive reduction
of the construction subsidy, the alternative of a fixed net
subsidy and lower railway rates would apparently have
resulted in an improvement in utilisation with no deterioration in the net financial position of either the State or
the concessionaire. But the appeal of these lump-sum
transfers that do not distort choices at the margin need not
survive as the analysis moves from a static context to a
dynamic one. Railway construction was a very long-term, risky
investment; a fixed net transfer would have put all of the
risk on the concessionaire, while the actual sliding scale
transferred much of it back to the state. The premium
necessary to compensate the concessionaire for a much
increased risk would have taken the form of a higher subsidy
(and therefore higher taxes elsewhere) or a higher net
operating income (and therefore higher railway rates): a
priori, one cannot say that the distortions produced by the
risk-sharing marginal tax rates would not have been exceeded
by the distortions produced by the risk-concentrating fixed
payments (46).

In the second place, railways have a military and strategic
significance as well as a commercial one; it may thus be
entirely rational for the state to build them even if they
are not to see much peacetime use, and reduce current net
income rather than increase it. These military-strategic
considerations seem always to have been important in Italy,
and never more so than in the first wave of railway

construction after 1861: the Franco-Piedmontese victories over
the Austrians that paved the way for national unification had
been due precisely to the use of railways to achieve a rapid
concentration of forces, and the early national governments
faced the need to consolidate their hold on a South that was
still often hostile (47). In the third place, of course, even
wasteful railway construction may be politically rational as
a pork-barrel project with which to favour one's constituents.
The Left's spendthrift ways, its ear for business interests,
and its reputation for dubious financial practices all suggest
that such considerations may have been particularly
significant during the second wave of railway construction,
after 1880, when public funds were poured into projects often
of purely local interest (48). But here too one cannot be sure
that sordid motives produced social waste; at a minimum, as we
shall see, the local lines built after 1880 were altogether
more useful than the trunk lines built in the preceding twenty
years.

7. THE IMPACT OF THE RAILWAY: AN ASSESSMENT

A comprehensive assessment of the overall impact of the railway
would of course evaluate the effects of railway transportation
together with those of railway construction. The unsurmounted
empirical difficulties discussed above in connection with the
effects of construction are equally relevant to the effects
of transportation; and where the former have received at least
an exploratory quantification, not even that much can be
claimed for the latter (49). Nor is it possible, in the context
of international factor mobility, to provide even a summary
'social saving' measure of the increase in national income
attributable to the reduction in transport costs. On the one
hand, the resources saved by transport improvements may simply
emigrate, so that the income gain accrues to the broader
international economy rather than to the small part of it in
which we happen to be interested. On the other hand, as noted
above, the reduction in transportation costs will typically
induce resource *immigration*, as the area now more cheaply
served is correspondingly more attractive to internationally
mobile activities; the income gain of the domestic economy
then includes both the 'social saving' and the income lost
by the rest of the world. In either case, the domestic gain
from transport improvements cannot be measured without
evidence on the transportation-elasticity of the domestic
resource base (50).

   For the present, all that can be hazarded is an overall
assessment of the extent to which the cost of building the

railways was actually warranted by the resulting reduction in
current transportation costs (51). The sample calculations in
Table 3.11 (rows 1-4) suggest that the internal rate of
return, including both the state's and the companies' net
income from operations, equalled just 3 per cent per annum in
the mid 1870s, and declined to roughly 2 per cent per annum
in the early years of the present century (col 4). The global
rate of return, which includes the surplus accruing to the
consumers, is of course very difficult to pin down; but some
plausible upper-bound estimates can be obtained on the
assumption that demand curves were linear, and that prices
were so set as to maximise total revenue (52).

Prices that maximise revenue are lower than those which
maximise profits (and therefore allow a larger consumers'
surplus); such prices were plausibly imposed by a state whose
own direct income from railway operations was, before
nationalisation, a given fraction of total revenue. After
nationalisation, the state's direct income is the operating
profit, so that nationalisation would if anything lead to
higher prices rather than lower ones; but there is no
evidence of a broadly-based rate increase before 1910 (53).
To be sure, the state might impose lower fares, not least
because it was able, in principle, to capture consumers'
surplus as well as producers' surplus; as seen above,
however, the fact that it taxed railway revenue at all
suggests that its ability to capture consumers' surplus was
in fact severely limited. Moreover, prices would have to
exceed the revenue-maximising level wherever demand was
relatively elastic even at the lowest price that would cover
marginal costs. The assumption that prices maximised revenue
may therefore somewhat overstate the price level and understate consumers' surplus; but not, presumably, by very much.
In any case, any downward bias on this score is plausibly
more than offset by the likely overstatement of consumers'
surplus that results from the assumption that demand curves
were linear. Whatever the shape of the demand curves for
transportation in general, the demand curves for railway
transportation in particular are likely to be convex from
below, as possible substitutes for the railway become
attractive at higher railway rates. In practice, then, the
assumption that consumers' surplus equalled half of total
revenue (which is what the present combination of assumptions
amounts to) seems a more than generous one, and the global
rates of return calculated on that basis are more likely to
be too high than too low (54). The actual global rate of
return thus seems to have averaged under 6 per cent per
annum (col 5): no more, and perhaps less, than the internal
rate earned by capital invested elsewhere at comparable risk

Table 3.11: *Sample rates of return on the investment in railways*

	(1) Total investment (end of year) (b)	(2) Total operating revenues (b)	(3) Total operating costs (b)	(4) Internal rate of return (a)	(5) Global rate of return (a) Upper bound (c)	(6) Global rate of return (a) Best estimate	(7) Total length of lines (d)
1. Total network: in 1875	2 296	155.2	90.1	2.8	6.2		
2. in 1890	4 139	271.8	173.4	2.4	5.7		
3. in 1901	5 604	347.3	247.2	1.8	4.9		
4. in 1910	6 962	604.0	452.4	2.2	6.5		
Components of the network in 1910:							
5. major Po Valley lines	1 822	226.8	142.0	4.7	10.9	9.0	2 483
6. other major lines	2 107	191.2	164.3	1.3	5.8	3.1	4 114
7. minor lines	3 032	186.0	146.1	1.3	4.4	4.4	11 328
Minor lines earning per kilometre, in 1910:							
8. less than 10 000 lire	833	32.3	30.2	0.3	2.2	2.2	4 866
9. more than 10 000 lire	2 199	153.7	115.9	1.7	5.2	5.2	6 462

(a) per cent per annum
(b) million lire
(c) calculated by adding half of total revenue to the operating surplus
(d) kilometres

Source: See the Appendix to this chapter.

levels (55). The capital invested in Italy's railways seems
to have yielded barely enough to cover its own cost, if that.
   Two glosses may here be in order. In the first place, of
course, the marginal social profitability of railway investment implies a negligible 'social saving'; but this does not
quite imply a negligible impact on the size of the domestic
resource base. While the railways did not reduce the social
cost of transportation, they did transfer much of that cost
from user charges to public debt-service costs; the latter
were covered by taxes, and could therefore be imposed, unlike
user charges, without regard to benefits received. If these
costs were imposed on internationally immobile resources
('land'), mobile resources might be attracted into Italy by
the lower user charges alone; in the opposite case, of
course, the net losers would be the mobile resources, and
these would accordingly tend to emigrate. The resulting
resource movements (in either direction) are perhaps unlikely
to have been significant; but they cannot be excluded a priori.
In the second place, the present calculations of the railways'
benefits do not take their strategic or political value into
account. As noted above, these benefits may warrant railway
construction even if the 'social saving' is negative; or, to
put the same point in different terms, a 'social saving'
measure that included the saving of alternative spending on
defence and pork-barrel projects would presumably be positive.
To the extent that these benefits represent no more than the
increased military and electoral security of a ruling estate,
however, they do not appear as benefits to the internationally
mobile resources; the size of the domestic resource base is
thus more likely to respond to the narrower 'social saving'
considered above (with all the indicated caveats) than to the
broader one considered here.
   The social profitability of the successive waves of
expansion of the Italian railway network cannot be gauged from
the changes in cumulative investment and in total surplus,
since the former also reflects the improvement of older lines,
and the latter also reflects system-wide changes in operating
conditions; but a rough surrogate is provided by a measure of
the rate of return earned on different parts of the network
near the end of the period at hand. The tentative estimates
in Table 3.11 (rows 5-7) disaggregate the network into three
parts: the major lines of the Po Valley, with their principal
links to the sea and to foreign rail lines; the major lines
in the peninsula and the islands; and the minor lines. These
correlate, somewhat loosely, with the lines originally built
before 1861; the lines built in 1861-80; and the lines built
after 1880 (and, mostly, by 1895) (56).
   The first striking result of these calculations is that the

internal rate of return of the investment in minor lines was
no lower than that of the major lines outside the Po Valley,
as their relatively low gross earnings per kilometre were
accompanied by low current costs per kilometre and especially
by low capital costs per kilometre (rows 6-7, cols 1-4 and 7).
The traditional evaluations that consider only relative gross
earnings per kilometre, and attribute relatively high capital
costs to the minor lines, seem correspondingly wide of the
mark (57). Those major lines admittedly outperform the minor
lines if one adds half of gross revenue to the operating
surplus (rows 6-7, col 5); but there is here a strong
presumption that the comparison is vitiated by the figures'
differential bias. The minor lines were overwhelmingly inland
routes, typically with no competition beyond that provided by
relatively inefficient horse-drawn road vehicles. Since
interlocal price discrimination was surely subject to political and administrative constraints, this limited intermodal
competition also increases the likelihood that prices were
below the level that would have maximised revenues on those
particular routes; as a result, the nominal upper bound is
here actually a relatively conservative best estimate. The
major lines outside the Po Valley were instead overwhelmingly
coastal or transpeninsular routes, and thus typically subject
to efficient waterborne competition. There is no doubt that
that competition bit deeply into the demand for railway
transportation: while the railway's superior speed and
comfort gave it a margin of superiority over the coasting
trade in carrying passengers and express freight, it found
it extremely difficult to win over other freight traffic
without the aid of special discounts (58). A best estimate
might allow these lines a consumers' surplus equal to 20
(rather than 50) per cent of gross revenue; the result is a
global rate of return that is quite low both with respect to
that earned by the minor lines (rows 6-7, col 6) and with
respect to the likely cost of capital.

The major drain on the global profitability of the Italian
rail system thus appears to have been the trunk system in the
peninsula and the islands, and not, as is widely thought,
the large mileage of minor lines. No doubt, the latter
included a conspicuous wasteful fringe, as the approximately
5000 kilometres earning less than 10 000 lire per annum
appear to have yielded a global rate of return below even
that of the peninsular trunk lines (rows 6 and 8, cols 4-6).
But the loss on these fringe lines was only about half that
incurred on the major lines outside the Po Valley, and the
other 6500 kilometres of minor lines seem to have come close
to covering their costs (row 9, col 6) (59). A breakeven
return may also have been earned on the cheaper portions of

the peninsular trunks, for instance along the Adriatic coast;
and even apparently unprofitable lines may actually have paid
for themselves by enhancing traffic and surplus on the rest
of the system. But with all due allowance for the weakness of
the present measures, the locus of socially costly construction seems to have been the trunk system much more than the
local lines. This result, though at odds with the prevailing
evaluations of the Italian railways, should come as no
surprise. A cheaply built rail line may represent a major
improvement in the accessibility of a land-locked site; but
there is no commercial advantage to drilling through a
mountain if one can sail around it (60).

This re-evaluation of the peninsular trunks and minor lines
points naturally to a re-evaluation of the railway-
construction policies of the Right and of the Left. The trunk
lines built by the Right in the immediate aftermath of
national unification seem to have done little to lower
transport costs; to the extent that one can judge from their
rate of return many years later, their cost had to be
justified at least as much by military and strategic benefits
as by commercial ones. The early flurry of railway construction thus appears not as the progressive fulfilment of a
precondition for economic growth but as a drag on development,
no different, in this light, from 'investment' in a large
standing army. The Left was responsible for that final and
most wasteful link in the peninsular trunk system, along the
western coast of southern Italy; but a majority at least of
the local lines built in the 1880s and 1890s seem to have been
warranted by their commercial benefits alone. The reduction
in transport costs per unit of railway investment thus
plausibly increased, rather than decreased, around 1880; and
whatever limited modernisation was induced in the peninsula
by the fall in transport costs before the diffusion of the
internal combustion engine seems better attributed to the
later minor lines than to the earlier trunks. Again, perhaps,
not surprisingly, the railways resulting from the Right's
high-minded pursuit of what it took to be the national
interest seem to have done altogether less to improve the
material conditions of the population than the railways
resulting from the Left's rather corrupt pliancy to the
wishes of its constituents (61).

The major Po Valley routes, largely laid out before 1861
(and substantially extended and improved, of course, in later
decades), were clearly the most valuable parts of the Italian
railway system. Their internal rate of return equalled nearly
5 per cent per annum, or over three times the average earned
on the rest of the system (rows 5-7, col 4). The upper-bound
estimate of their global rate of return is in the neighbour-

hood of 11 per cent per annum; and the present best estimate, at 9 per cent per annum, is handsomely above both the return to the rest of the network and the likely cost of capital. This best estimate is based on a ratio of consumers' surplus to revenue equal to 35 per cent, midway between the 50 per cent allowed the minor lines and the 20 per cent allowed the other major lines, to reflect the availability of natural and artificial navigable waterways from the Lombard lakes to the Venetian lagoon. These remained in use, providing some competition for the railways, despite near-total public neglect; and they had apparently allowed the first development even of the Piedmontese textile industry, in the area adjoining the Lombard lakes, before the coming of the railway (62).

The existence and possible development of this water-based alternative suggests that the railway made its greatest contribution to the upper reaches of the Po Valley and to the Ligurian ports. In the Upper Po Valley, navigable waterways were not available, and water resources were probably too limited to allow for navigation without sacrificing irrigated agriculture (63). Limits on the local water supply, and the difficulty of the terrain, similarly seem to have ruled out canal links across the Ligurian Apennines from Genoa and Savona to the Po; While these were planned in the early nineteenth century, they were never built, and these ports remained largely without a hinterland until the coming of the railway (64). Lower in the Po Valley and along its Adriatic shore, the increased availability of waterways limited the gain from the railway, and the trade created by the development of the upper valley was balanced, wholly or in part, by the diversion of trade to the Ligurian ports. Had transport improvements been pursued by improving navigation rather than by building railways, the focus of Italy's industrial growth would no doubt have been located rather lower in the valley than it actually was, and served through Venice rather than through Genoa. The limits to this counterfactual industrial development depend, of course, on the long-run supply curve of internal navigation. If the latter could have been cheaply and abundantly expanded, the net effect of choosing railways over waterways would be little more than a westward shift in the location of industry and a redirection of trade; if the waterways' potential was instead extremely limited, a large portion, as well as the location, of Italy's industrial growth may be attributed to the railway. In either case, however, the industrial development of the Upper Po Valley, and its primary orientation to the western Mediterranean, remain the work of the railway.

The infrastructure that most mattered to Italian industrial
growth as it actually took place was thus the regional network
in northwest Italy, largely laid out in the 1850s. From a
national point of view, the extension of the railway network
throughout the peninsula after 1861 may have been of doubtful
value; from a regional point of view, the gain from the
railway construction launched by the pre-unification
Piedmontese state was undoubtedly large.

NOTES AND REFERENCES

I wish to thank the Ente per gli studi monetari, bancari, e
finanziari 'Luigi Einaudi' and the National Science Foundation
(grant no. SES79-13427) for their financial support, and
V. Ceriani, P. Ciocca, K. Kimbrough, J. Pincus, the members of
the 1979 Renfe seminar and the Triangle Economic History
Workshop, and the editor of this volume for their helpful
comments and suggestions. Responsibility for the views
expressed here is of course mine alone.

1. There is a vast and varied literature on Italy's railways.
    The histories by A. Crispo, *Le ferrovie italiane* (Milan,
    1940) and F. Tajani, *Storia delle ferrovie italiane*
    (Milan, 1939) are old but still useful; so too the
    detailed account in I. Sachs, *L'Italie: ses finances et
    son développement économique* (Paris, 1885). The present
    chronology of railway construction is derived initially
    from R. Ispettorato generale delle strade ferrate,
    Relazione sull'esercizio delle strade ferrate italiane
    (henceforth *Relazione SFI)*, e.g. 1899 pp. 60-90, and
    subsequently from Direzione generale della statistica,
    Annuario statistico italiano (henceforth *Annuario)*,
    e.g. 1913 p. 231.
2. The rapid growth of the Istat index in the late 1860s and
    early 1870s was not confirmed by my subsequent index. The
    indices are described in A. Gerschenkron, *Economic
    Backwardness in Historical Perspective* (Cambridge, Mass.,
    1962) pp. 367-421; Istituto centrale di statistica
    (Istat), *Annali di statistica,* series 8, vol.9:*Indagine
    statistica sullo sviluppo del reddito nazionale
    dell'Italia dal 1861 al 1956* (Rome, 1957; henceforth
    Reddito nazionale) pp. 98-9; S. Fenoaltea, 'Public Policy
    and Italian Industrial Development, 1861-1913',
    unpublished PhD dissertation, Harvard University
    (Cambridge, Mass., 1967) chs. 1-3. See also S. Fenoaltea
    'Decollo, ciclo, e intervento dello Stato', in
    A. Caracciolo (ed), *La formazione dell'Italia industriale*

2. *Continued*

(Bari, 1969) pp. 96-9, and S. Fenoaltea, 'Railroads and
Italian Industrial Growth, 1861-1913', *Explorations in
Economic History,* IX (1972) 349. My own effort to extend
and improve the available information base is currently
under way: see S. Fenoaltea, *Italian Industrial Production, 1861-1913: A Statistical Reconstruction*
(incomplete typescript, 1980; forthcoming, Cambridge
University Press).

3. Gerschenkron, *Economic Backwardness;* A. Gerschenkron,
Continuity in History and Other Essays (Cambridge,
Mass., 1968); R. Romeo, *Risorgimento e capitalismo*
(Bari, 1959); R. Romeo, *Breve storia della grande
industria in Italia* (Bologna, 1961).

4. Romeo, *Risorgimento e capitalismo,* pp. 17-18.

5. Gerschenkron, *Economic Backwardness,* pp. 5-30, 353-64.

6. Fenoaltea, 'Public Policy and Italian Industrial
Development'; Fenoaltea, 'Decollo'; S. Fenoaltea,
'Riflessioni sull'esperienza industriale italiana dal
Risorgimento alla prima guerra mondiale', in G. Toniolo
(ed), *Lo sviluppo economico italiano 1861-1940* (Bari,
1973). The popularity of stages-of-growth models peaked
with W. W. Rostow, *The Stages of Economic Growth*
(Cambridge, Mass., 1960), as much of the work inspired
by that dramatic essay failed to find empirical support
for its generalisations.

7. On the familiar accelerator principle, the demand for
durables depends not on the desired level of capacity but
on the change in that level; an increase in the desired
level of capacity leads to a *temporary* increase in the
demand for durables. The domestic demand for metal goods
had in fact begun to fall by 1913; but its likely
continued decline was turned into a sharp increase by
the outbreak of war (which had the advantage, from the
point of view of the metalworking industries, of turning
their products into current consumables).

8. In the case of the new industries, one should strictly
speaking say 'not untrue' rather than 'true', since
there is no proof that the response to new opportunities
would have been equally prompt in earlier years. There
is also some question as to whether the introduction of
the sugar beet induced the increased protection against
imported sugar, or vice versa; but this issue is here
immaterial.

9. On the time path of public works construction, see
Fenoaltea, *Italian Industrial Production*. The benefits
of railway transportation are discussed in sections 6

9. *Continued*

and 7 below.

10. It has recently been pointed out that the growth of German-style banks came largely at the expense of other financial instruments, so that even their absolute contribution to capital accumulation in industry would be limited to their superiority over existing institutions – a superiority which is typically taken for granted, but the extent and institutional basis of which have yet to be established. See A. M. Biscaini Cotula and P. Ciocca, 'Le strutture finanziarie: aspetti quantitativi di lungo periodo (1870-1970)'. in F. Vicarelli (ed), *Capitale industriale e capitale finanziario: il caso italiano* (Bologna, 1979).

11. *Annuario,* 1913 p. 46. See also J. D. Gould, 'European Inter-Continental Emigration. The Road Home: Return Migration from the USA', *Journal of European Economic History,* IX (1980) 41-112.

12. Istituto centrale di statistica (Istat), *Sommario di statistiche storiche italiane, 1861-1955* (Roma, 1958; henceforth *Sommario*). pp. 152, 172.

13. Over the last few decades, for example, the German and Swiss economies have notoriously been characterised by a flexible resource base, as the number of 'guest workers' responded elastically to domestic demand; these economies therefore combined low unemployment figures (even when employment had been falling) with the lack of resource constraints commonly attributed to underemployed economies. See J. C. Lambelet and K. Schiltknecht, *On the Importance of an Elastic Supply of Labor and Capital: Simulation Results for the Swiss Economy* (Zurich, 1973).

14. These tables cover tramways as well as railways, since much of the basic evidence (on employment, production and international trade) does not distinguish between them.

15. The similar effect one would have expected around 1865 may have been masked by the more rapid relative growth of the entire railway network.

16. These figures are obtained as follows. Value added in construction, from Table 3.3, cols 3-4. Value of construction, value added divided by 0.55. Land value, 3 per cent of value in construction. Value of rails, value added (Table 3.6, col 2) divided by 0.29; value of accessories, engineering value added (Table 3.4, col 6) divided by 0.50. The rest of the value of construction is distributed as follows: 30 per cent, value added in processing construction materials; 45 per cent, value added in quarrying; 25 per cent, value of fuel. Value

16. *Continued*

added in engineering, from Table 3.4, cols 2 and 6.
Value of engineering, value added in freight cars
(Table 3.5, col 6) divided by 0.66, and other value
added divided by 0.50. Value of metal consumed in
engineering, value added (Table 3.6, col 3 plus col
6 minus col 4) divided by 0.32. The rest of the value
of engineering is attributed, for simplicity, to fuel
and natural resources. Value added in metalmaking, from
Table 3.6, col 8 minus col 4. Value of metalmaking, value
of rails plus value of metal consumed in engineering, as
above. Value of metalmaking raw materials: 80 per cent
scrap and 20 per cent fuel, or 40 per cent ore and 60
per cent fuel. Total value, value of construction plus
value of engineering. See also the appendix to this
chapter summarising the derivation of the estimates in
the tables, and Fenoaltea, *Italian Industrial Production.*
Strictly speaking, of course, scrap metal was not a
'natural' resource, and coal costs, in Italy, consisted
largely of international transportation.

17. The lower figures are based on certain domestic production (Table 3.4, col 1 and Table 3.6, col 1), while the
higher ones include possible domestic production, i.e.
the consumption that cannot be allocated between domestic
production and imports (Table 3.4, col 6 and Table 3.6,
col 3 plus col 5 minus col 4); the metal content of
imported rolling stock (Table 3.6, col 6 minus col 5) is
assumed to have been imported.

18. In the early years, in fact, the repair shops appear to
have accounted for a significant proportion of the
domestic production of vehicles as well as for their
maintenance.

19. The actual estimates are 14 per cent and 19 per cent if
the metal content of imported rolling stock is included
in total consumption (col 8), and 16 per cent and 21 per
cent if it is not (col 7).

20. The corresponding shares of the total railway demand for
engineering (fabricated metal and machinery: cols 5 plus
6) are 53 per cent in 1861–95 and 48 per cent in 1896–
1913.

21. These ratios are based on a simple comparison of the
changes in railway production (Table 3.3, col 8) to the
changes in, or initial levels of, total production (col
9); they thus entirely ignore possible indirect effects.
The latter are returned to below.

22. In the present case, the industry totals are all defined
to exclude shipbuilding and the production of wood road

22. *Continued*

    vehicles.

23. The distinction between new production and maintenance is admittedly arbitrary; in the present case, the maintenance of fabricated metal is the largest single component of the engineering industry because it is taken to include the entire large blacksmithing sector, the size of which appears related to the stock, rather than to the flow, of fabricated metal. Any transfer of engineering value added from maintenance to new production would of course reduce the size of railway demand relative to current new production.

24. The comparisons to all metalmaking would be even closer to the comparisons to semi-finished ferrous metalmaking if railway metal were assumed to have been manufactured from ore rather than from scrap; see Table 3.6, note (a).

25. See R. A. Mundell, *International Economics* (London, 1968), ch. 18 and Fenoaltea, 'Railroads and Italian Industrial Growth', to which the reader is referred for a more complete discussion.

26. To an extent, this problem stems from the static nature of the model, which forces the full effect of any cause into a single time period; more generally, it is the usual result of joint causation, no more paradoxical than the hanging of twelve men for a single murder.

27. With realistically finite elasticities, the displaced production would not be quite the same in the two cases: in a demand-limited context, it would probably include a more than proportionate share of other investment; in a supply-limited context, it would probably include a more than proportionate share of other construction (and of other activities using unskilled labour). But the essential point remains.

28. This assumes that interest rates varied across risk classes, and that government bonds became riskier as public debt increased. The government thus faced a rising cost-of-borrowing curve even though it did not affect 'the' interest rate (i.e. the interest rate within each risk class).

29. Three sources of dissatisfaction with the model in Fenoaltea, 'Railroads and Italian Industrial Growth' may be pointed out, beyond the obvious ones implicit in its static nature and small size. The first one, which addresses the entire model, is the fact that the parameters are very crudely guessed, and not directly measured. The second one is the neglect of construction materials, which are also industrial products, in the

29. *Continued*

composition of railway investment. The third and most
troubling one is the lack of an explicit formulation of
the determinants of domestic prices, real wages and
international labour movements. These were neglected on
the understanding that the flexibility in labour employment levels stemmed from significant domestic
unemployment; I am now sceptical of the latter (since
the one million industrial workers counted by the 1911
demographic census but missed by the simultaneous
industrial census seem to have been not so much
unemployed as self-employed in artisanal operations:
Fenoaltea, 'Railroads and Italian Industrial Growth',
328n), and incline to stress international mobility
instead. See also note 49 below.

30. Venice, the Netherlands and England are obvious cases in
point. For an analysis of a negative example, where the
possible density of resources was limited by poor
transportation, see D. R. Ringrose, 'Transportation and
Economic Stagnation in Eighteenth-Century Castile',
Journal of Economic History, XXVIII (1968) 51-79.

31. The state railways' total shipments (39 million tons),
seaport loadings (11 million tons, disaggregated by port),
and rail imports (2 million tons) are reported in
Direzione generale delle ferrovie dello Stato,
*Relazione dell'amministrazione delle ferrovie esercitate
dallo Stato* (henceforth *Relazione FS*), 1911-12 pp. 293-9.
An estimate of the other railways' total shipments (6
million tons) is based on the preceding year's figure in
Ufficio speciale delle ferrovie e tramvie e degli
automobili, *Relazione sull'esercizio delle strade ferrate
concesse all'industria privata* (henceforth *Relazione SFC*),
1910 p. 319; since these railways were very largely
confined to the country's interior, their direct seaport
loadings and rail imports are here considered negligible.
The combined shipments of the state and other railways
(45 million tons) are reduced by 5 million tons to allow
for double-counting; this figure includes some 3 million
tons transshipped from the state to the other railways,
and some 2 million tons transshipped in the opposite
direction. The former transshipments are estimated as 1.3
times the latter, from the evidence on the directional
imbalance at the domestic rail transshipment points in
Direzione generale delle ferrovie dello Stato,
Statistica dell'esercizio (henceforth *Statistica FS*),
1911 part 2 pp. 439-43; the latter transshipments are
instead obtained as the difference between the state

31. *Continued*

railways' loadings from all other rail systems on the one
hand, and from foreign rail systems only on the other
(*Relazione FS*, 1911-12 pp. 292, 299). Loadings in the
interior are obtained by deducting seaport loadings and
rail imports from estimated total shipments.

32. *Sommario*, pp. 144, 146.

33. In 1973, overland shipments by modern means totalled 1168
million tons (89 per cent of them by road, 6 per cent by
pipeline, and 5 per cent by rail: Ministero dei
trasporti, *Compendio di statistiche sui trasporti*, 1977
pp. 59, 62, 94, 102). Imports totalled 217 million tons
(*Annuario*, 1976 p. 271); domestic shipments by modern
overland means thus equalled (at least) 951 million tons,
or about 33 times the comparable level in 1911. Total
commodity production, in turn, increased in value from
some 14.1 thousand million lire to some 40.8 million
million lire; these estimates are obtained as domestic
value added in commodity production plus half the value
of imports (*Sommario*, pp. 152, 213; *Annuario*, 1976 pp.
271, 413), on the assumption that the other half of
imports were consumed directly or in the production of
services. Since the wholesale price index increased from
1.00 in 1911 to 429 in 1973 (*Annuario*, 1971 p. 307,
1975 p. 313), physical commodity output in 1973 was only
about 6.7 times the comparable level in 1911. Shipments
per ton of commodity output grew as the ratio of the
growth in total shipments to the growth in physical
commodity output (33/6.7), or approximately five-fold
from 1911 to 1973.

34. Seaport loadings for cereal and various other major items,
but not lumber, are reported in the *Relazione FS*,
1911-12 p. 306. However, the international trade
statistics suggest that roughly half of Italy's lumber
imports arrived directly by rail from Austria-Hungary
and Switzerland. See Direzione generale delle gabelle,
Movimento commerciale del Regno d'Italia (henceforth
Movimento commerciale), 1900 pp. 196-7, 1911 part 1 p. 168.

35. Sand is here a partial exception, in that the proportion
of output moved by rail seems unusually high for a good
whose value per ton was under half that of bricks and
tiles, and perhaps one tenth that of lime and cement. A
likely explanation is the availability of a special low
rate, as suggested (with all due allowance for possible
variations in the average haul) by railway revenues of
about 2 lire per ton of sand, against a typical range of
4 to 10 lire per ton (*Relazione FS*, 1911-12 p. 312).

36. See e.g. Comitato d'inchiesta industriale, *Atti* (10 vols, Florence and Rome, 1873-4), *Deposizioni orali* category 8 sub 1 - 2 - 3 instalments I pp. 2, 8, instalment III pp. 2, 9, instalment VI p. 3; R. Corpo delle miniere, *Rivista del servizio minerario* (henceforth *Rivista mineraria),* 1898 p. 238. Coal freight rates suggest that the cost of sea transport from England to Italy was typically equivalent to the cost of rail transport over 300 to 600 kilometres, while the distance from Turin to Naples is nearly 1000 kilometres. See E. A. V. Angier, *Fifty Years' Freights* (London, 1920); R. Commissione per lo studio di proposte intorno all'ordinamento delle strade ferrate, *Atti* (10 vols, Rome, 1903-6; henceforth *Atti CSO),* vol. 5 parts 1-2 p. 100. The South's relatively inefficient industry, built up behind the prohibitive tariff walls of the Kingdom of Naples, was thus largely destroyed by foreign competition when the low Piedmontese tariff was extended to the entire peninsula in 1860; what survived does not appear to have been affected by the completion of the first all-rail route to the North in 1866. See G. Luzzatto, *L'economia italiana dal 1861 al 1914,* vol. 1 (Milan, 1963) pp. 27-35; also E. Sereni, *Capitalismo e mercato nazionale in Italia,* 2nd edn (Rome, 1974) pp. 71, 93. Sereni's view that the railways were the means by which Italy's ruling bourgeoisie welded the local markets into a national one is undermined both by the evidence of limited inter-regional transportation presented in Table 3.9 and, more directly, by the evidence that the peninsular trunk lines did little or nothing to reduce interregional transport user charges; see Sereni, *Capitalismo,* pp. 69-76 and note 58 below.

37. See for instance G. Baglioni, *Per la riforma ferroviaria* (Milan, 1910); M. Diegoli, 'La trazione a vapore', *Ingegneria ferroviaria,* XVI (1961) 671-80; M. Maroni, 'L'armamento del binario', *Ingegneria ferroviaria,* XVI (1961) 595-600. In fact, the incidence of curves and gradients reflects a trade-off between capital and current costs, and therefore expected utilisation levels, just as much as the equipment standard for the existing lines; the only difference is that the construction of the basic right of way involves a relatively longer time horizon. In either case, improvements allow for marginal costs inclusive of additional capital costs lower than marginal costs with the existing track and equipment.

38. The pruning of off-peak capacity to raise load factors tends to raise costs per unit of capacity, since the variable costs saved by such adjustments are a relatively small part of total costs; the labour force, in particular,

38. *Continued*

   remains relatively constant, and is simply underutilised
   at off-peak times. The superior solution is, of course,
   the systematic use of discriminatory pricing to offset the
   fluctuations in demand and 'flatten the load curve';
   but this seems to be a relatively recent development.
   See J. R. Nelson (ed), *Marginal Cost Pricing in Practice*
   (Englewood Cliffs, NJ, 1964).

39. Relative fuel costs are probably best compared on the
   basis of ton-kilometres of gross weight actually hauled
   (within rounding error, row 19 times row 23 divided by
   row 21), since these seem least affected by extraneous
   factors (input substitution, traffic composition and so
   on). The possible impact of relative fuel costs is better
   gauged by scaling fuel costs up on the foreign systems
   than by scaling them down on the Italian systems: in the
   presence of input substitution, the former estimate
   provides an upper bound, the latter a lower one. Relative
   fuel costs are stressed e.g. in *Atti CSO*, vol. 5 parts
   1-2 pp. 119-20; see also *Relazione FS*, 1906-7 p. 12 and
   Baglioni, *Per la riforma ferroviaria*, p.14.

40. Unlike fuel costs, other non-labour costs are scaled up
   by an ad hoc allowance because they seem so highly subject
   to input substitution that none of the available comparisons can reveal the influence of relative prices and
   terrain-related consumption levels alone. The estimated
   cost levels of the French and German systems are in
   principle upper bounds, since they neglect the savings
   that could have resulted from substitution among inputs.

41. Marginal cost is difficult to evaluate directly, since the
   time-series evidence is here more than usually ambiguous.
   Traffic rose relatively constantly from 1898 to 1913; but
   measured productivity (train-kilometres per employee)
   rose from 1898 to 1905, then fell sharply to 1907, and
   then recovered. The main influence here was the reduced
   hiring by the private companies in the last few years of
   their contracts, the 28 per cent increase in staff in the
   two years after nationalisation, and the subsequent
   virtual freeze on hiring. Service also deteriorated to
   notoriously poor levels early in this century, and
   apparently did not recover until the state railways had
   digested their new personnel, and improved their
   equipment, after a few years of operation. See
   Relazione FS, 1910-11 pp. 8-15; also e.g. Baglioni,
   Per la riforma ferroviaria, p. 42 and Tajani, *Storia delle
   ferrovie italiane*, pp. 115-23. The international comparisons in row 29 indicate that the ratio of operating

41. *Continued*

revenues to current costs was even higher on the major
French and German systems than on the Italian ones.
However, their lower average revenues suggest lower
prices (rows 26-7; see also the sample rates in *Atti CSO*,
vol. 5 parts 1-2 pp. 99-117), and their high utilisation
levels (row 4) suggest that marginal costs may have
exceeded average costs. On the Nord and the Preussische-
Hessische, especially, one cannot say from the evidence
at hand that prices were obviously too high.

42. The 28 per cent-72 per cent revenue split discussed here
applied to the main lines of the Rete Mediterranea and
Rete Adriatica, on which they earned some 95 per cent of
their revenue. On the minor lines, they received a small
fixed subsidy per kilometre of line, and operating
revenues were shared with the state on a 50-50 basis
(equivalent to a 100 per cent excise tax). See *Atti CSO*,
vol. 4 part 2 pp. 8-10; *Relazione SFI*, 1898 cols 933,
944-5; Sachs, *L'Italie*, pp. 1061-4. The state could waive
its share of revenue to allow special low rates, but this
was very rarely done. See R. Ispettorato generale delle
strade ferrate, *Relazione intorno all'esercizio delle
strade ferrate delle reti Mediterranea, Adriatica,
e Sicula dal 1º luglio 1885 al 1900* (4 parts in 6 vols,
Rome, 1901), part 3 pp. 209-29; also *Atti CSO*, vol. 3
p. 556. In addition to thus sharing revenue, the state
levied explicit excise taxes at the rate of 13 per cent
on passenger and 'grande velocità' freight, and 2 per
cent on 'piccola velocità' freight; e.g. *Annuario*, 1904
p. 494.

43. These arrangements were relatively complex, since they
covered construction as well as operation. Taxes on
revenue were imposed as a reduction in the construction
subsidy, normally on a sliding scale; a 50 per cent
marginal rate, equivalent to a 100 per cent excise, seems
to have applied to the Romane, the Meridionali and the
recent lines of the Alta Italia. The old Piedmontese
state lines were instead sold to the Alta Italia, so that
the state could immediately obtain the capitalised
operating surplus allowed by the fares specified in the
act of sale; these fares were in any case the same as
those applicable on the lines subject to tax. The railway
reorganisation of 1885 was accompanied by a significant
reduction in railway rates, apparently on the companies'
initiative; since cost levels changed relatively little,
the reduction in fares is plausibly attributed to the
lower marginal tax rates introduced by the new conventions.

43. *Continued*

The fiscally optimal fare level was also probably reduced
by the elimination of the state's former interest in the
maximisation of expected net revenue on the lines it sold
to the Alta Italia, and the consequent generalisation of
its interest in the maximisation of the railways' gross
revenues. See *Annuario*, 1878 part 1 p. 140, 1905–7 p. 669;
E. Corbino, *Annali dell'economia italiana*, vol. 3 (Città
di Castello, 1933) p. 305; *Raccolta ufficiale delle leggi
e dei decreti del Regno d'Italia*, XI (1865) pp. 696, 765,
768, 819, 855; Sachs, *L'Italie*, pp. 966–7.

44. *Annuario*, 1913 p. 242; *Relazione FS*, 1910–11 pp. 10–11.

45. See e.g. *Relazione SFI*, 1898 pp. 8–9 and *Relazione FS*,
1910–11 pp. 23–4.

46. A similar argument applies to the possibility of a lump-
sum tax in operating contracts. In fact, the decline of
the state's typical share of revenue from 50 per cent to
28 per cent suggests that growing experience reduced
uncertainty and allowed the companies to shoulder a
greater portion of the remaining risk. Taxes on profits
were also possible in principle; in practice, however,
they were difficult to administer, and would blunt the
incentive to control costs about as much as they would
redistribute risk. Public operation would let the state
bear the risk directly, but would encounter similar cost-
control problems; moreover, though practised as a last
resort, it was politically infeasible as a permanent
solution in the 1880s, and then legally infeasible until
the expiration of the twenty-year conventions signed in
1885. The likelihood that the prevailing system was the
result of rational choice is strengthened by the evidence
that the state was aware of the traffic-reducing
incentives associated with high marginal revenue tax
rates, and knowingly accepted them. See e.g. Commissione
d'inchiesta sull'esercizio delle ferrovie italiane, *Atti*
(3 parts in 7 vols, Rome, 1879–84; henceforth *Atti CIE*)
part 2 vol. 2 pp. 559–63; Corbino, *Annali dell'economia
italiana*, vol. 3, pp. 288–96.

47. See e.g. Luzzatto, *L'economia italiana*, pp. 24–6;
Tajani, *Storia delle ferrovie italiane*, p. 62; S. J. Woolf,
'La storia politica e sociale', in R. Romano and C. Vivante
(eds), *Storia d'Italia*, vol. 3 (Turin, 1973) p. 508. The
railway requirements of the military were considered in
Atti CIE, part 2 vol. 3 pp. 1237–96 and *Atti CSO*, vol. 3
pp. 9–38, 63–143.

48. E.g. Baglioni, *Per la riforma ferroviaria*, pp. 90–2; Corbin
Annali dell'economia italiana, vol. 3, pp. 218, 268, 309,

48. *Continued*

    313, 320-4, 342-3; A. Plebano, *Storia della finanza italiana*, vol. 2 (Turin, 1900) pp. 162-70.

49. A calculation of the effect of the post-1861 extensions of the railway network was admittedly presented in Fenoaltea, 'Railroads and Italian Industrial Growth', but the results of that tentative effort are of little value. On the one hand, in light of the evidence in Table 3.9, the metal import-substitution there attributed to railway transportation seems vastly overestimated. On the other, there is no attempt to measure what was surely the most immediate effect of the provision of railway transportation: namely, the reduction in the transportation provided by, and therefore in investment in, alternative transport modes. While the railways' apparent lack of superiority over these alternatives warranted neglecting the income effect, as it were, the substitution effect was plausibly significant.

50. A familiar analogy is provided by the impact of technical progress on a particular industry. If the elasticity of demand for its output is low, the decline in costs will lead to a decline in the volume of resources employed in the industry; at the limit, output remains constant, and all the resources saved by technical change migrate to other industries. An industry facing a highly elastic demand will instead recruit additional resources and expand its production by far more than the productivity gain alone would allow.

51. The railways' construction costs would not need to be deducted from their gross benefits to the Italian economy if Italy had had the wit to export those costs, as some did, by importing the needed capital and then defaulting on the debt.

52. A linear demand curve is elastic above its midpoint, and inelastic below it; the midpoint accordingly defines the price that maximises total revenue. With always positive marginal costs, the price that maximises profits falls necessarily in the elastic portion of the curve, i.e. above the price that that maximises total revenue. The operative demand curve is here the one that allows for induced resource movements; the total surplus defined by this demand curve and the railway transportation supply curve accordingly measures the world's gain from Italy's railways, and not Italy's own gain (which includes the transfer price of immigrant resources, or excludes that of emigrant resources).

53. E.g. *Relazione FS*, 1909-10 pp. 59-67. A general rate

53. *Continued*

increase was sanctioned by the law n. 310 of 13 April 1911
(arts. 14-15); but this seems to have been a response to
increasing costs rather than a switch to profit maximisation.
54. The essential point is that intermodal competition would
tend to reduce the ratio of consumers' surplus to railway
revenue; a convex demand curve, and a linear demand curve
that is highly elastic even at the lowest acceptable
price, are essentially alternative manifestations of the
same phenomenon. Price discrimination, which transformed
into railway revenue what would otherwise have been
consumers' surplus, would here have an equivalent effect.
Since railway rates were set for long periods, the
assumption that prices continuously maximised revenues
produces a cyclical variation in the bias of the present
year-specific estimates; by the same token, however, the
present rate-of-return figures may be considered partly
sheltered from cyclical disturbances.
55. That rate appears to have been close to 6 per cent per
annum until the mid-1880s; it then declined to about 5
per cent per annum by the mid-1890s, and remained near
that level up to the eve of the First World War (Biscaini
Cotula and Ciocca, 'Le strutture finanziarie', pp.
122-6). The global rate of return to railway investment
is properly compared to the internal rate of return to
alternative investment if the capital invested in
railways was imported or withdrawn from marginal projects
with negligible surplus.
56. The network length figures in Table 3.11, col 7, refer to
the 'operated network', which double-counts those segments
common to more than one line; the figure in Table 3.1,
col 5, refers instead to the unduplicated 'installed
network'. The two measures are reconciled e.g. in
Relazione SFC, 1910 p. 65, *Statistica FS*, 1910 pp. 58-60.
57. E.g. Baglioni, *Per la riforma ferroviaria*, pp. 90-2;
Relazione FS, 1906-7 pp. 12-13. The latter erroneously
measured the capital costs of the minor lines from the
secular growth in average investment per kilometre,
neglecting the improvement of older lines.
58. See e.g. *Atti CIE*, part 1 vol. 2 pp. 83 and 99, vol. 3
p. 306. Particularly significant is the railways' 1886
petition, which was denied, for special rates with which
to attract traffic from traditional sailing coasters.
See R. Ispettorato generale delle strade ferrate, *Annali
del consiglio delle tariffe delle strade ferrate*, 1886
pp. 56-7.

59. If the cost of capital is estimated as 6 per cent per annum, the capital loss incurred by the major lines in row 6 is 2107 million lire times (6.0 - 3.1)/6.0, or roughly 1000 million lire; that incurred by the minor lines in row 7 is 3032 million lire times (6.0 - 4.4)/6.0, or roughly 800 million lire, of which over 500 million from the low-yield lines in row 8. However, the minor lines were generally built later than the major lines, and thus benefited from lower interest rates (above, note 55); a conservative 5.5 per cent per annum would reduce the loss on the minor lines in row 7 to 600 million lire, of which all but 100 million are traceable to the low-yield lines in row 8.

60. In a similar vein, the varying availability of water-based competition meant that American railroads were attributed a greater 'social saving' in short-haul transportation than in long-haul transportation. See R. W. Fogel, *Railroads and American Economic Growth: Essays in Econometric History* (Baltimore, 1964) pp. 208-19.

61. It is tempting to view the measured losses incurred by the construction of minor lines in disadvantaged areas as a socially desirable transfer of resources to deserving groups; but one would need to show that these redistribution benefits were not nullified by the regressivity of the taxes imposed to pay for them.

62. See *Atti CSO*, vol. 5 parts 1-2 pp. 477, 480, 499, 526; Commissione per la navigazione interna, *Atti del comitato tecnico-esecutivo. Relazione riassuntiva* (Rome, 1908) pp. 76-89; *Enciclopedia italiana*, vol. 27 p. 182.

63. *Atti CSO*, vol. 5 parts 1-2 pp. 477, 521.

64. *Atti CSO*, vol. 5 parts 1-2 pp. 482-9.

APPENDIX

In Table 3.1, the area figures (col 1) are adapted from *Encyclopedia Britannica*, 11th edn, vol. 10 p. 775, vol. 11 p. 808, vol. 15 p. 527, vol. 25 p. 527, and vol. 27 p.599. The population and railway-mileage data (cols 2-5) are adapted from B. R. Mitchell, *European Historical Statistics 1750-1970* (London, 1975) pp. 20-4, 581-4, with the exception of the Italian railway-mileage figure for 1913, which is taken from *Annuario*, 1913 p. 231 (Mitchell's higher figure is equal to that in *Sommario*, p. 137, for the network within the borders of 1924).

In Table 3.2, the Gerschenkron index (col 1) is that first published in A. Gerschenkron, 'Notes on the Rate of Industrial Growth in Italy, 1881-1913', *Journal of Economic History*, XV

(1955) 362 and reprinted in Gerschenkron, *Economic Backward-ness*, p. 75. The Istat index (col 2) is that which appeared in *Reddito nazionale*, p. 218, and again in G. Fuà (ed), *Lo sviluppo economico in Italia*, vol.3 (Milan, 1969) p. 40. The Fenoaltea index (col 3) is from Fenoaltea, 'Public Policy and Italian Industrial Development'.

Tables 3.3-3.6 are based on preliminary calculations for Fenoaltea, *Italian Industrial Production*. In Table 3.3, value added in first construction (cols 1-2) is the sum of separate estimates for the (future) state railways, other railways, extra-urban tramways, electric urban tramways and horse-drawn urban tramways. Value added per completed kilometre is estimated at about 55 per cent of the corresponding value (excluding the value of improvements from that of the state railways) and distributed over five years (state railways), three years (other railways), or two years (tramways). Value added in improvements (col 3) is obtained by distributing 55 per cent of the estimated cumulative value of improvements (to the state railways) in proportion to rail consumption in excess of the amount needed for first construction. Value added in maintenance (cols 5-6) is estimated directly from expenditure data for each major type of system in 1909-11, and then extrapolated in proportion to system-specific indices of track use (total vehicle-kilometres or axle-kilometres). Value added in the construction industry as a whole (col 9) is obtained as the sum of separate estimates for railway construc-tion, other public works and private construction; the present figures are very rough and preliminary.

In Table 3.4, the rolling stock figures (cols 1-5) are the sums of the disaggregated estimates in Table 3.5. Track accessories (col 6) are such fabricated metal as spikes, fishplates, turntables and the like; only total consumption can be estimated here, in the absence of data on either output or imports. Value added is here estimated as 57 per cent of the value added in rail production plus imports (Table 3.6, col 2); this coefficient allows accessories and rails 25 per cent and 75 per cent, respectively, of their combined cost, and a ratio of value added to value equal to 29 per cent in the case of rails and 50 per cent (for fabrication only) in accessories. The industry-wide estimates (cols 7-12) are again very rough figures, obtained by interpolating direct estimates for 1862 and 1911. Value added in the production both of machinery (col 6) and of fabricated metal and machinery together (col 9) is indexed by the consumption of semi-finished ferrous metal other than rails. The estimates of value added in maintenance (cols 7 and 9) instead assume constant geometric growth in the maintenance of clocks and watches (from 6 million lire per annum in 1861-5 to 12 million

in 1911-13), of other non-railway machinery (from 7 million
lire per annum in 1861-5 to 68 million in 1911-13), and of
fabricated metal (from 257 million lire per annum in 1861-5
to 311 million in 1911-13), and add the resulting figures to
those for railway rolling stock (col 3).

In Table 3.5, the production and acquisitions figures (cols
1-6) are obtained as the product of vehicle-specific estimates
of tons produced or purchased on the one hand, and value added
per ton at 1911 prices (50 per cent of value for locomotives
and passenger cars, 66 per cent for freight cars) on the other
hand. Tons purchased are estimated from current evidence on
numbers purchased by each major type of system, and unit
weights specific to each year and type of system; tons produced
are estimated initially as a percentage of those purchased (in
the 1860s and 1870s, when year-specific import figures are not
available) and later by deducting reported imports from
estimated purchases. Value added in maintenance (cols 3-9) is
estimated initially for the state railways in 1906, from
particularly abundant information on employment in the railway's own repair shops, the share of subcontracted maintenance,
and relative expenditure for each type of vehicle; these
estimates are then extrapolated to other systems and to other
years on the basis of type-specific vehicle- or axle-kilometres.

In Table 3.6, the rail figures are obtained as the product
of tons produced (col 1), or tons produced plus imports (col
2), and value added per ton at 1911 prices (about 29 per cent
of value). Value added in the manufacture of (domestic or
imported) track accessories (col 3) is estimated as 18 per
cent of value added in rail production; this coefficient is
analogous to that underlying the figures in Table 3.4, col 6,
allowing a ratio of value added to value in accessories of 16
per cent (for metalmaking) instead of 50 per cent (for
fabrication). Value added in rolling stock metal is estimated
as value added per ton (about 32 per cent of a value figure
itself 58 per cent higher than the value of rails) times the
estimated tonnage of metal consumed in the maintenance (col 4)
and domestic manufacture (col 5 minus col 4) of railway
rolling stock, or in the manufacture of imported rolling
stock as well (col 6 minus col 5). Tons of metal consumed per
ton of rolling stock manufactured are assumed to equal 1.2
for locomotives; 0.14 for passenger cars in 1861-5, growing
linearly to 0.44 in 1876-80 and 0.50 in 1881 ff; and 0.43 in
freight cars in 1861-5, growing to 0.63 in 1866-70 and 0.75
in 1871 ff. Metal consumption for maintenance is estimated
from value added in rolling stock maintenance (Table 3.5,
cols 7-9), and ratios of metalmaking value added to engineering
value added equal to half those obtained for new construction.
The total-market figure in col 7 is the sum of cols 2, 3 and 5;

that in col 8 is the sum of cols 2, 3 and 6. The estimates for
the entire industry in col 9 cover the manufacture of rails
and other semi-finished metal, including castings, from pig or
scrap; col 10 further covers the manufacture of pig iron from
ore; and col 11 further covers the manufacture of other ingot
metal from ore and other semi-finished metal from ingot.

  Tables 3.7 and 3.8 are based on Tables 3.4 and 3.6. In both
of these, the first set of estimates compares the average
level of railway-related value added to the average level of
total value added: e.g. Table 3.7, col 1 (0.13 in 1861-95) is
the ratio of Table 3.4, col 1 (an average of 5.4 million lire
per annum in 1861-95) to Table 3.4, col 7 (an average of 40.9
million lire per annum in 1861-95). The second set of estimates
compares the period-to-period changes in railway-related value
added to the changes in total value added: e.g. Table 3.7,
col 1 (0.29 from 1876-80 to 1886-90) is the ratio of the change
in Table 3.4, col 1 (13.7 million lire per annum from
1876-80 to 1886-90) to the change in Table 3.4, col 7 (48
million lire per annum from 1876-80 to 1886-90). The third
set of estimates compares that same period-to-period change
in railway-related value added to the total value added in the
initial period, and reduces the result to an annual rate:
e.g. Table 3.7, col 1 (0.04 per annum, obtained as the
equivalent of 0.44 in 10 years, from 1876-80 to 1886-90) is
obtained from the ratio of the change in Table 3.4, col 1
(13.7 million lire per annum from 1876-80 to 1886-90) to the
level of Table 3.4, col 7 in the initial period (31 million
lire per annum in 1876-80).

  In Table 3.7, as indicated, col 1 is derived from Table 3.4,
cols 1 and 7. Col 2 is derived from Table 3.4, col 2 on the
one hand and col 7 plus the difference between cols 2 and 1
on the other. Col 3 is derived from Table 3.4, cols 4 and 9.
Col 4 is derived from Table 3.4, col 5 on the one hand and
col 9 plus the difference between cols 5 and 4 (or 2 and 1)
on the other. Col 5 is derived from Table 3.4, col 1 plus col
6 on the one hand, and col 10 on the other. Col 6 is derived
from Table 3.4, col 2 plus col 6 on the one hand, and col 10
plus the difference between cols 2 and 1 on the other. Col 7
is derived from Table 3.4, col 4 plus col 6 on the one hand,
and col 12 on the other. Col 8 is derived from Table 3.4, col
5 plus col 6 on the one hand, and col 12 plus the difference
between cols 5 and 4 (or 2 and 1) on the other.

  In Table 3.8, col 1 is derived from Table 3.6, cols 1 and 9.
Col 2 is derived from Table 3.6, col 2 on the one hand and
col 9 plus the difference between cols 2 and 1 on the other.
Cols 3 and 4 are analogous to cols 1 and 2, substituting
Table 3.6, col 11 for col 9. Col 5 is obtained from Table 3.6,
col 1 plus the product of col 12 and the sum of cols 3 and 5

on the one hand, and col 9 on the other. Col 6 is obtained from
Table 3.6, col 2 plus col 3 plus col 6 on the one hand, and
col 9 plus the difference between col 2 plus col 3 plus col 6
and col 1 plus the product of col 12 and the sum of cols 3 and
5 (i.e. 9 + ((2 + 3 + 6) − (1 + 12 (3 + 5)), where these
figures are the column numbers) on the other. Cols 7 and 8 are
analogous to cols 5 and 6, with the substitution of Table 3.6,
col 11 for col 9.

In Table 3.9, the railway-shipment figures (col 1) are
obtained as the average of the 1910/11 and 1911/12 figures in
Relazione FS, 1910-11 pp. 305-6, 1911-12 pp. 311-12, with the
animal head count converted to weight (row 12) at the rate of
0.15 tons per head (from the stock proportions and unit live
weights in *Annuario*, 1913 p. 144, 1977 p. 153). The import and
export figures (cols 2 and 3) are from *Movimento commerciale*,
1911 part 1 pp. 23-58. The domestic production figures (col 4)
are typically extremely rough estimates, obtained from a
variety of sources. Rows 1, 16, 18-19, 22 and 26 are from
Fenoaltea, *Italian Industrial Production*. Row 21 is based on
that same source, allowing 1.1 tons per ton of rails and 1.2
tons per ton of other semi-finished ferrous metal, and deducting
imports. Rows 2 and 17 are from *Sommario*, p. 118, multiplying
the 1911 figures by the ratio of the 1932 figures to the 1931
figures (to convert potential to actual yields) and by
specific gravities equal to 0.65 and 0.35, respectively. Rows
3-5 are estimated as 1.67 times the 1901 figures reported in
Rivista mineraria, 1901 pp. CI, CVIII. Rows 6-9, 11-15, and
27-9 are from *Sommario*, pp. 106, 108, 110, 113-14, 124, 126,
134. Row 10 is from *Annuario*, 1913 p. 132. Row 23 is estimated as 90 per cent of fibre consumption; net imports are
obtained analogously to cols 2 and 3, and domestic production
(rows 24 and 25) from *Annuario*, 1913 p. 132 and *Sommario*,
p. 115.

In Table 3.10, the line track figures in row 1 are calculated from the track-length figures in *Atti CSO*, vol. 6 cols
10-14; single-track lines are counted once, double-track lines
twice, and so on, and service track is excluded. The traffic
per kilometre figures in rows 2 and 3 are obtained from row 1
and traffic figures obtained as follows. For the Italian
systems, the source is *Relazione SFI*, 1898; aggregate
passenger-kilometres are transcribed from col 622, and
aggregate freight ton-kilometres are estimated as 10 per cent
of col 705, plus 40 per cent of col 717, plus col 770, plus
20 per cent of col 780, plus 200 per cent of col 783, plus
col 822. For the French systems, the source is Direction des
chemins de fer, *Statistique des chemins de fer français*, 1898
part 1 (henceforth *Statistique CFF*); aggregate passenger-
kilometres are transcribed from p. 170 col 3, and aggregate

freight ton-kilometres are estimated by scaling up the
'petite vitesse' figures in p. 183 col 13 in proportion to
the ratio of total freight capacity to 'petite vitesse'
capacity alone (see below). For the German system,
passenger-kilometres and freight ton-kilometres are transcribed from *Atti CSO*, vol. 6 cols 150 and 160. The total
traffic per kilometre figures in row 4 are obtained from
row 1 and the sum of passenger-kilometres and freight ton-
kilometres; within rounding error, they equal the sum of the
partial figures in rows 2 and 3. The shares of freight in
total traffic in row 5 are the ratios of row 3 to row 4. The
passenger load factors in row 6 are the ratios of passenger-
kilometres (as above) to seat-kilometres; the freight load
factors in row 7 are the ratios of freight ton-kilometres
(as above) to freight capacity ton-kilometres. The Italian
systems' capacity figures are obtained from *Relazione SFI*,
1898; passenger capacity is the sum of cols 378 and 381, and
freight capacity is the sum of cols 384, 387 and 390. The
French systems' capacity figures are calculated from
Statistique CFF. Passenger capacity is estimated as the product
of average seats per car and passenger car-kilometres; the
former are calculated from the distributions in p. 152 cols
3-14, and the latter are reported in p. 200 col 12. Total
freight capacity is obtained as the sum of separate figures
for 'grande' and 'petite vitesse', each of which is estimated
as the product of average freight capacity per car (p. 152
cols 18 and 21) and car-kilometres (p. 200 cols 13-14). The
German system's capacity figures are from *Atti CSO*, vol. 6;
passenger capacity is the product of cols 113 and 134, and
freight capacity the product of cols 123 and 136. The overall
load factors in row 8 are the ratio of the sum of passenger-
kilometres and freight ton-kilometres to the sum of seat-
kilometres and freight capacity ton-kilometres. The average
loads per passenger train in row 9 are the ratio of passenger-
kilometres to passenger-train kilometres. The latter are
reported in *Relazione SFI*, 1898 col 264 for the Italian
systems, *Statistique CFF*, p.189 col 14 for the French systems,
and *Atti CSO*, vol. 6 col 128 for the German system; the
Italian and French figures include, but the German one excludes
the mileage of mixed trains. The average loads per freight
train in row 10 are the ratio of freight ton-kilometres to
freight train-kilometres. For the Italian systems, these
ratios relate total freight ton-kilometres (as above) less
those at 'grande velocità' (*Relazione SFI*, 1898, 10 per cent
of col 705 plus 40 per cent of col 717) to freight train-
kilometres (exclusive of mixed trains' mileage) (*Relazione SFI*,
1898 col 268). For the French systems, these ratios relate
'petite vitesse' freight-kilometres to 'petite vitesse'

freight train-kilometres (*Statistique CFF*, p. 183 col 13,
p. 188 col 18). For the German system, these ratios relate
total freight ton-kilometres to total freight and mixed
train-kilometres (*Atti CSO*, vol. 6 cols 129, 160). Because of
this different treatment of mixed trains, the German figures
in rows 9 and 10 are not strictly comparable to the others:
that in row 9 is rather too high, and that in row 10 rather
too low. The average loads per train in row 11 are the ratios
of total traffic units (the sum of total passenger-kilometres
and total freight-ton kilometres, as above) to total train-
kilometres (for the Italian systems, *Relazione SFI*, 1898 col
269; for the French systems, *Statistique CFF*, p.189 cols 14
plus 18; for the German system, *Atti CSO*, vol. 6 cols 128
plus 129).The average loads per locomotive in row 12 are the
ratios of those same total traffic units to total locomotive-
kilometres; the latter are reported in *Relazione SFI*, 1898 col
172 for the Italian systems, and in *Statistique CFF*, p. 195
col 9 for the French systems. The employment figures in rows
13-15 are normally those reported in *Atti CSO*, vol. 6 cols 228
(row 13), 232 (row 14), and 236 plus 240 (row 15), divided by
total traffic units. Exceptionally, the very low French
figures in col 228 are re-estimated as follows: administrative
labour costs are estimated as 55 per cent of the total
expenditure for administration (col 188), and divided by unit
labour costs in administration (the ratio of col 229 to col
228). The employment totals in row 16 are the sum of rows
13-15. The labour costs per employee in row 17 are normally
the ratio of total labour costs to total employment (*Atti CSO*,
vol. 6 cols 246 and 248). Exceptionally, the administrative
employment and labour costs of the Paris-Lyon-Méditerranée are
re-estimated as above, and the figure for the Nord simply
repeats that obtained for the Paris-Lyon-Méditerranée. This is
preferred to the much lower figure (1200 lire per employee)
obtained as the ratio of labour costs to employment (re-
estimated as for the Paris-Lyon-Méditerranée), since major
elements of the labour cost figures on the Nord seem peculiarly
low (possibly because of subcontracted maintenance and the like;
the employment figures seem less affected, either because
indirectly employed workers were included in total employment,
or because of an offsetting bias from part-time employment).
The current costs per traffic unit in rows 18-21 are obtained
by dividing total traffic units into total current cost figures
obtained as follows. Total labour costs (for row 18) are taken
as reported (*Atti CSO*, vol. 6 col 248) for the Italian and
German systems, as re-estimated above for the Paris-Lyon-
Méditerranée, and as the product of estimated total employment
and estimated labour costs per employee (as above) on the
Nord. Total fuel costs (for row 19) are taken as reported in

Relazione SFI, 1898 col 1039 for the Italian systems, and in
Statistique CFF, p. 236 col 5, for the French systems; the
figure for the German system assumes the same percentage
distribution of non-labour costs as on the Paris-Lyon-
Méditerranée. Other current costs (for row 20) are simply the
difference between total current costs and labour plus fuel
costs; total current costs (for row 21) are themselves taken
as reported *(Atti CSO,* vol. 6 col 200). The total current
costs per capacity unit in row 22 are those same total current
costs, divided by the sum of seat-kilometres and freight
capacity ton-kilometres. The total current costs per actual
weight unit are those same total current costs, divided by
estimates of the total ton-kilometres of gross weight actually
hauled. These estimates are obtained by assuming tare weights
of 0.21 tons per passenger seat and 0.56 tons per freight
capacity ton (from the figures for the major French systems
together, *Statistique CFF,* p. 152 cols 3-21), and payload
weights of 0.10 tons per passenger and (obviously) 1.00 tons
per freight tons. Total weight units in passenger operations
are obtained as total passenger-kilometres times actual weight
units per passenger-kilometre; the latter equal to the payload
weight (0.1 tons) plus the tare weight (0.21 tons per seat
divided by the load factor). Total weight units in freight
operations are estimated in the same way, and the sum of the
passenger and freight figures yields the desired totals. In
rows 24-6, total costs per traffic, capacity and actual weight
unit are re-estimated on the basis of Italian wages and
materials costs. The figures for the Italian systems (cols
1-2) simply repeat those in rows 21-3; the others are obtained
as follows. Foreign labour costs per employee are scaled down
to the average Italian level (1280 lire), and foreign fuel
costs per thousand actual weight units are scaled up to the
average Italian level (3025 lire); since the latter were
probably little affected by input substitution, they can be
taken to reflect the influence of fuel prices and terrain
features (fuel consumption) alone. Other foreign costs are
simply increased by two thirds; a suitably direct indicator of
relative prices and consumption levels does not seem to be
available, since consumption levels may have been heavily
influenced by input substitution. The revenues per passenger-
kilometre in row 27 are the ratio of passenger revenues to
total passenger-kilometres; the revenues per freight ton-
kilometre in row 28 are, analogously, the ratio of freight
revenues to total freight ton-kilometres. The revenue figures
are obtained, for the Italian systems, from *Relazione SFI,*
1898 (passengers, col 895; freight, cols 898 plus 901 plus
904); for the French systems, from *Statistique CFF* (passengers
p. 212 col 3; freight, p. 210 col 10 plus p. 224 col 3);

for the German system, from *Atti CSO*, vol. 6 (passengers, col 170; freight, col 179). The ratio of operating revenues to current costs is the ratio of passenger and freight revenues together to current costs (all as above).

In Table 3.11, the total investment figures in col 1 correspond in principle to cumulative, undepreciated expenditure on capital account. The total operating revenues in col 2 include the excise taxes imposed by the laws n. 1945 of 14 June 1874 and n. 101 of 22 March 1900. The internal rate of return in col 4 is the difference between these total revenues and the corresponding total costs in col 3, divided by col 1; it is thus a ratio of surplus to total investment with both numerator and denominator gross of depreciation allowances, as if the investment were perpetual. The upper-bound estimates of the global rate of return in col 5 are based on the surplus obtained by deducting col 3 from 1.50 times col 2. The corresponding best estimates in col 6 are based on the surplus obtained by deducting col 3 from, respectively, 1.35 (row 5), 1.20 (row 6), and 1.50 (rows 7-9) times col 2. The length of the lines reported in col 7 refers to 'operated length', and double-counts segments common to more than one line. The figures in cols 4-6 are thus obtained from the other entries in the table; cols 1-3 and 7 are instead obtained as follows. In rows 1-3, cols 1-3 are obtained directly from aggregate data. Col 1 is transcribed from *Annuario*, 1878 part 1 p. 133, 1904 p. 498. Row 1, cols 2 and 3 are obtained from *Relazione SFI*, 1875 p. 329, the one as 1.13 times cols 14, 15 and 17, plus 1.02 times col 16, the other as 0.621 times col 19. Row 2, cols 2 and 3 are obtained from *Relazione SFI*, 1888-1889-1890 vol.1 part 3 pp. 210-12 (1.13 times cols 183 and 186, plus 1.02 times cols 189 and 192, plus the reimbursements reported on p. 212) and 224 (col 239). Row 3, cols 2 and 3 are obtained from *Relazione SFI*, 1901 pp. 320-7 (1.13 times cols 980 and 983, plus 1.02 times cols 986 and 989, plus col 1006, plus the surcharges on the Rete Mediterranea, Rete Adriatica and Rete Sicula equal to 0.03 times cols 980 and 983 and 0.01 times cols 986 and 989) and 383 (col 1122). Row 4 is obtained as the sum of separate figures for the state railways and for other railways. The state railways' total investment is estimated as the average of the mid-1910 and mid-1911 figures in *Relazione FS*, 1909-10 p. 25, 1910-11 p. 24. These figures probably exclude the equipment no longer in the railways' inventory, but include the value of current stocks of raw materials; the resulting net bias appears to be very slight (compare also the increment between rows 3 and 4 to the 1911-price gross investment implied by Tables 3.3 and 3.4, allowing for the roughly 35 per cent increase in

unit construction costs from 1901 to 1910; Fenoaltea,
Italian Industrial Production). Their total revenues and costs
are estimated from *Statistica FS*, 1910 part 1 pp. 308-9 (1.13
times cols 5, 8 and 9, plus 1.02 times cols 10 and 11, plus
cols 12, 20 and 24) and 369 (col 53). The other railways'
investment, revenue and cost figures are obtained from
Relazione SFC, 1910 pp. 108 (col 203), 326-7 (1.13 times cols
980 and 983, plus 1.02 times cols 986 and 989), and 359 (col
1088). Rows 5-7 are a disaggregation of row 4, obtained as
follows. The major Po Valley lines are those identified in
Statistica FS, e.g. 1910 part 1 pp. 152-289, by the numbers
1-2, 17-18, D.18, 21, 27-8, 34-5, 41-2, 44, 47-8, 61-3, 70,
72-4, 84, 90-2, 94, 96-7, 97.I-II, D.97-8, 103, 108 and 128;
they cover the Modane-Turin-Novara-Milan-Venice-Udine-
Pontebba line, with the spurs from Novara to Luino and from
Milan to Domodossola and to Chiasso; the Turin-Savona, Milan-
Genoa, Milan-Piacenza-Bologna-Ancona, Parma-Spezia and
Venice-Bologna lines; and the lines radiating from Alessandria
to Novara, Turin, Savona, Genoa (via Acqui and via Novi Ligure),
and Piacenza. The other major lines are those identified by
the numbers 100-2, 104-5, 109-11, 116, 118-20, 129-30, 134,
141-4, 150, 159-64, 166-9, 193-4, 198 and 201; these cover the
entire west coast line from the French border to Reggio
Calabria, the east coast line from Ancona to Lecce, the Ionian
coast line from Brindisi to Taranto and Reggio Calabria, the
Sicilian coast lines from Messina to Palermo and Catania, the
transpeninsular routes from Rome to the Adriatic, Naples to
the Adriatic, and Naples to the Ionian, and the inland routes
from Florence to Bologna, Pisa (via Pistoia and via Empoli),
and Rome. The minor lines are the residual. The lengths of the
corresponding operated networks (col 7) are obtained as
follows. The figures in rows 5-6 are obtained directly by
cumulating the line-specific data in *Statistica FS*, 1910 part
1 pp. 152-289 col 5; that in row 7 is the reported total of
those state railways figures (14 329 kilometres), less those
of the major lines (6597 kilometres, for a balance of 7732
kilometres), plus the reported total for the private railways
(3596 kilometres: *Relazione SFC*, 1910 p. 65 col 17). Capital
costs (col 1) are distributed by allowing the private railways
their reported total, equivalent to 159 000 lire per operated
kilometre, and the minor state railways twice that average,
or 318 000 lire per operated kilometre; the resulting estimate
leaves the major railways a total of 3930 million lire (row 4
minus row 7), for an average 596 000 lire per operated
kilometre. This pattern of average capital costs is broadly
confirmed by the cost data in *Relazione SFI*, 1903 pp. 123-9,
which yield an average capital cost of over 400 000 lire per
kilometre for the most significant 8817 kilometres (summing

over groups A1.1.Aa, A1.1.AbI, A1.1.B, A1.1.Da, A1.2.Aa,
A1.2.AbI, A1.2.Ba, and A1.3.Aa), and under 230 000 lire per
kilometre for the residual 6895 kilometres; one notes that the
more expensive group includes some 2200 kilometres of what are
here considered minor lines, and that both rolling stock and
subsequent improvement expenditures were presumably concentrated on the major lines (e.g. Baglioni, *Per la riforma
ferroviaria,* p. 42). The major lines' estimated capital cost
is here distributed between rows 5 and 6 in proportion to the
two groups' total axle-kilometres (respectively 1142 million
for the major Po Valley lines and 1321 million for the other
major lines, against 3283 million in all; *Statistica FS,* 1910
part 1 pp. 152-289 col 61) rather than to their operated
lengths; while this procedure allows for the likely relative
incidence of double-tracking and other improvements, it
probably tends to overestimate the cost of the Po Valley lines
and underestimate that of the others. Total operating revenues
(col 2) are distributed as follows. For simplicity, the major
Po Valley lines (row 5) and the other major lines (row 6) are
attributed the same share of the estimated total revenues of
the state railways (564.1 million lire, entering row 4) as of
reported revenue net of tax (respectively 40.2 per cent and
33.9 per cent of 535.7 million lire: *Statistica FS,* 1910 part
1 pp. 312-57 col 17); row 7 is obtained as row 4 minus rows 5
and 6. Total operating costs (col 3) are distributed as
follows. The private lines are allowed their reported total
(30.5 million lire, as in row 4), equivalent to some 0.141
lire per axle-kilometre (allowing 108.3 million vehicle-
kilometres, *Relazione SFC,* 1910 p. 123 col 264, and 2 axles
per vehicle); the other minor lines are allowed that same unit
figure for each of their 820 million axle-kilometres (the
reported total less the major lines' figures, as above), or
another 115.6 million lire. The major lines are thus allowed
a total of 306.3 million lire (row 4 minus row 7), equivalent
to 0.124 lire per axle-kilometre; these costs are also
distributed between rows 5 and 6 in proportion to the axle-
kilometres reported above. Since traffic density (axle-
kilometres per kilometre was over 50 per cent higher on the
state railways' minor lines than on the other minor lines,
and over 50 per cent higher on the major Po Valley lines than
on the other major lines, the results of the present
procedure plausibly overestimate the operating costs of the
minor lines and underestimate those of the major lines
outside the Po Valley, while the figure for the major Po Valley
lines is subject to opposite biases. Rows 8-9, finally, are
a disaggregation of row 7, obtained as follows. Row 8 refers
to those minor lines earning less than 10 000 lire per
kilometre, net of tax, in 1910; these are the lines identified

in *Statistica FS*, 1910 by the numbers 3, 11-13, 15-16, 20, 24, 49, 75, 79, 123, 125, 135-37, 140, 145, 147, 152, 154-8, 171-3, 179-81, 183-4, 186, 188-92, 196, and 206 (pp. 312-57, col 18) and in *Relazione SFC*, 1910 by the numbers 6-9, 16-17, 21-4, 26-30, 33-6, 39, 41-2, 44-55, 59-63, and 67 (pp. 329-31, col 1010). The figures in row 8, cols 1-3 and 7 are accordingly obtained by summing over separate estimates for the appropriate groups of state and private lines. The private lines totalled 2492 kilometres in operation, 358 million lire of capital costs (equivalent to 144 000 lire per kilometre), 13.9 million lire of revenues net of tax (36.6 per cent of the reported total 38.0 million lire), and 14.0 million lire of operating costs *(Relazione SFC*, 1910 pp. 101-8 col 203, 324-31 cols 17 and 1009, 356-9 col 1088). For simplicity, their total operating revenues are estimated as 36.6 per cent of the 39.9 million lire entering row 4, col 2 for all the private lines together, or 14.6 million lire. The state group totalled 2374 kilometres in operation, 16.8 million lire of revenues net of tax (3.14 per cent of the reported total 535.7 million lire), and 115.1 million axle-kilometres *(Statistica FS*, 1910 part 1 pp. 152-289 cols 5 and 61, 312-57 col 17). For simplicity, their total operating revenues are here estimated as 3.14 per cent of the 564.1 million lire entering row 4, col 2 for all the state railways, or 17.7 million lire; their total operating costs are estimated, as above, on the basis of 0.141 lire per axle-kilometre, for a total of 16.2 million lire; and their capital costs are estimated on the basis of 200 000 lire per kilometre, for a total of 475 million lire. The figures in row 9, cols 1-3 and 7 are the difference between those in row 7 and those in row 8.

4 Germany

RAINER FREMDLING

1. INTRODUCTION

There seems to be no doubt among scholars assessing its modern
economic growth that in the period from the middle of the 1830s
to the early 1870s, the German economy gained momentum for an
unprecedented rate of growth. Thus according to Hoffmann's
figures, between 1850 and 1913 net domestic product grew at an
average yearly rate of 2.6 per cent; from 1850 to 1871 it was
somewhat lower but still well above 2 per cent. The per capita
figures were around 1.5 per cent a year (1).
 The hero of this take-off, or big spurt (or let it simply be
called the beginning of accelerated growth) was born in the
mid-1830s, with the opening of a four-mile railway line
between Nuremberg and Fürth, although this particular line
never became part of the national railway network. It was the
construction of trunk lines between the major commercial
cities from 1836 onwards, which formed the nucleus of the new
railway system. Whereas in 1840 nearly 500 kilometres of track
were in operation, a decade later the mileage had grown more
than tenfold, and it doubled again by 1860. In the following
decades railway investment remained very high compared with
other sectors of the German economy. In consequence of these
expenditure flows the share of railways in the economy's
total stock of capital came to almost 12 per cent in its
peak years from 1879 to 1884 compared to a modest 3 per cent
in the early 1850s (2).
 Before turning to an analysis of the connections between
railways and economic growth, let me make some remarks on the
driving forces behind the beginning of railway construction (3).
The traditional historiography of railways has emphasised the
active role played by the state in promoting the introduction
of this new means of transport. Historians have argued that
during the 1830s the relatively backward German economy had
not generated enough demand for transportation services to
permit the running of profitable privately-owned railways.
Having decided to mobilise the necessary funds for this
capital-intensive and costly enterprise, governmental
authorities had the choice of either subsidising private rail-

way construction or running the lines themselves. Furthermore, the actual involvement of German states with railways leads to the impression that they played a positive and decisive role in their promotion. At that time, the 1830s and 1840s, the entity which 1871 became the German Empire still comprised 39 separate sovereign states. The extent of their involvement differed widely: some governments (e.g. Hanover, Brunswick, Baden and Württemberg) built state-owned systems; whereas in states like Prussia and Saxony privately-owned railways dominated the rapidly expanding system right from its beginnings. In these latter cases governmental influence on privately-owned companies spanned a spectrum of relationships from examples where the state was a major shareholder to cases where the governments guaranteed minimum returns on private share capital. In some states civil servants even ran privately-owned companies when they had performed inefficiently

Nevertheless, and in contrast to the impression that states played a positive role in the development of railways, a systematic analysis of the evidence reveals that state inter-vention often hindered the development, especially during the 1830s. States adopted a negative attitude to railways when they thought they caused 'trade diversion' instead of 'trade creation'. Thus several governments rather reluctantly granted concessions to private companies which planned lines that crossed state borders. Such lines usually followed existing trade routes, and merely linked well-established and major commercial centres. Ironically it was this very attitude, which jealously viewed railway construction in terms of a zero sum game, that actually led to accelerated growth in the 1840s. As soon as a railway line was being built in a neighbouring state its rival felt compelled to construct one as well, in order to counteract the assumed 'trade diversion' effects. But by and large, railway construction by states or public support of private companies did not compensate for the obstacles placed by governments on private initiatives. And the breakthrough into a railway network must be attributed mainly to the efforts of private enterprise. The fact that railways were in general lucrative investments from the beginning suggests that their construction followed an existing demand for their services. The earliest railway paid for themselves even in the short run. It could be argued that without interference from governments concerned with particularistic aims, and with private companies allowed to determine the shape of their respective networks, a comparable, and probably superior, railway system would have emerged. State financial support might never have been necessary, and railway construction would have taken off somewhat earlier and proceeded more rapidly than it actually did under a regime of bureaucratic interference and delay.

In the following sections I will concentrate on three aspects
of the connections between railways and economic growth: first,
on the backward linkage effects, particularly the impact of
railway construction on the iron industry and import substitution; secondly, on the forward linkage effects, particularly
the significance of railways for coal consumption outside the
mining areas; and finally on structural connections between
heavy industries and railways from the 1840s to the 1860s.

2. RAILWAYS AND THEIR BACKWARD LINKAGE EFFECTS (4)

Before analysing connections with the iron and engineering
industries the pattern of railway investment will be outlined
in order to show its significance for the entire German
economy. Reliable data on gross investment by railways do not
exist, but estimates for capital stock and net investment
flows nevertheless make clear the overall importance. Table 4.1
shows net investment in 'Gewerbe' (the 'modern' sectors of the
economy) and the economy as a whole. 'Gewerbe' includes mining,
manufacturing and handicrafts, trade, banking, insurance and
transport (with the exclusion of railways and post). Railways'
share in the economy's total stock of capital grew from a
modest 3 per cent in the early 1850s to almost 12 per cent
over the years from 1879 to 1884 (5). During the same period
the ratio of capital invested in railways compared to that of
'Gewerbe' grew from about 0.15 to more than 0.62. Between 1845
and 1848 railway investment was probably more important than
it was in the late 1870s, when it was 2.46 times the investment
of the 'Gewerbe' sector (6).

When the constructions of railways began about 1835, Germany's
engineering and iron industries were hardly capable of producing
rails and locomotives. This was due both to technological
backwardness and to the lack of capacity. Thus in 1837 more
than 90 per cent of Prussian pig iron and nearly 70 per cent
of the bar iron was still produced with charcoal fuel (see
Table 4.2).

Throughout the early years of railway construction, foreign,
i.e. mainly British, suppliers dominated the market and
maintained their strong position into the 1840s (7). But
gradually a process of import substitution was initiated.
German firms then quickly adopted foreign technology,
particularly for the production of locomotives. In Table 4.3
the 729 locomotives running on Prussian railways in 1853 are
listed according both to the country of origin and to the year
in which they had been bought. Increasing import substitution
can be clearly seen: after 1854 all locomotives (except a few
from Austria) were supplied by German producers (8). This

Table 4.1: *Net investment flows in railways (R) in 'Gewerbe'*
(G), and in the entire German economy (D) 1851–1913
(annual averages)

	R	G	D	R as ratio of G	R as percentage of D %
	(Million of marks at current prices)				
1851–54	88	113	738	0.78	11.9
1855–59	134	170	678	0.79	19.7
1860–64	142	246	1 204	0.58	11.8
1865–69	201	178	1 148	1.13	17.5
1870–74	425	718	2 282	0.59	18.6
1875–79	503	204	1 946	2.46	25.8
1880–89	165	840	1 973	0.20	8.4
1890–99	214	1 643	3 533	0.13	6.1
1900–13	489	2 498	6 086	0.20	8.0

Note: 'Gewerbe' includes mining, manufacturing and handicrafts,
trade, banking, insurance and transport (with the
exclusion of railways and post).

Sources: R. Fremdling, *Eisenbahnen und deutsches Wirtschafts-*
wachstum, 1840–1879 (Dortmund, 1975) pp. 29, 31;
W. G. Hoffmann et al., *Das Wachstum der deutschen*
Wirtschaft seit der Mitte des 19. Jahrhunderts
(Berlin, 1965) pp. 259–60.

table is a good indicator of the development of Germany's
ability to satisfy her own needs for engineering products,
particularly for steam engines (9).
    Research on backward linkages has concentrated on railway
demand for iron products. Until Fogel and Fishlow reinter-
preted this issue in their American case studies (10), the
impact of railway construction on the iron industry had been
exaggerated (11). Several methods for measuring backward
linkage effects are available. Two points should be emphasised:
first, railways not only demanded iron but supplied it as well,
and that is why the replacement of rails only partly generated
an additional demand for pig iron: scrapped rails were

Table 4.2: *Iron production in Prussia 1837–65*

	Blast furnace output		Bar iron output	
	Metric tons (000 s)	From charcoal %	Metric tons (000 s)	From mineral fuel %
1835	99.5	90.4	58.7	31.8
1842	101.0	82.0	79.3	39.5
1850	135.0	75.1	130.4	63.6
1855	301.4	44.4	247.5	80.9
1860	394.7	24.1	265.7	89.7
1865	771.9	7.8	403.9	>95

Sources: W. Oechelhäuser, *Vergleichende Statistik der Eisenindustrie aller Länder und Erörterung ihrer Ökonomischen Lage im Zollverein* (Berlin, 1852) p. 35; W. Oechelhäuser, *Die Eisenindustrie des Zollvereins in ihrer neueren Entwicklung* (Duisburg, 1855) p. 14; E. Althans, 'Zusammenstellung der Statistischen Ergebnisse des Bergwerks-, Hütten- und Salinenbetriebes in dem preussischen Staate während der zehn Jahre von 1852 bis 1861', *Zeitschrift für das Berg-, Hütten- und Salinenwesen in dem preussischen Staate,* Suppl. vol. 10 (1863) pp. 85, 101; H. Marchand, *Säkularstatistik der deutschen Eisenindustrie* (Essen, 1939) pp. 37-9, 88, 128.

recycled into the iron industry and used for manufacture of iron products (12). Secondly, the importation of railway iron led to income and employment effects only in the exporting country (mainly Britain). Those same imports, however, showed potential domestic suppliers the opportunities available in their own market. Table 4.4 shows the influence of German railway construction on pig iron production and consumption.

Disregarding the iron demand from locomotives, wagons, buildings and bridges, the consumption of pig iron in five-year averages for rails and initial rail fastenings amounted to between 22 per cent and nearly 37 per cent of the domestic

Table 4.3: *Distribution of the locomotives on Prussian railways by year of purchase and country of origin in 1853*

	Total number	Germany number	Germany %	Great Britain number	Great Britain %	Belgium number	Belgium %	USA number	USA %
1838	7	0		6	85.7	1	14.3	0	
1839	12	0		12	100	0		0	
1840	12	1	8.3	11	91.7	0		0	
1841	20	0		19	95.0	1	5.0	0	
1842	22	6	27.3	12	54.5	2	9.1	2	9.1
1843	35	11	31.4	13	37.1	3	8.6	8	22.9
1844	17	7	41.2	8	47.0	1	5.9	1	5.9
1845	50	26	52.0	21	42.0	3	6.0	0	
1846	80	56	70.0	20	25.0	4	5.0	0	
1847	106	72	67.9	14	13.2	20	18.9	0	
1848	74	57	77.0	11	14.9	6	8.1	0	
1849	24	23	95.8	0		1	4.2	0	
1850	53	42	79.2	5	9.4	6	11.3	0	
1851	54	54	100	0		0			
1852	58	56	96.6	1	1.7	1	1.7	0	
1853	105	99	94.3	0		6	5.7	0	

Source: Prussia, Ministerium für Handel, Gewerbe und Öffentliche Arbeiten, *Statistische Nachrichten von den Preussischen Eisenbahnen,* 1 (Berlin, 1855) pp. 72-143.

production and to between 16 per cent and 26 per cent of the
domestic consumption of pig iron in Germany between 1840 and
1859. This is well above the measured impact on the iron
industries of the United States and Great Britain (13). Although,
surprisingly enough, British studies have neglected the
effects of foreign railway construction on the British iron
industry, railway iron exports constituted a major part of
British iron exports from the 1830s onwards (14).

Table 4.4: *Railway-derived demand for iron (in pig iron
equivalents) in Germany 1840–59*

	As percent of total domestic production and consumption	
	%	%
1840–44	22.1	15.9
1845–49	32.1	24.3
1850–54	36.5	26.2
1855–59	31.5	22.9

Source: R. Fremdling, 'Railroads and German Economic Growth: A
Leading Sector Analysis with a Comparison to the
United States and Great Britain', *Journal of Economic
History*, XXXVII (1977) pp. 590, 602 f.

During the first decade of German railway construction,
1835–45, most rails were imported, but by the beginning of the
1840s import substitution had been initiated (15). Many iron-
processing plants using modern British technology were
established, and existing firms enlarged their capacities,
which enabled domestic producers to meet a growing proportion
of local demand for rails and other finished iron products.
By the 1850s most of the rails were produced in Germany (16).
Table 4.5 shows how rapidly this import substitution proceeded.
It took no more than two decades to reverse the relation
between domestic and foreign produced rails on Prussian railways. The German iron-processing industry, almost incapable
of producing rolled rails at the beginning of the railway era,
experienced an astonishing increase in capacity from 1840–60.
Not only did it supply an expanding domestic market for railway iron, it also exported more iron products, including rails,
than were imported (17). During the 1860s and 1870s these
backward linkages remained extremely strong. This was due both
to further expansion of the railway network and to the steady

replacement of rails (18).

Table 4.5: *Origin of the stock of rails on Prussian railways 1843-63 (percentage)*

	Germany %	Great Britain %	Belgium %	Austria %
1843	10.2	88.1	1.8	–
1853	48.4	51.0	0.6	–
1858	61.5	37.8	0.8	–
1863	85.4	13.3	0.7	0.6

Source: Fremdling, 'Railroads and German Economic Growth', pp. 590, 603 f.

Since the speed of the modernisation process differed widely in the different branches of the iron industry it is necessary here to distinguish between the two stages of primary iron production, namely the smelting process and the refining process (puddling and rolling). The refining branches producing bar iron and rails had caught up rather early with British technology, but these modern German rail mills used mainly imported coke pig iron as their input. That is why, throughout the period, imported pig iron smelted with coke played a major role, and the substitution of foreign rails was accompanied by increased imports of pig iron. Domestic pig iron output, which continued to be produced mainly in charcoal-using blast furnaces, stagnated in the 1840s (19) because rails and other iron inputs used by the new network mainly required the cheaper pig iron produced by coke-using blast furnaces. Thus in the early years of railway construction, when the technology of coke-using blast furnaces was too difficult to adopt and too expensive to use in Germany, pig iron was imported from Britain and Belgium. Not until 1851-60 did domestic production of coke-smelted pig iron accelerate and eventually dominate this industry (20). Although the 1850s saw the Ruhr with its heavy industries emerging as Germany's major industrial area (21), Belgian and Scottish pig iron remained competitive, and it was still imported in large quantities (22). Nevertheless the erection of modern coke-using blast furnaces in the Ruhr from the beginning of the 1850s stimulated coal mining, and coal production from the Ruhr experienced an important expansion from 1851 onwards (23).

Naturally, the expansion of the German iron industry affected British iron exports. From 1815-70 Britain could be

called 'ironmaster of the world' and exported increasing
proportions of her iron production. From a British point of
view Hyde seems right to state that British ironmasters
'maintained and perhaps strengthened the strong international
competitive position they had established in the early part
of the century' (24). But from a Continental point of view the
gap was closing, and Britain's *relative* position, in
particular in European markets, deteriorated during the middle
decades of the nineteenth century. This is particularly true
for exports to Germany. Tables 4.6 and 4.7 exemplify the

Table 4.6: *German shares of British iron exports 1830-69*
(annual averages in percent)

	Pig iron		Bar iron (including rails until 1855)		Railroad iron (changing composition)	
	Germany	Holland	Germany	Holland	Germany	Holland
1830-34	3.0	7.6	5.8	6.9		
1835-39	4.5	13.9	5.6	6.9		
1840-44	14.9	33.0	14.9	9.9		
1845-49	10.6	15.1	15.1	3.1		
1850-54	14.9	9.0	4.6 (a)	2.2 (a)		
1855-59	20.8	17.7	7.1 (b)	4.0 (b)	5.5 (c)	1.7 (c)
1860-64	17.0	14.4	5.1	3.3	3.9 (d)	3.0 (d)
1865-69	15.4	14.4	4.3	2.6	3.2	2.1

(a) 1850-5. (b) 1856-60. (c) 1856-61. (d) 1862-4.

Sources and Notes: The iron export data are to be found in the
respective yearly volume of the Parliamentary
Papers. From 1856 on railroad iron got
special attention; the headings of the
respective separate statistics, which are
here lumped together as 'Railroad iron',
are: 1856-61, Railroad Iron of all Sorts;
1862-4, Railroad Rails and Chairs;
1865-9, Rails and Tie Rods.

import-substitution process in Germany, and measure the changing importance of the German market for British iron exports. British export statistics classify countries according to the sea port a cargo was sent to: iron imports of the Rhineland from Britain, which were sent up the Rhine, therefore appear in the British statistics as exports to Holland. This is why Holland is included in both tables.

In Table 4.6 the importance of the German market is seen from a British viewpoint. Germany saw her first boom of railway construction in the 1840s and bought vast quantities of British iron (e.g. from 1840 to 1844 nearly 50 per cent of all British pig iron exports, and nearly a quarter of all British bar iron exports, including rails). And the subsequent shares show that Germany remained an important consumer of British-produced pig iron (25), but she purchased less and less British-produced bar and railroad iron.

On the Continent the process of puddling and the rolling of bar iron diffused faster than coke-smelting. As a result, the comparative advantages Britain possessed at the second stage of manufacturing iron diminished earlier than those of the first stage. In other words, the Continent first caught up with Britain in the processes of refining (e.g. puddling), whereas Britain managed to hold her dominant position in coke-smelting far longer. The ratios of bar to pig iron in columns 5 and 6 of Table 4.7 reflect this shift in the comparative advantage Britain had against her competitors from the 1830s to the 1860s (26).

To conclude: nearly all the iron products required for the early phases of railway construction in Germany had to be imported, but thereafter were increasingly supplied by domestic producers. Import substitution proceeded first through the replacement of foreign by domestic locomotives; second through the replacement of rails (puddled and rolled iron) using imported pig iron; and third through a relative replacement of imported with domestically produced coke-smelted pig iron. The sequence and rapidity of import substitution sketched above received strong impetus from the peculiar character of the Zollvereins's tariff policy: the tariff on iron products clearly favoured the import of coke-smelted pig iron as a raw material and at the same time protected the wrought iron industry, including rail production, by levying heavy duties on all processed iron products (27). And the new tariff of 1844 reinforced these tendencies.

Table 4.7: British iron exports to German states 1830-69 (annual averages in metric tons)

	Pig iron		Bar iron (including rails)		Ratios of bar iron (including rails) to pig iron	
	Germany	Holland	Germany	Holland	Germany and Holland	All countries
1830-34	516	1 315 (a)	4 041	4 809 (a)	6.53	4.99
1835-39	1 832	5 697	5 885	7 258	2.36	3.22
1840-44	14 595	32 369	26 427	17 686	1.17	2.27
1845-49	16 039	22 932	36 971	7 692	1.43	2.02
1850-54	36 571	22 151	25 208	10 753	0.83	2.85
1855-59	74 010	63 099	54 115	22 575	0.69	1.72
1860-64	72 898	61 635	25 781	16 977	0.40	1.94
1865-69	89 984	84 075	26 758	17 030	0.31	1.60

(a) From 1830 to 1832 the United Netherlands, i.e. including Belgium.

Sources and Notes: See Table 4.6; The figures for bar iron were converted by a multiplier of 1.25 to become comparable to those of pig iron. On this basis the ratios were calculated.

3.   RAILWAYS' FORWARD LINKAGE EFFECTS (28)

This section will concentrate on the effects of lower railway
fares on coal sales outside the mining areas in northern
Germany, where initially British coal monopolised markets.
But first let us tabulate the development of freight rates
from 1840 until the eve of the First World War.

Table 4.8: *Railway freight transportation and freight rates
in Germany 1840-1913*

	Output (millions of ton-kilometres)	Rates (pfennig per ton-kilometre)
1840	3	16.9
1845	51	13.6
1850	303	10.1
1855	1 095	8.2
1860	1 675	7.9
1865	3 672	6.0
1870	5 876	5.6
1875	10 625	5.3
1880	13 039	4.4
1885	15 965	4.1
1890	22 237	3.9
1895	25 116	3.9
1900	34 699	3.7
1905	41 936	3.7
1910	51 815	3.7
1913	61 744	3.6

Source: Fremdling, *Eisenbahnen und deutsches Wirtschaftswachstu*
pp. 17-19, 57.

Evidently, the average rate per ton-kilometre had declined
dramatically by 1880. This was mainly due to considerable
improvements in productivity, which coincided, especially in
long-distance haulage, with intense competition among
different railway companies. From 1880 until 1913 relatively
slight decreases can be observed in the mainly nationalised
system, but this does not imply that there were no further
gains in productivity. Output still increased faster than

input, but these gains were simply not passed on to the consumers of railway services - rather they became instead a major source of state revenues. They clearly served as a substitute for an appropriate tax system, and it is no exaggeration to state that from the 1880s to 1913 the Prussian state budget depended heavily on the then nationalised railways (29). To sum up, the average rate per ton-kilometre in Germany declined by 74 per cent from 1840 to 1880, whereas it declined by only 18 per cent from 1880 to 1913. Our table also reveals how rapidly the output of German railways grew from 1840 to 1913.

Within Germany's mining areas sales of pit coal depended more and more on the fuel consumption from the growth of local iron and steel industries. Whereas outside the coal fields it was transportation costs which determined whether or not domestic pit coal could compete with imported British coal.

Until the middle of the last century the sales from German coal mines were mainly confined to their local markets. The exceptions, where collieries had direct access to navigable rivers (e.g. the Ruhr), do not alter the overall picture (30). Around 1840, when the average rate per ton-kilometre for coal transported by cart was 40 pfennig, railway lines charged between 11 and 14 pfennig. The rates imply that the price of coal was doubled after a journey of 13.5 kilometres by road or 38 to 50 kilometres by rail (37). Thus the complete dominance of British coal in northern and central Germany, outside mining areas, was no surprise, because it was due entirely to cheap transportation by ship from England right into the heart of Germany, for example to Berlin or even further up the Elbe to Saxony, although the rapidly growing railway network could have facilitated long-distance haulage of coal by railway as early as the second half of the 1840s. Berlin, for instance, had rail connections to the Ruhr as well as to Upper Silesia even at that time, but prohibitively high rates still directed a rapidly expanding demand to British suppliers. Once again, British dominance at a local market acted as a stimulus to local producers, and when railway freight rates finally fell the German firms could sell vast quantities of coal.

The relationship between coal shipments and freight rates is reflected in Table 4.9. As late as the early 1850s the level of freight rates did not allow any significant coal transportation by railway. Only a successful campaign for the introduction of the 'Einpfennigtarif' (i.e. a special low rate for coal transportation) helped to surmount this obstacle (32). The special tariff was originally designed to make Upper Silesian pit coal competitive on the Berlin market, and the price differential between British coal in Berlin and

Table 4.9: *Coal transportation on Prussian railways*

		Rate per ton-kilometre (in pfennigs)		Coal transportation as share of all ton-kilometres (percentage)		All ton-kilometres (millions)
		pit coal alone	pit coal, lignite, coke	pit coal alone	pit coal, lignite, coke	
until	1848	11.2				
	1850			1		194.2
	1853	8.2				412.5
	1858	5.0	4.71		30.7	876.6
	1860		4.63	14	30.9	963.7
	1863	2.2	3.88		39.4	1637.5
	1865		3.67		45.1	2244.0
	1870		3.42	27	38.3	4176.6

Sources: On pit coal alone see E. Engel, 'Das Zeitalter des Dampfes in technisch-statistischer Beleuchtung', *Zeitschrift des Königlich Preussischen Statistischen Bureaus*, special issue (1879) 141, 146; on the other figures cf. Fremdling, *Eisenbahnen und deutsches Wirtschaftswachstum*, pp. 17, 69.

Upper Silesian coal at the pit-head determined the rate. Special trains delivered domestic coal to the Berlin market already in 1849, and political pressure compelled the Upper Silesian Railway Company to keep those special trains with this special tariff running regularly from 1852 onwards, because the Prussian Minister of Trade had threatened to run state-owned trains along the company's network - an action allowable under the legislation of 1838, but never actually implemented (33).

Only the establishment of special rates for domestic coal enabled German mines to undermine British dominance of the rapidly expanding Berlin coal market, and Upper Silesian coal could then match the prices of British coal on this most important market outside local mining areas (34). This process of substitution, which coincided with the replacement of railways for ships, can be traced in Table 4.10 (35).

Table 4.10: *Coal transportation to Berlin*

	1846	1860	1862	1865	1871	1881
British pit coal						
(000s) of metric tons	95	203	181	134	247	75
Market share in %	100	57.4	41.9	20.6	23.0	4.9
of which transportation by ship in %	100	98.9	99.9	99.9	100	99.6
Upper Silesian pit coal						
(000s) of metric tons	-	66	139	352	562	769
Market share in %	-	18.5	32.1	53.9	52.4	49.8
of which transportation by railway in %	-	85.1	99.9	100	99.1	99.9
Total of metric tons (000s) (a)	95	354	432	652	1073	1546
of which transportation by railway in %	0	23.0	47.3	72.9	72.4	92.0

Note: The total includes Bohemian and other German pit coal and lignite.

Continued

Table 4.10 - *continued*

Sources: Prussia, Königlich Preussischer Minister der
       Öffentlichen Arbeiten, *Berlin und seine Eisenbahnen
       1846-1896*, vol. II (Berlin, 1896) pp. 355 f.;
       Königlich Preussisches Ministerium für Handel,
       Gewerbe und Öffentliche Arbeiten, *Erläuterungen zu
       der Karte über die Production, Consumtion und
       Circulation der mineralischen Brennstoffe in
       Preussen während des Jahres 1860* (Berlin, 1862)
       p. 37; 1862 pp. 37 f., 1865 pp. 42 f., 1871 pp. 33
       ff., 1881 pp. 37 f.

The introduction of the special rate for coal transportation, the 'Einpfennigtarif', from Upper Silesia to Berlin
served as a model for the demands of colliery owners in
other mining areas, such as the Ruhr. Although their demand
was supported both by public opinion and by state authorities,
it was, nevertheless, the increasing profits - due to
economies of scale and a high price elasticity of demand for
coal and thus its transportation - which really prompted
private railway companies to cut these freight rates (36).
Slightly falling prices outside the mining areas in the 1860s
were not the only factor behind the expansion of the coal
market; railways also transported coal to places which
formerly had been excluded from supplies - hence they *created*
new markets.
    A similar pattern of import substitution occurred in several
other cities besides Berlin with comparable results (37),
but British coal maintained a strong position up to the First
World War, especially in coastal cities like Hamburg (38).
Indeed, and in spite of this process, British coal exports
to Germany even increased in absolute terms from the 1840s
up to 1913. Nevertheless their market share declined from the
1860s onwards. The German market remained very important for
British coal exports and, from the 1840s to about 1880, it
absorbed about 15 per cent of exports, and ranked second only
to France (39).

4. GERMANY'S LEADING SECTOR COMPLEX

Looking at German economic growth from the viewpoint of
unbalanced growth theory there seems to be no doubt that from
the 1840s to the late 1860s the interplay between the railway
and heavy industries formed a leading sector complex of German
industrialisation.
    In order to reveal the close interconnections between heavy

industries and railways over time I utilised data to
guestimate the changing input-output relations between these
sectors.

For three different periods (in each case related to the
early years of the respective decades) the coefficients or
percentages indicate how much of sectoral output (including
imports minus exports) was delivered to the sector named at
the top of a given column (40). In row one, for example: in
the early 1840s 0 per cent of the railway's output went to
coal mining, that is to the transportation of coal; in the
early 1850s it was 1 per cent; but during the early 1860s it
rose to 25 per cent. These figures prove beyond any doubt how
closely these two sectors were linked. They also reveal how
important agricultural demand for iron products was from the
1840s to the 1860s (field 3/5), while import substitution at
the level of iron processing becomes evident in field 3/6,
and field 4/6 indicates the continued dependence of Germany
on imported pig iron. Finally the rapidly changing magnitude
of most of the coefficients reflects structural changes
occurring in the German economy during these years. The most
independent sector within the leading sector complex was the
railway: its growth depended far less on the growth of the
other two sectors. Whereas the increase both of domestic coal
mining and of the domestic iron industry depended heavily on
the linkage effects of the other two leading sectors, the
growth of the railway was determined mostly exogenously,
especially in its beginning (41). So, in applying 'the hero
theory of history ... to things rather than persons' the
railway deserves to be labelled the hero of Germany's
industrial revolution.

5. CONCLUSIONS AND SOME BRIEF REMARKS ON THE SOCIAL
   SAVINGS (42)

Compared to transportation by inland waterways the railway
peaked in the 1870s. Until the First World War both means of
transportation (measured in ton-kilometres) grew roughly at
the same rate, and the ratio between railways and inland
waterway transportation remained constant at around 4 (43).
Not by accident did discussions on whether or not major canals
should be constructed coincide with a point of time when
railways maximised their share of internal transportation.
In 1882, when the Prussian government decided to build a
canal that linked the Ruhr area to the North Sea on German
territory, the 'Dortmund-Ems-Kanal', its alleged aim was to
facilitate the transportation of bulky commodities like coal
and iron ore (44). This waterway was opened in 1899. And

Table 4.11: *Input-output relations between some sectors in Germany or the Zollverein, or Prussia from the 1840s to the 1860s (coefficients in percent of consumption)*

Delivery (including foreign trade) to / from	(1) railway	(2) coal-mining	(3) iron-processing	(4) blast furnace production	(5) agriculture	(6) consumption = output + (imports + exports)
(1) railways						
1840s		0				100
1850s		1				100
1860s		25				100
(2) coal-mining						
1840s	0	7				100 = 106-6
1850s	2	7				100 = 102-2
1860s	3	7				100 = 109-9
(3) iron-processing						
1840s	32		5		30	100 = 70+30
1850s	36		12		26	100 = 96+4
1860s	27		30		20	100 = 113-13
(4) blast furnace production						
1840s			84			100 = 72+28
1850s			88			100 = 72+28
1860s			92			100 = 82+15

Source: R. Fremdling, 'Modernisierung und Wachstum der

before 1914 the construction of Germany's most important
canal, the 'Mittelland-Kanal' began - a canal flowing in a
west-east direction, which connected major German rivers.
It seems that at the end of the nineteenth century not only
bulky commodities could be transported cheaper on inland
waterways than on railways, but that *at that time* canals and
navigable rivers, supplemented by the necessary wagon
transportation, were a feasible alternative to railways. The
cost differences between both means of transportation (water
and rail) were marginal, and a social saving calculation for
around 1900 would probably not come to more than 5 per cent
of GNP, a comparable result to Fogel's estimate for the United
States. This apparently low percentage of GNP does not,
however, imply that railways were a relatively unimportant
component of German economic growth from the 1830s to the
1870s. While adjectives such as vital or indispensable are not
literally applicable to the German case, it is nevertheless
extremely difficult to conceive of growth without railways
because the increased use of natural waterways, and above all
the construction of canals, was not a viable alternative to a
railway system at the time when German economic growth gained
its momentum (45). Throughout these decades the direct and
indirect effects of the railway were of paramount importance
for economic growth.

The level and structure of demand for transportation
services made it possible to start railway construction with
profitable small lines between neighbouring major commercial
cities within the borders of one state. In 1850 still more
than 50 per cent of railway revenues came from passenger
transportation, and furthermore goods with high value-weight
ratios dominated freight transportation, whereas bulky
commodities such as coals (which were soon to become so very
important) barely reached 1 per cent of total railway revenues
during the early 1850s. The same is probably true for the
shipment of another sort of bulky commodity, namely grain (46).
Of course, goods such as coal, grain, etc. (which had low
value in relation to weight) were and could be shipped
cheaper on rivers, canals and on the sea; the point is,
however, that from the 1830s to the 1850s the volume of this
kind of transportation was clearly below the critical minimum,
which would have induced the construction of canals as a
feasible substitute for the emerging railway system.

The particularism of 39 independent states had delayed the construction of railway lines crossing state borders, because of the supposed trade diversion effects. But railway construction could start on a small scale within small states. And in the mountainous regions of the middle and southern parts of Germany, where it would have been very expensive anyway to link the navigable parts of the major rivers (Rhine, Danube, Weser, Elbe, Oder) the particularistic aims of the numerous medium-sized and petty states would have blocked and delayed a canal construction far longer than they actually did in the case of the cheaper railway (47). The same holds true for northern Germany, where a desirable west-east connection of the major rivers could have been built without any heavy technical problems, but here too, the political superstructure (e.g. the hostility and rivalry between Hanover and Prussia) would have been an important obstacle. To find out how these institutional restraints actually worked (apart from trans-portation systems) one could study the problems involved in the founding and development of the German custom union, the 'Zollverein' (48).

The fact that there was no flourishing canal construction before the railway era in Germany - in contrast to Britain and the United States - lends strong support to this opinion: it was not before the demand for the transportation of bulky commodities had developed sufficiently (and such demand was partly a response to the railway) that resources could be saved by building canals, and then (i.e. towards the end of the century) they were built. German railways were not only sufficient but also necessary for the provision of the cheap transportation required for German industrialisation (49).

NOTES AND REFERENCES

This paper was first presented in the Seminar in International Economic History at St Antony's College, Oxford, Hilary Term 1979. I would like to thank the participants of this seminar for their critical and therefore helpful comments. The final draft of this paper profited much from suggestions by Antonio Gomez-Mendoza and Patrick O'Brien.

1. W. G. Hoffmann et al., *Das Wachstum der deutschen Wirtschaft seit der Mitte des 19. Jahrhunderts* (Berlin, 1965) p. 13; on population data ibid., pp. 172-4; on value added figures ibid., pp. 454 f.
2. On the railway mileage see R. Fremdling, *Eisenbahnen und deutsches Wirtschaftswachstum, 1840-1879: Ein Beitrag zur Entwicklungstheorie und zur Theorie der Infrastruktur*

2. *Continued*

(Dortmund, 1975) p. 48; on the railways' share in the
economy's capital stock, ibid., p. 30.
3. A broad discussion of the following issues is to be found
ibid., pp. 107-63. The early history of railway construction, its driving forces in the context of Germany's
level of economic development with a special emphasis on
the role of governmental authorities versus the bourgeoisie,
represented by agents of merchant capital, has recently
been exemplified by P. Beyer, *Leipzig und die Anfange des
deutschen Eisenbahnbaus. Die Strecke nach Magdeburg als
zweitälteste deutsche Fernverbindung und das Ringen der
Kaufleute um ihr Entstehen 1829-1840* (Weimar, 1978). The
scope of this study is much broader than the title
suggests; Beyer complements and moreover revises the
works by Marxist scholars, e.g. Mottek and Eichholtz. He
underlines the hindering role of state bureaucracy, but
he sets forth the key role commercial bourgeoisie played
in promoting the first long-distance railways.
4. In this paragraph I draw mainly on R. Fremdling,
'Railroads and German Economic Growth: A Leading Sector
Analysis with a Comparison to the United States and Great
Britain', *Journal of Economic History*, XXXVII (1977) pp.
583-604; furthermore see Fremdling, *Eisenbahnen und
deutsches Wirtschaftswachstum*, pp. 74-83.
5. Capital stock is defined as cumulative net investment.
For the data on railway capital stock since 1840 see
Fremdling, *Eisenbahnen und deutsches Wirtschaftswachstum*,
p. 28; for capital stock of Germany since 1850 see
Hoffmann, *Das Wachstum der deutschen Wirtschaft*, pp. 251 f.
6. On capital formation in Prussia during the 1840s see
R. H. Tilly, 'Capital Formation in Germany in the Nineteenth
Century', *Cambridge Economic History of Europe*, VII (1978)
pp. 382-441. According to his estimates, railway investment far exceeded that of manufacturing and was about the
same level as agricultural investment and non-agricultural
construction.
7. See for example H. Wagenblass, *Der Eisenbahnbau und das
Wachstum der deutschen Eisen- und Maschinenbauindustrie,
1835-1860* (Stuttgart, 1973) pp. 23 ff.
8. Prussia, Ministerium für Handel, Gewerbe und Öffentliche
Arbeiten, *Statistische Nachrichten von den Preussischen
Eisenbahnen*, vols. 1-27 (Berlin, 1855-80). All newly
purchased locomotives are referred to in a special section
of each volume.
9. The significance of locomotive construction for the whole
engineering sector is shown by their increasing proportion

9. *Continued*

of all steam engines. Measured by horse power, the locomotive shares were as follows (in percentages): 1840 = 2.8
1846 = 35.7; 1855 = 55.0; 1861 = 56.5; 1875 = 74.0.
Source: E. Engel, 'Das Zeitalter des Dampfes in technisch-
statistischer Beleuchtung', *Zeitschrift des Königlich
Preussischen Statistischen Bureaus* (1880) p. 122.

10. R. W. Fogel, *Railroads and American Economic Growth:
Essays in Econometric History* (Baltimore, 1964) pp. 147-9(
A. Fishlow, *American Railroads and the Transformation of
the Antebellum Economy* (Cambridge, Mass., 1965) pp.
132-49.

11. For example in the 1973 published work on the backward
linkage effects of the German railway by Wagenblass, *Der
Eisenbahnbau*, pp. 268-270; he relied on the contemporary
estimates done by Oechelhäuser for his 1852 publication:
W. Oechelhäuser, *Vergleichende Statistik der Eisen-
Industrie aller Länder und Erörterung ihrer ökonomischen
Lage im Zollverein* (Berlin, 1852) pp. 129-31.

12. In the second issue of his book Oechelhäuser stressed the
growing importance of railways as suppliers of iron:
'... dass wir bereits bedeutende Walzwerke haben, die
mehr Stabeisen und Schienen aus altem Eisen als aus
Roheisen darstellen' (There are important rolling mills
which produce more bar iron and rails from scrapped iron
than from pig iron). W. Oechelhäuser, *Die Eisenindustrie
des Zollvereins in ihrer neueren Entwicklung* (Duisburg,
1855) p. 64; see also ibid., p. 74.

13. Cf. Fishlow, *American Railroads*, p. 142; Fogel, *Railroads
and American Economic Growth*, p. 132; G. R. Hawke,
*Railways and Economic Growth in England and Wales, 1840-
1870* (Oxford, 1970) p. 240; W. Vamplew, 'The Railways and
the Iron Industry: A Study of their Relationship in
Scotland', in M.C. Reed (ed), *Railways in the Victorian
Economy* (New York, 1968) pp. 66, 74; see also B. R.
Mitchell, 'The Coming of the Railway and United Kingdom
Economic Growth', in M. C. Reed (ed), *Railways in the
Victorian Economy* (New York, 1968) pp. 13-32.

14. For a preliminary estimate of these experts see Fremdling,
'Railroads and German Economic Growth', p. 600.

15. Wagenblass's detailed analysis at the level of single
iron-processing plants supports the results presented in
this article.

16. Wagenblass, *Der Eisenbahnbau*, pp. 85, 171 f.; see also
T. C. Banfield, *Industry of the Rhine* (London, 1848, rpt.
New York, 1969) pp. 48, 236 f.

17. See M. Sering, *Geschichte der preussisch-deutschen*

17. *Continued*

Eisenzölle von 1818 bis zur Gegenwart (Leipzig, 1882)
pp. 292 f., 300 f.; for rails the relation between
imports and exports of the Zollverein was as follows
(source, ibid.):

	Thousands of metric tons	
	1860-5	1866-71
(1) Imported rails	10.2	23.6
(2) Exported rails	23.6	149.9
(3) (1) as ratio of (2)	0.43	0.16

18. Cf. Fremdling, 'Railroads and German Economic Growth',
     p. 591; and Fremdling, *Eisenbahnen und deutsches
     Wirtschaftswachstum*, pp. 82 ff.
19. On pig iron production see H. Marchand, *Säkularstatistik
     der deutschen Eisenindustrie* (Essen, 1939) p. 115. It was
     not before 1855 that coke-smelted pig iron exceeded
     charcoal-smelted pig iron in Prussia, where nearly all
     German coke-using blast furnaces were located, ibid.,
     p.39.
20. As shown by Spree in his analysis of the cyclical pattern
     of non-agricultural output in Germany between 1840 and
     1880, the railway was the dominating cycle-maker.
     R. Spree, *Die Wachstumszyklen der deutschen Wirtschaft
     von 1840 bis 1880* (Berlin, 1977) pass., in particular
     pp. 261-312.
21. For coal mining see C.-L. Holtfrerich, *Quantitative
     Wirtschaftsgeschichte des Ruhrkohlenbergbaus im 19.
     Jahrhundert* (Dortmund, 1973).
22. On the quantities of pig iron imports versus blast
     furnace production of the Zollverein from 1834 to 1879
     see Sering, *Geschichte der preussisch-deutschen
     Eisenzölle*, pp. 294 f.
23. Holtfrerich, *Quantitative Wirtschaftsgeschichte*, p. 24.
24. C. K. Hyde, *Technological Change and the British Iron
     Industry, 1700-1870* (Princeton, 1977) p. 173.
25. It should be mentioned at this point that Belgian pig
     iron exports significantly reduced the British share of
     German imports since the 1840s. This might mainly be
     attributed to the introduction of the new tariff on pig
     iron from 1 September, 1844 onwards. Belgium got a
     special treatment: only half of the duties which British
     pig iron had to bear were levied on the Belgian product.
     From foreign trade statistics of the Zollverein and

25. *Continued*

Belgium Sering calculated the following shares Belgium
had in the total pig iron import of the Zollverein:

	%
1842	16
1843	18
1844	31
1845	58
1846	22
1847	42
1848	42
1849	51
1850	69

Cf. Sering, *Geschichte der preussisch-deutschen Eisenzölle*
p. 79.

26. Unfortunately, British export statistics for years before
1856 hide the railroad iron exports under the heading of
'Bar Iron', which formed the bulk of British iron exports.
The overwhelming importance of this single item is
revealed when from then on railway iron gets special
attention. At least a hint at its former importance
within the category of bar iron may be seen in the
percentage of the later railroad iron in relation to bar
iron plus railroad iron from 1856 to 1859: it made up
64.6 per cent. Sources as for Table 4.7.

27. Cf. Fremdling, 'Railroads and German Economic Growth',
pp. 595-7; Sering, *Geschichte der preussisch-deutschen
Eisenzölle*, pp. 19 ff.

28. In this paragraph I draw mainly on Fremdling, *Eisenbahnen
und deutsches Wirtschaftswachstum*, pp. 55-73; see also
R. Fremdling, 'Modernisierung und Wachstum der
Schwerindustrie in Deutschland, 1830-1860', *Geschichte
und Gesellschaft* (1979) pp. 201-27.

29. R. Fremdling, 'Freight Rates and State Budget, The Role
of the National Prussian Railways, 1880-1913', *Journal
of European Economic History*, IX (1980) pp. 21-39.

30. E. Adolph, *Ruhrkohlenbergbau, Transportwesen und
Eisenbahntarifpolitik* (Berlin, 1927) p. 120.

31. Calculated from F. Ulrich, 'Die fortschreitende
Ermässigung der Eisenbahngütertarife', *Jahrbücher für
Nationalökonomie, und Statistik*, 3 series, I (1891)
p. 58, table 5; Holtfrerich, *Quantitative
Wirtschaftsgeschichte*, p. 22 .

32. K. Bloemers, 'Der Eisenbahntarif-Kampf', in K. E. Born
    (ed), *Moderne deutsche Wirtschaftsgeschichte* (Köln, 1966)
    pp. 151-70; Martini, 'Die Einführung des Einpfennigtarifs
    für die Beförderung oberschlesischer und westfälischer
    Kohlen nach Berlin', *Archiv für Eisenbahnwesen* (1890)
    pp. 533-52.

33. *Archiv für Eisenbahnwesen,* p. 533; Prussia, Königlich
    Preussischer Minister der Öffentlichen Arbeiten, *Berlin
    und seine Eisenbahnen, 1846-1896,* vol. 2 (Berlin, 1896)
    pp. 356 ff. The state controlled the other railway
    company involved.

34. For price data see: Prussia, Königlich Preussisches
    Ministerium für Handel, Gewerbe und Öffentliche Arbeiten,
    *Erläuterungen zu der Karte über die Production, Consumtion
    und Circulation der mineralischen Brennstoffe in Preussen
    während des Jahres 1871* (Berlin, 1873) Appendix C.

35. Ibid. These detailed statistics were published for 1860,
    1862, 1865, 1871, 1881. They comprised information for
    up to several hundred cities in the last edition for 1881.
    Later, however, British coal was able to slightly increase
    its market share again. On this see Fremdling, *Eisenbahnen
    und deutsches Wirtschaftswachstum,* p. 63.

36. The price elasticity of demand for coal obviously was
    higher than 1. This in combination with decreasing trans-
    portation costs led to increasing sales for domestic coal
    the farther the coal was transported. Cf. *Erläuterungen*
    (1865) pp. 18 f.

37. Cf. the special issues of the *Erläuterungen* between 1860
    and 1881.

38. See R. Heidmann, *Hamburgs Kohlenhandel* (Hamburg, 1897)
    pp. 5 f., a. pass.; in 1913 Ruhr coal had a market share
    of 39.2 per cent, whereas British coal delivered the
    remaining 60.1 per cent to Hamburg. H. Schoene, *Der
    Wettbewerb zwischen Eisenbahn und Rheinschiffahrt und
    sein Einfluss auf die Kohlenzufuhr nach Baden, Württemberg
    und dem Rechtsrheinischen Bayern,* Doctoral Dissertation
    (Köln, 1923) p. 1.

39. Later years were not checked. For confirmation of this
    statement see *Parliamentary Papers* (House of Commons),
    vol. 52 (1854/55) and the respective volumes of each
    year containing the 'Annual Statement of the Trade and
    Navigation of the United Kingdom with Foreign Countries
    and British Possessions in the Year: [1853 ff.] '. For
    Prussian coal production see Holtfrerich, *Quantitative
    Wirtschaftsgeschichte,* p. 16 f.

40. The coefficients are based on physical units. For
    calculation methods and sources see Fremdling,
    'Modernisierung und Wachstum', pp. 255 f.

41. See also Holtfrerich, *Quantitative Wirtschaftsgeschichte*, pp. 149-54.
42. The general discussion on the issue of social savings is comprisingly summarised by P. O'Brien, *The New Economic History of the Railways* (London, 1977) pp. 22-54. For recent assessment see now the Presidential address to the Economic History Association by R. W. Fogel, 'Notes on the Social Saving Controversy', *Journal of Economic History*, XXXIX (1979) pp. 1-54.
43. For the respective ton-kilometres see Hoffmann, *Das Wachstum der deutschen Wirtschaft*, pp. 403 f. and Fremdling, *Eisenbahnen und deutsches Wirtschaftswachstum*, pp. 17 f., 86.
44. See for example W. v. Nördling, *Die Selbstkosten des Eisenbahn-Transportes und die Wasserstrassen-Frage in Frankreich, Preussen und Österreich* (Wien, 1885) pp. 155 ff.
45. 'Railroads were indispensable, however, in regions where waterways were not a feasible alternative', Fogel, 'Notes on the Social Saving Controversy', p. 50.
46. R. Fremdling and G. Hohorst, 'Marktintegration der preussischen Wirtschaft im 19. Jahrhundert-Skizze eines Forschungsansatzes zur Fluktuation der Roggenpreise zwischen 1821 und 1865', in R. Fremdling, R. H. Tilly (eds), *Industrialisierung und Raum* (Stuttgart, 1979) p. 64 f.
47. In the early nineteenth century no systematic network of canals was constructed which could have supplemented the navigable rivers, and the few canals which existed had mainly been built in the middle of the eighteenth century. On this subject see E. Sax, *Land- und Wasserstrassen. Post, Telegraph, Telefon. Die Verkehrsmittel in Volks- und Staatswirtschaft*, vol. 2 (Berlin, 1920) p. 328 f. and Nördling, *Die Selbstkosten*, pp. 134f.
48. On this see the recent contribution by R. H. Dumke, *The Political Economy of German Economic Unification: Tariffs, Trade and Politics of the Zollverein Era* (Doctoral dissertation, University of Wisconsin-Madison, 1976).
49. The introduction of the railway in Germany during the nineteenth century has recently been used as a paradigm or guide to assess the potential effects of a future high-speed and long-distance transport system by P. B. Huber, *Die deutsche Eisenbahnentwicklung: Wegweiser für eine zukünftige Fernschnellbahn?*, Deutsche Forschungs- und Versuchsanstalt für Luft- und Raumfahrt (Köln, 1978). In the context of the debate on the historical importance

49. *Continued*

of railway construction Huber's conclusion is remarkable:
'A detailed comparison of the supply and demand conditions
prevailing on the introduction of the railway and of a
potential future high-performance system yields the
conclusion that neither the success of the railroad nor
its importance is likely to be duplicated in the fore-
seeable future.' This conclusion is drawn by taking a
full and moreover sympathetic account of the revisionis-
tic approach through which New Economic Historians
defined the role railways had played.

5 Spain

ANTONIO GOMEZ-MENDOZA

1. HISTORIOGRAPHY

Recent studies on the development of the Spanish economy in the nineteenth century have argued that the social costs for the provision of a railway network were excessive and may have exceeded its long-term benefits (1). This view is based on the postulated negative effects of the General Railway Law of 1855 which offered incentives to investors in order to attract foreign capital into railways. According to Tortella, the 1855 law diverted scarce savings away from alternative manufacturing investments. His estimates show that in 1865 the ratio of railway to manufacturing investments was 6.6 (2). Furthermore, because the government exempted the inputs required for the establishment of a railway system from customs duties, the potential feedbacks from railway construction to the domestic iron industry were limited. This fact led Nadal to argue that the state policy missed 'a great opportunity' of promoting the growth of Spanish metallurgy (3) Finally the construction is held to have started too late and the network radiating from Madrid to the peripheral towns of Spain was not designed to meet the requirements of an expanding economy, but to serve the interest of foreign mining enterprises rather than internal trade. In this sense, the railways became 'an instrument of surplus extraction' which boosted mining in the 1870s (4).

I wish to make an alternative case and will argue that:

(a) Given the depression of trade and the general backwardness of the Spanish economy in the 1850s, foreign capital would not have flowed into Spain without the incentives offered by the 1855 law. Deprived of foreign capital, railway construction would have proceeded at a slower pace, perhaps at the pace of the 1840s when only 260 miles were laid down in a decade.

(b) In the 1850s the Spanish iron industry did not possess and could not install the capacity required to meet the massive inflow of iron demanded by railways and supplied from abroad. This would have delayed even further the

148

construction of the railway and would have raised
construction costs (5).

My argument will proceed in four stages. Section 2 will
attempt to measure the costs of delaying construction by
utilising a social saving estimate. Section 3 will deal with
possible objections to social saving estimated for relatively
backward economies with underemployed labour. Section 4
quantifies the feedbacks from railways to Spain's iron and
coal industries and section 5 explores the implications of
counterfactual policy which would have compelled railway
companies to buy only Spanish iron and Spanish coal.

2. SOCIAL SAVINGS FOR 1878

If railways had been built with domestic capital and supplied
with inputs by the local industry, the start of the construction would have been postponed and the actual pace of
construction would have faltered. The dependence of the
economy on its traditional transportation system would have
been protracted. These social costs will be assessed through
a social saving calculation.

Social savings measure the extra cost of moving the actual
railway traffic by a combination of the best alternative
means of transport in a counterfactual situation where railways have been shut down for one year (6). It presupposes
that both the volume and distribution of railway traffic
will remain unchanged in spite of the expected price increase
in transportation. Moreover, the railway and the traditional
transport system are assumed to be perfectly competitive and
all factors of production to be fully employed. In this sense,
social savings measure the contribution of railways to
economic growth or the loss in GNP because when railways are
shut down additional resources must be reallocated to a
transport system of lower efficiency. My estimate refers only
to the goods traffic carried by Spanish railways in 1878 and
excludes the benefits from the higher speed and regularity of
railways over alternative means of transport.

In the pre-rail years goods were moved around Spain by a
combination of coastal shipping and road transportation.
Inland navigation was rare and precarious because the
climatic conditions and mountainous topography of the
Peninsula rendered rivers shallow and prevented the building
of canals. An exception was the Canal of Castile, only 200
miles in length, which provided an outlet for Castilian grain
surpluses by cutting high transportation costs by road. It
permitted the haulage of foodstuffs during most seasons,

except for periods of drought, at prices which had cut normal costs by a factor of 5. I have estimated that only 1 per cent of railway freight traffic could have been taken over by water transport in 1878 (7).

The compact shape of Spain conferred a natural advantage to coastal shipping over land transport over long distances. However, the potentialities of coastal shipping were not developed because of the poor state of Spanish harbours, the prevalence of sailing over steam well into the nineteenth century and a number of legal restrictions which obstructed coastal trade. When it comes to the question of how much railway traffic could have been diverted to the sea route in the counterfactual economy, it must be borne in mind that owing to the radial shape of the railway network, railways and coastal shipping were complementary except along the Mediterranean seaboard. In 1878 railway traffic in competition with the sea route came to 9 per cent of aggregate freight output for that year (8). Compared to road costs, the extremely low freight rates would have ensured that this railway traffic would have taken the sea route in spite of increased transshipment costs. Thus, in the event of a railway closure in 1878, only 10 per cent of the actual rail-way freight would have been moved by the cheap alternative of water. The bulk of the goods traffic would have been moved by carts and pack animals along the roads of Spain.

Professor Ringrose has analysed this 'traditional' system for the second half of the eighteenth century (9). Given the persistence of a subsistence agriculture and the lack of technological improvements in road transportation, the system described by Ringrose remained in operation up to the intro-duction of railways. A significant share of road transport was supplied by part-time carriers whose main activity was in agriculture and for whom transport provided a secondary source of income during slack seasons. They operated short hauls required for intraregional trade. In addition, the system included professional carriers engaged in transporta-tion for the whole year except when roads remained impassable in the winter. They provided specialised services on long-distance interregional trade.

Therefore, the traditional road transport system depended heavily upon agriculture to release surplus labour and animals and as a result the supply of transport services was highly seasonal. When farmers were fully engaged in agriculture, especially at harvest and sowing times, the supply of transport was restricted to professional carriers. The price of transport was competitively determined and part-time carriers could compete by charging below ruling prices and encouraged the haulage of bulky commodities of little value.

As a result of the unprecedented population increase in the first half of the nineteenth century, disentailed marginal land came under cultivation. But the lack of improvement in labour productivity meant that demand for labour increased. Pressure was put on pasture land to the disadvantage of professional carters who relied upon the availability of the 'reserved grazing areas'. Furthermore, urbanisation required the provision of additional transportation services at a time when more agricultural capital and other resources were required to work the land. In brief, the agrarian system was becoming a bottleneck on the supply of transport services which could not easily be augmented to meet the requirements of the expanding economy of Spain. The transfer of resources from agriculture into the carrying trade was restrained by the low capital-labour ratio in agriculture. Its reallocation would have resulted in the loss of output.

Railways helped to surmount these obstacles to Spanish economic development by gradually eliminating the seasonal re-deployment of labour and animals between agriculture and transport. With the construction of railways, the flow of freight could be ensured without a massive transfer of resources from agriculture in the off peak season. However, the point is not simply to describe the advantages of railway over traditional transportation but to attempt to measure their actual contribution to economic growth.

The social savings on the freight carried by Spanish railways in 1878 have been estimated and set out in Table 5.1. The distinction between the saving of financial charges and social savings proper derives from the fact that published railway rates incorporate an element of monopoly pricing. The social saving estimate attempts to measure 'true' resource saving by eliminating this monopoly pricing. On the other hand, saving of charges involves an income transfer from suppliers to consumers of transport services.

My social saving estimate is, however, not original. As early as 1866, Spanish railway companies considered that the saving accruing to transport users was not less than 75 million pesetas annually (10). And in the 1880s the managing director of one of the leading companies claimed that ' ... if the freight receipts of Spanish railways are one hundred million pesetas each year, agriculture and industry are benefiting from an annual saving of 200 million pesetas ... ' (11). My estimate shows, however, that railways contributed more to economic growth than the sums suggested by these two early estimates. A railway shutdown in 1878 would have resulted in the loss of 536 million pesetas or 11.9 percentage points of Mulhall's income estimate for

Table 5.1: *Freight social savings for 1878*

(1)	Railway output	863.2 10^6 TKm
(2)	Railway charges	0.08537^P/TKm
(3)	Railway cost	0.02165^P/TKm
(4)	Canal output	8.0 10^6 TKm
(5)	Canal cost	0.1403^P/TKm
(6)	Coastal shipping output	68.4 10^6 TKm
(7)	Coastal shipping cost	0.04053^P/TKm
(8)	Road output	669.0 10^6 TKm
(9)	Road cost	0.8234^P/TKm
(10)	Saving of charges	481.2 10^6 Ptas
(11)	Social savings	536.2 10^6 Ptas

Notes and Sources:

Row (1): Railway freight output in millions of ton-kilometres.
It is based upon my estimate of the freight output of Spanish
railways, 1868–1913, see Appendix A of Chapter 2 of *Thesis*.
Row (2): Railway freight rate in pesetas per ton-kilometre
as an average of the rates charged in 1878 by the two leading
railway companies, see Compañía de los Caminos de Hierro del
Norte de España, *Historia, Actuacion, Concesiones* (Madrid,
1940) vol. II, Table 10 (hereafter, Norte) and Compañía de
los Caminos de Hierro de Madrid a Zaragoza y Alicante
(hereafter, MZA), *Memoria del Consejo de Administración*
(Madrid, 1879) (hereafter, *Memoria*).
Row (3): Railway marginal cost in pesetas per ton-kilometre
of freight. Railway companies were not competitive and they
enjoyed strong monopolistic positions along certain routes.
The use of actual railway rates (in row (2)) as a proxy for
marginal costs will understate social savings. This departure
from marginal costs can be obviated by the use of this
railway cost which is an accounting rate applied by the
companies to the shipment of their own goods. It is based
upon MZA's internal rate for 1878, see *Memoria* for 1878.

Table 5.1: *Continued*

Row 4: Canal output in millions of ton-kilometres of freight
is the railway freight which hypothetically would have been
transferred to internal waterways during a railway shutdown,
see chapter 2 in *Thesis*.

Row 5: Canal cost in pesetas per ton-kilometre of freight is
the average rate for the shipment of grain and flour along
the Canal of Castile, being the two main local staples, see
Compañía del Canal de Castilla, *Bases y Condiciones de
Aplicación para las Tarifas de Transporte por el mismo*
(Madrid, 1884). The Sarda price index was used as a deflator.

Row (6): Coastal shipping output in millions of ton-
kilometres is the railway freight which would have been
transferred to coastal shipping. It involves freight moved
by the Tarragona-Barcelona-Francia and Almansa-Valencia
railway companies in 1878, see Dirección General de Obras
Públicas, *Memoria relativa a Ferrocarriles, 1873-80* (Madrid,
1882).

Row (7): Freight rates in pesetas per ton-kilometre were
deduced from rate quotations for the shipment of coal from
Asturias in 1867, see *Información sobre el Derecho
Diferencial de Bandera* (Madrid, 1867) vol. III, p. 23. In
order to reflect the gradual shift to steam navigation,
North's ocean freight index was applied, see D. North,
'Ocean Freight Rates and Economic Development, 1750-1913' in
Journal of Economic History, XVIII (1958) p. 537.

Row (8): Overland road output in millions of ton-kilometres
measures the railway freight output reallocated to road
transport as a difference between (1) and (4) ÷ (6).
Distances by railway were adjusted to reflect the higher
'roundaboutness' of railways over more direct road links.
The adjusting factor was estimated by comparing the distance
from Madrid to the major provincial towns by rail and by
road. Distances by rail were on average 15 per cent longer
than by road, Renfe, *Distancias Kilométricas* (Madrid, 1944)
and Dirección General de Obras Publicas, *Memoria de
Carreteras, 1873-81* (Madrid, 1883).

Row (9): Road rate in pesetas per ton-kilometre of freight.
It is a compound of carting and pack animals under the
assumption that carting would have provided 80 per cent of
the road transport supply. See Appendices C and D to
Chapter 2 in *Thesis* for details of calculation.

Row (10): Saving of charges (in million pesetas) for
railway users when railway average rates are applied, i.e.

$$\big[(4) \times (5) \quad (6) \times (7) \quad (8) \times (9)\big] - \big[(1) \times (2)\big]$$

that is the difference in cost between railway transport
and the combination of alternative means. *Continued*

Table 5.1: *Continued*

Row (11): Saving of real resources (in million pesetas) using
real costs for railway transport instead of railway charges,
that is (3) *in lieu* of (2) in the above expression.

---

that year (12). Social savings amount to more than the total
value of imports in 1878. Thus, foreign capital in the form
of railway investment boosted Spanish domestic product by about
12 per cent. This contribution should be modified by taking
into account the interest paid by railway companies to foreign
creditors. The two leading companies (Norte and MZA) paid 35.6
million pesetas in 1878. These two companies carried 72 per
cent of the freight output transported by the Spanish network
over that year. It is, therefore, possible to estimate that
foreign investment in Spanish railways boosted Spain's national
income (the income accruing to Spanish nationals) by not less
than 10.2 per cent (13).

However, by 1878 the railways had been in operation for only
20 years and about half of the final network had been laid
down. The full benefits of railway construction came only in
later years. In 1912, the freight social savings amounted to
2340 million pesetas or 23 per cent of Spain's GNP for that
year (14).

An alternative way of looking at the contribution of railways
to economic growth is to consider the amount of land required
to feed the additional draught animals required to carry the
freight by road. Table 5.1 indicates that 669 million ton-
kilometres diverted onto roads would have required an extra
half million mules and horses to cope with the goods carried
by railways (15). In order to feed this large addition to the
animal population, over 30 per cent of the acreage devoted to
wheat would have been required to grow animal feedstuffs (16).
This, of course, is a lower bound of the costs of coping
without railways given that it does not include capital and
labour costs. In fact, the value of the lost wheat output
would have amounted to 247 million pesetas or over half my
social saving estimate (17).

3.   UNDEREMPLOYED RESOURCES FOR TRANSPORTATION

Toniolo has recently criticised the use of social saving
estimates in the context of backward economies (18). He argued
that in countries with large subsistence sectors where the
supply of labour at the prevailing subsistence wage was
probably highly elastic, the implications of estimates of

social savings for economic growth are not clear. If some of the resources which must be diverted from other sectors in order to provide transport services in the counterfactual scenario are otherwise underemployed or unemployed, prevailing wage rates will then fail to reflect the true opportunity costs of labour (and capital) and as a result social savings will be overstated.

Nineteenth-century Spain provides a good case study for this particular objection. If valid, it would strengthen the argument that delays in railway construction would not be costly because supply in the traditional transport system was elastic. The country's labour-intensive agriculture absorbed high inputs of labour during determined seasons of the year. For the rest of the year the release of resources from agriculture would not affect agricultural output. That is to say the marginal productivity of labour (and of animals) at that time of the year was close to zero. Therefore, under these special circumstances, it would have been possible to expand the supply of transport at very low opportunity costs. Seasonal unemployment in agriculture implies that the cost of road transportation which has been used to calculate social savings in Table 5.1 fails to reflect the true opportunity costs of the resources devoted to transportation in the part-time sector. Indeed, among peasant carriers, maintenance costs for animals are fixed unless animals are rented out (19). But if farmers decided to engage in transportation during the slack season, they would incur some extra costs in the form of the additional food required by animals when working, higher depreciation rates on animals and carts, higher costs of shoeing plus some compensation for moving away from his home and land.

To deal with Toniolo's argument I will set out three possible alternatives to the railway shutdown which take into account underemployment in agriculture. They involve a discussion of the seasonal nature of labour and capital employed in agriculture and the use of alternative, or 'shadow' prices for road transportation which truly reflects social costs. I will distinguish two limiting cases and an intermediate solution:

Any increase in the demand for transport will be entirely satisfied from the pool of unemployed peasant carriers. I will call this the 'Inventory Solution' because it assumes that the Spanish economy could cope without railways by holding inventories until commodities could be moved around in the slack season at low transportation costs.

The second limiting case can be identified with the social saving estimate set out in Table 5.1. There, railway traffic was taken over by a second best combination of the means of transport; peasant carriers were treated as professionals as far as the price of transportation was concerned.

An 'Intermediate Solution' establishes a distinction between part-time and professional carriers, by adjusting their relative prices to reflect true opportunity costs. Goods will be moved by professional carriers during the agricultural year and by peasant carriers during the rest of the year.

A. THE INVENTORY SOLUTION

The farmer and his animals were tied to the land for 210-20 days on average, leaving 3 idle months each 'working' year (20). Farm animals required at least two months to rest each year (21). Even if the farmer worked on some of the feast days, or if the above figures are overstated because work animals were not required for such activities as hoeing, three idle months seem still to be a fair estimate because of the impassability of roads in the rainy season. The bad state of roads was very often denounced in contemporary works as a major impediment to the smooth and continuous operation of the economy. It can be assumed that roads were impassable for at least another two months each year and in many regions for much longer (22). But since railways were laid down along the highways less liable to suffer from flooding, two months would seem to be a valid average. In summary, animals and men were otherwise unemployed for three to four months each year and fully employed during the rest of the year (23).

Up to 50 per cent more nutrients were required by farm animals for hard draught work than when idle (24). Converted into the cost of grain equivalents this ratio shows that the extra feeding costs involved in working a farm animal over a full working year amounted to an additional 22 per cent for a mule or horse, 23 per cent for a donkey and 17 per cent for a ream of oxen (25). Related to their relative transport capacities, we obtain the variable costs of peasant transport which reflect true social opportunity costs. These new prices are, however, lower bounds as they exclude the costs met by peasants while away from home for lodging and purchased food. Furthermore, these figures should also be adjusted upwards to reflect underutilised transport capacity (26).

When the real marginal cost of using farm transport is substituted into the calculations of Table 5.1, social savings from railways are reduced to 40 million pesetas, or around 1 per cent of the national income.

B. THE INTERMEDIATE SOLUTION

This possibility departs from the normal social savings
calculation in the sense that it makes a distinction between
'working' and 'off peak' seasons of the year. The degree to
which unemployed resources might be expected to respond to the
demand for transport depends obviously upon the nature and
timing of seasonal unemployment. During the work season, of
six to seven months, demand for transportation could be met
only by professional carriers and during the remaining three
to four months peasant carriers would take over much of the
freight. Indeed, peasant carriers could, at that time of the
agricultural year, compete and undercut professional carriers.
When this intermediate solution is estimated, resource saving
due to the introduction of railway comes to 326 million
pesetas or 63 per cent of the original social saving estimate.
This is 7.5 per cent of Spain's income in 1878.

The possibility of having some underemployed resources in
the subsistence sector at certain times of the year has led
us to analyse the hypothetical alternatives open to the
Spanish economy. The most efficient way in which the counterfactual economy could have coped without railways involved
the haulage of goods for just four months of each year. Under
this situation, the economy would have been forced to hold
stocks of raw materials and final products in order to secure
its consumption and production needs during the remaining
eight months. Such a solution would have minimised the direct
costs of closing down the railway network. But huge indirect
costs would arise from holding hypothetical but vast amounts
of capital tied up in stocks. Finally, the 'Inventory
Solution' also required the mobilisation of over one million
mules and horses and 230 000 donkeys which exceeded the
draught animals employed on farms in 1878 by 30 per cent (27).
The supply of these animals could only be met by rising
costs, at least in the short run.

The 'Intermediate Solution' appears as the most plausible
with peasant carriers competing with professional carters
during the off peak season. On this basis my social saving
estimate in Table 5.1 becomes an outer bound of the true
social savings which should be somewhere in between 7.5 and
12 per cent of Spain's national income for 1878.

4. FEEDBACKS TO IRON AND COAL

Table 5.2 estimates feedbacks from railway demand for permanent
way iron to the Spanish iron industry. As shown in the table,
demand for rails over the period 1855-72 was entirely met by

Table 5.2: *Railways and the iron industry, 1855-1913 (000' T)*

	(1) C^T	(2) D^T	(3) ND^T	(4) $\%\ ND^T \over pig\ iron$	(5) $\%\ ND^T \over steel$
1855-6/1871-2	494	–	–	–	–
1872-3/1889-0	776	54	– 31	–	–
1890-1/1901-2	346	173	143	4.3	9.5
1902-3/1913-14	373	370	380	8.0	8.1

Notes and Sources: See Tables 5 and 6 in Chapter 3 of *Thesis*, pp. 138, 142.

Column (1): Consumption of rails in thousand tons.

Column (2): D^T is the gross demand for domestic rails expressed in pig iron equivalent. It is the result of $(C^T - M^T)$ x 1.35 where M^T is rail imports and 1.35 is the pig iron equivalent of one ton of rails, see Dirección General de Minas, *Estadística Minera de España* for 1815, p. 84.

Column (3): ND^T is net railway demand for pig iron after deducting from D^T sales of scrap rails to the domestic iron industry and adding rail exports from Spain. For scrap sales, see Chapter 3 in *Thesis* and for rail exports, see Dirección General de Aduanas, *Estadística del Comercio Exterior de España,* 1903-14.

Column (4): Net demand for pig iron as share of pig iron output.

Column (5): Net demand for steel as share of steel output.

foreign suppliers, Britain contributing 62 per cent to total imports, Belgium 30 per cent and the rest coming from France. The predominance of British rails is interesting given the close financial links between Belgium and France and the Spanish railway companies.

Between 1873 and 1890, demand for rails totalled 776 000

tons. Yet, 25 per cent less railway track was laid than in the
former period. The explanation is that steel rails which were
gradually used on new lines after 1870, were being substituted
for worn out iron rails on most lines. Only 5 per cent of the
rail consumption was satisfied by domestic iron mills, as the
new railway companies went on making use of their right to
import railway material free of duty. However, after 1880 the
small Biscayan iron industry benefited from the inflow of
domestic (and foreign) capital at a time when the new technological developments in the manufacture of pig iron had freed
it from the long-standing constraint of high fuel costs.
Finally, the table shows that when sales of scrap rails are
taken into account, Spanish railways become net suppliers of
pig iron to the iron industry.

In the 1890s, when the Spanish iron industry was protected
by tariffs and a depreciation of the exchange rate, its
capacity expanded rapidly. Purchases of rails from domestic
manufacturers amounted to 37 per cent of total rail consumption.
However, the share of the pig iron output which went into rail
manufacture was relatively small whereas in terms of the output
of steel, feedbacks were quite significant.

In the 1900s, the position enjoyed by the Biscayan iron mills
in the internal and external markets was secured by the merger
in 1902 of Bilbao's three main iron works to form 'Altos Hornos
de Vizcaya'. The new works succeeded in exporting steel rails
for the first time. In the domestic market, sales totalled
274 000 tons which covered 3/4 of total demand for rails. In
terms of output, 8 per cent of the pig iron and of the steel
manufactured in Spain over this period was delivered to the
rail rolling mills.

Part of the demand for coal was also satisfied through
imports. But railway companies used far less imported coal
than imported railroad iron. Foreign coal, chiefly from Britain,
was preferred for its lower cost but also for its better
quality. After 1880, which marks the growth of mining industry
in Spain, British coal was cheaper than Asturian coal (which
supplied half of Spanish coal) in all the markets of the
periphery. Price differentials in favour of British coal were
up to 30 per cent in Cadiz in 1882 (28). At the pit-head,
British coal was already cheaper. Coal seams were thin and
uneven in Spain, producing a high output of 'small' coal. In
addition, British coal was shipped to Spain at very low
freight rates as a return cargo in the ships engaged in the
transport of Spanish mineral ores to Britain and other parts
of Western Europe. As a result, increasing shares of the
domestic coal consumption were satisfied by imported coal.
Excluding coke imports, the share of imported coal into
domestic consumption increased steadily between 1865-94 from

40 to 53 per cent. Then, this ratio decreased sharply to 38
per cent owing to the protectionist policies of the 1890s and
the better integration of the coal market in Spain.

Evidence on coal purchased by railroad companies suggests
that their preferences were determined by the price of coal.
In the interior of Spain where domestic coal was protected by
high transportation costs, railway companies found it more
profitable. Thus, it is not surprising to find that the
leading railway companies (Norte, MZA and Andaluces), the
lines of which traversed extensive coal-fields, satisfied up
to 75 per cent of their fuel requirements from domestic coal
despite the exemption from customs duties on coal imported for
railways. Coastal lines continued, however, to rely upon
foreign coal benefiting from its cost differential. Such lines
which expanded after 1900 accounted for 20 per cent of the
total cost consumed by railways. In summary, around 40 per
cent of the coal consumed by railways after 1900 came from
abroad, compared to only one third before the turn of the
century.

As Table 5.3 shows, around one fifth of the Spanish consumption of coal was absorbed by the railways. Indeed, the railway
share kept fairly stable over the whole period, except for
1885-1904 when coal output grew at higher rates than the
railway consumption of coal. Feedbacks from railways to coal
mining were very important given that almost one fourth of
Spain's coal output was supplied to the railway industry.
Their impact was particularly significant in the periods 1875-
84 and 1905-14 when 45 and 32 per cent of the incremental
growth in coal output was due to the demand for coal from the
railways.

Nadal has estimated that one fifth of the forged iron and
steel output between 1904 and 1913 was absorbed in the
manufacture of rails. He states '... railway demand weaker than
in previous periods gave birth to steel production in the late
19th century. This fact reinforces a fortiori the lost
opportunity argument for the pig iron and steel industries ...
that could have taken place thirty years before' (29).

The first part of the argument is confirmed by my calculations. Gross demand for steel from railway companies came to
13.6 per cent of output in the 1890s, but after the turn of
the century gross demand was hardly one third of Nadal's
estimate. By deducting scrap sales in the home market, this
disparity is further emphasised. Thus, the development of the
steel industry after 1890 cannot be explained by demand from
railways.

Table 5.3: *Railways and the coal industry, 1865-1914 (annual averages in thousands of metric tons)*

	(1) Consumption	(2) Output	(3) (1)/(O ÷ M)	(4) DC/O	(5) ΔDC/ΔO
1865–74	177	571	18	21	–
1875–84	368	852	22	29	45
1885–94	441	1 212	17	24	13
1895–04	655	2 377	16	18	12
1905–14	1 287	3 565	22	21	32

Notes and Sources:

Column (1): Railway consumption of coal in thousands of metric tons, see *Thesis*, pp. 160-1.

Column (2): Spanish output of coal in thousands of metric tons, see J. Nadal, *El Fracaso de la Industrialización en España, 1814-1913* (Barcelona, 1975) App. 5.

Column (3): Railway consumption of coal as share of Spain's domestic consumption of coal. Coal imports which exclude coke imports from Dirección General de Aduanas, *Estadística del Comercio Exterior, 1865-1914*.

Column (4): Railway consumption of domestic coal as share of Spain's coal output. It was assumed that one third of railway fuel requirements were met through imports before 1900 and 40 per cent afterwards; for coefficient see text.

Column (5): Incremental railway consumption of domestic coal as share of incremental coal output.

5. THE PROTECTIONIST MODEL

My estimates of feedbacks from railways to the iron and coal industries show that between 1855-72 the demand for iron rail was met entirely through imports. Had the capacity of the local iron industry expanded to meet railway demand, the output of pig iron might have doubled over this period. Adding the pig iron equivalent for rail fastenings, it would

have increased by 120 per cent. Furthermore, additional supplies
of coal would have been required by the iron works. My
calculations suggest that an additional 2.5 million tons of
coal would have been consumed by 1864. This figure represents
an increase of 130 per cent in the output of Asturian coal-
fields. Despite the slump in railway construction after 1865,
a 20 per cent increase would have been required between that
year and 1872.

These figures lead us to question the arguments for
protection and this section will examine the implications for
the iron and railway industries of the imposition of a
prohibitive tariff on the eve of railway construction.

If such a tariff had been introduced, Spanish ironmasters
would have responded to higher prices and would have increased
their output to meet demand for rails. A basic assumption of
the protection model is that the pattern of railway construction would have been unaltered, that is to say, demand for
permanent way iron was completely inelastic. Furthermore, the
model also implicitly assumes that the supply of iron rails
would not have been affected by capital or technical
constraints. These assumptions guarantee that the construction
of the railway network would have started and proceeded without
substantial delays.

The protectionist model also assumes that foreign investment
in railways would have remained unaffected. However, foreign
capital might have been deterred by a rise in construction
costs which would have certainly lowered expectations for
profits. Even if foreign capital had continued to flow into
Spanish railways a considerable inflow of domestic savings
would have been required not only to finance the expansion of
the iron industry but coal and iron mining as well.

For iron consumers, the cost of protection would have
consisted of a 'production cost' (30). This production cost
is the bill paid by the railway companies for their iron rails
in the domestic market in excess of their cost under free
trade. Given that no iron rails were manufactured on a large
scale in Spain in those years, the price of local pig iron
is used as a proxy for the price of rails. Then, the price of
rails can be estimated by applying the ratio of pig iron to
rail prices in England to the price of pig iron in the
Asturian iron mills. Since it would be quite unrealistic to
assume that Asturian iron works would have been as efficient
as their English rivals these hypothetical prices for iron
rails made in Spain must be viewed as lower bound estimates.
My calculations indicate that the average excess cost of
Spanish rails over the price of English rails would amount to
100 pesetas per ton of rails. Under a protectionist policy,
railway companies would have paid additional costs of around

50 million pesetas for their purchases of rails alone. For the MZA company, the additional bill would have amounted to 10 million pesetas, or a 32 per cent increase in the company's total expenditure on permanent way materials.

Under the protectionist assumptions, capacity in the local iron industry would have increased in line with the annual demand for iron rails. Given the low levels of pig iron output in Spain in the middle of the nineteenth century, it implies a twelve-fold expansion in capacity between 1855 and 1864, reaching a peak of 155 000 tons of pig iron output in that year. Furthermore, railway construction in Spain proceeded in cycles. And the level of demand for railroad iron attained in 1855-66 was not reached again until the early 1880s when a second cycle in railway construction coincided with the substitution of steel for iron rails. For the iron industry, such a high level of dependency on railway developments would have meant idle capacity after 1865 of around 60 per cent of total output. Problems of excess capacity would have persisted year after year given the limited linkages from the iron industry itself to the rest of the economy. Perhaps that level of peak capacity would not have been utilised again until the 1880s when demand for railroad iron increased once more.

6. CONCLUSIONS

Spanish economic historians have speculated about the 'lost opportunities' from their country's pattern of railway development in the nineteenth century. Implicit in their arguments is a protectionist model in which feedbacks from the construction of railways could have promoted a higher rate of long-run development of the economy. They have criticised governments of the day for their liberal trade policy and for expanding the market for railway securities to the detriment of alternative investments.

Given the backwardness of the Spanish iron industry at the start of the era of railway construction, a protectionist policy could have seriously delayed and increased the construction costs for the railway network. In my research, I have tried to show that railways were extremely important for Spanish economic development because they solved the transport bottleneck which had afflicted the economy for generations before 1855. The possible cost of delayed railway construction can be assessed with reference to the social saving estimate for 1878. National income could have fallen by somewhere between 7.5 and 12 per cent, had railways been shut down in that year. Furthermore, the subtraction from these social gains of the private earnings accruing to foreign creditors would take away only one percentage point from the estimate. The gains which accrued to Spain from foreign investment in her railways were far higher than the price she paid to foreigners for financing their construction. Whatever may have happened in the mineral sector, foreigners did not 'exploit' Spain by investing in Spanish railways.

Alternatively, something like a 43 per cent decrease in land under wheat would have been necessary to provide capacity for road transport to cope with the level of freight traffic attained in 1878. At a time when rising population was pressing on arable land and given that the potential response of agriculture was seriously constrained by soil and climatic conditions, the release of this amount of cultivated land would seem to be unlikely.

It must be recognised, however, that my social saving estimates could overstate the contribution of railways to the economy because of seasonal underemployment of capital (draught animals and carts) and labour in agriculture. I have shown that an inventory solution to the transport bottleneck was feasible only at the cost of moving goods for just four months in each year. However, this hypothetical alternative could only have reduced the efficiency of the traditional transport system still further. Furthermore, it is difficult to understand how the economy could have developed by operating its transport system for just one third of the year. After all, the Spanish economy in the 1850s was not run in that way.

My estimates also show that a twelve-fold increase in capacity over ten years was required by the iron industry to match demand from railways. Such a performance can be compared to that of the German iron industry. Fremdling has shown that at the start of railway construction in the 1830s the German iron industry was relatively backward. None the less, in 1837 its pig iron output was seven times higher than Spanish production in 1855. Between 1837-65, railways expansion in Germany was accompanied by an eight-fold increase in the capacity of her iron industry. The possibility that Spain could have created a modern iron industry in less time than Germany seems quite dim. Even this reading 'a la lettre' of the protectionist model introduces implausible assumptions such as the invariable pattern of railway development.

The lost opportunity argument was also supported by referring to the performance of the Spanish iron industry after 1890. According to Nadal, 21 per cent of the steel manufactured in Biscay between 1904 and 1914 was delivered to the rail rolling mills. My estimates indicate that feedbacks from railways in that period were much more modest, though quite substantial. Protected by tariffs and the fall of the peseta, pig iron output increased 2.5 times between 1890 and 1913. From these

late developments in the iron industry, we might point to the
potential benefits from an alternative government policy
based on the German example. While the British iron industry
enjoyed a strong comparative advantage because of the
availability of cheap and good quality coke, it may well have
paid Spain to liberalise the import trade of coke pig iron
while protecting its rolling mills. As the market for iron
products was enlarged and the fuel requirements in iron
manufacturing cut, a gradual protection of the local iron
industry in the first stages of iron production might well
have promoted its steady growth.

A final comment must be made about the positive impact of
railways on the spread of the market. By cutting transportation costs by a factor of 9, and releasing internal
communications from the restraint of seasonality, railways
afforded higher marketing opportunities for local surpluses
and this led to a gradual integration of the home market.

Table 5.4 shows how the share of domestic consumption of
grain, flour, wine and coal carried on trains increased over
the period 1882–1913. In all cases, the process was
accompanied by long-distance shipments from the surplus area
of the interior to deficit areas of the periphery.

Table 5.4: *The commercialisation of grain, flour, wine and
coal by rail, 1881-1913 (%)*

	Grain	Flour	Wine	Coal	Year
1882	25	16	–	14	1865/74
1886	22	16	10	28	1875/84
1901	24	18	33	34	1885/94
1905	32	32	52	43	1895/04
1909	31	28	69	46	1905/14
1913	47	34	65		

Sources and Notes: All columns indicate the share of domestic
consumption carried by railways. See
Thesis, pp. 187, 189, 226, 234.

Railways opened up new coal-fields and created new trade for
the mines of Central Spain to supply local markets with coal
as a substitute for charcoal or imported coal. However,
railways were unable to promote the substitution of English
for Spanish coal at the peripheral markets because Spanish
coal was already too costly at the pit-head.

Thus, in the 1880s domestic coal and grain were uncompetitive

at the periphery because production costs at the core were
too high. But when tariffs were levied in the 1890s, railways
contributed to the process of import substitution by hauling
large volumes of coal and grain from Central Spain at costs
well below those obtainable by road. Without railways a much
higher protection of the domestic grain would have been
required to allow it to be sold at the periphery. Import
substitution depended critically on the availability of
railways.

The analysis of internal trade flows suggests that railways
met the requirements of the Spanish economy. To those who
perceive railways as an instrument for promoting Spanish
dependency on foreign capital we should point out that the
haulage of mineral ores was but a small part of the freight
carried by the major railway networks. For MZA and Norte, it
came to only 5 per cent of their freight traffic. Furthermore,
the pattern of flows indicates that only one third of the
mineral ores carried by Norte in 1878 was intended for export.
The resource saving in this mineral ore traffic attributed to
these two companies in 1878 represented only 8 per cent of
their total social savings. Even on the unrealistic assumption
that all the ores were exported it cannot be concluded that
social savings from railways were exported in the form of
cheap ores.

Furthermore, the export statistics show that mineral ores
and wine were already exported before the advent of railways.
The original spurt in these export trades was caused by an
expansion in world demand which boosted world prices and
compensated for high transport costs in Spain. The export of
ores, and wine, would have proceeded without assistance from
railways because the country's major ore deposits and vineyards were located near the coast. And except for the sherry
wines, Spain's wine industry was in the hands of nationals:
benefits from the availability of cheap railway transport
reverted fully to the Spanish economy.

NOTES AND REFERENCES

This chapter draws upon my doctoral dissertation at Oxford
University, *Railways and Spanish Economic Growth in the late
19th Century* (D.Phil. Oxford, 1981; hereafter referred to as
Thesis). I would like to thank Patrick O'Brien, Rainer
Fremdling, Gianni Toniolo and Gabriel Tortella for their
helpful comments.

1. J. Nadal, *El Fracaso de la Revolución Industrial en
    España, 1814-1913* (Barcelona, 1975) 2 and 6 (hereafter,

1. *Continued*
   Fracaso), G. Tortella, *Los Orígenes del Capitalismo en España* (Madrid, 1973), ch. 5 (hereafter, *Orígenes*). There is an abridged English version of Nadal's work in C. M. Cipolla (ed), *The Fontana Economic History of Europe* (London, 1973) vol. 4 (2) pp. 532-626. For a recent survey of these views, see J. Harrison, *An Economic History of Modern Spain* (Manchester, 1978) pp. 48-54.
2. Tortella, *Orígenes*, p. 178.
3. Nadal, *Fracaso*, pp. 161-3 and pp. 183-7.
4. Ibid. p. 74.
5. In an unpublished work on the Spanish economy in the nineteenth century, Tortella appears to have revised his views, see G. Tortella, *La Economía Española, 1830-1900* Valencia, 1980), in particular, chs 5 and 7.
6. For a useful survey of the social saving literature, see P. K. O'Brien, *The New Economic History of Railways* (London, 1977) and R. Fogel, 'Notes on the Social Saving Controversy', *Journal of Economic History*, XXXIX (1979) pp. 1-54.
7. See Row (4) in Table 5.1.
8. See Row (6) in Table 5.1.
9. D. R. Ringrose, *Transportation and Economic Stagnation in Spain, 1750-1850* (Durham, 1970).
10. 'Exposicion de las Compañías de Ferrocarriles', *Gaceta de los Caminos de Hierro*, XI (1866) 113-15.
11. Compañía de los Caminos de Hierro de MZA, 'Datos Estadísticos facilitados por MZA' in *La Crisis Agrícola y Pecuaria* (Madrid, 1887) vol. VI, p. 122 (hereafter, *Crisis*).
12. Mulhall states that Spanish income in 1879 was 175 million pounds or 4375 million pesetas, see M. Mulhall, *Progress of the World* (London, 1880) p. 437.
13. Tedde has estimated that in the 1870s 60 per cent of the capital of railway companies was held by foreigners, see P. Tedde, 'Las Compañías Ferroviarias en España (1855-1935)' in M. Artola (ed), *Los Ferrocarriles en España, 1844-1943* (Madrid, 1978) vol. II, pp. 38-43. Thus, interest paid to France amounted to 30 million pesetas or 7 per cent of Spain's income.
14. See *Thesis*, pp. 70-1 for calculations. National income estimate from Instituto de Estudios Fiscales, *Datos Básicos para la Historia Financiera de España* (Madrid, 1978) p. 1142. There is an alternative estimate by the *Consejo de Economía Nacional* which is 24 per cent lower, boosting social savings up to 23 per cent, see B. R. Mitchell, *European Historical Statistics* (1978) Table J1, p. 415.

15. I assumed that carriers would have operated for 8 months
     each year; see below, Section 3. For capacity calcula-
     tions, see *Thesis*, Appendix C pp. 108-10.
16. The feeding allowance for a mule over.one year is 30.9
     Hls of barley. It includes a one-year maintenance ration
     of 23 Hls plus an extra feeding of 7.9 Hls while at work.
     For calculations, see *Thesis*, Table 6, pp. 83-4. Thus,
     total consumption of barley would have amounted to 16.04
     million Hls or 1.12 million Has of land, for yield of
     barley see Junta Consultiva Agronómica, *Avance
     Estadístico sobre el Cultivo Cereal y de Leguminosas
     Asociadas* (Madrid, 1891), vol. III, pp. 597-8. There
     are two estimates for the acreage under wheat in 1891.
     The first one was produced by the *Junta*, pp. 595-6. The
     second was estimated by E. de la Sotilla, 'Produccion y
     Riqueza Agrícola de España en el último decenio del
     siglo XIX y primero del XX ', *Boletín de Agricultura
     Técnica y Económica (1911)*.
17. Wheat yields come to 9.5 Hls/Ha, same source as barley
     yields, see footnote 16. Wheat prices for 1878 as given
     in N. Sanchez Albornoz, *Los Precios Agrícolas durante la
     2ª mitad del siglo XIX* (Madrid, 1975) Table 3.2, p. 180.
18. G. Toniolo, 'Railways and Economic Growth in Southern
     Europe: Some Methodological Remarks', unpublished paper
     delivered at the conference on *Railways and Western
     Economic Development* (Madrid, 1979).
19. Maintenance costs represent the costs of keeping the
     farm animals alive during one calendar year.
20. The 'working' year was assumed to be 300 days, see
     Crisis, vol. V, p. 745.
21. A. D. Thaer, *The Principles of Agriculture* (London, 1844)
     p. 74.
22. For instance, the Belmez coalfields in Cordoba could be
     mined only during the summer, *Interrogatorio sobre el
     Derecho Diferencial de Bandera* (Madrid, 1867) vol. III,
     p. 73.
23. This final estimate has been weighted to reflect the size
     of the 1878 crop which was slightly below average.
24. See F. B. Morrison, *Feeds and Feeding. A Handbook for the
     Student and the Stockman* (New York, 1936) Table III in
     the Appendix, and Tables 6 and 7 in Chapter II of *Thesis*.
25. See *Thesis*.
26. Railway companies operated with 25 per cent of empty
     return cargoes. Given that in the counterfactual economy
     the distribution of traffic is assumed to be constant,
     the effective capacity of traditional means must be
     weighted by a similar ratio.
27. I have estimated the farm animal population in 1878 by

27. *Continued*
assuming a linear trend between the 1865 and 1891 livestock censuses and a constant share of farm animals over
this period. For livestock census, see J. Sanz et al.,
'Contribucion al Analisis Historico de la Ganaderia
Española, 1865-1929', *Agricultura y Sociedad*, X (1979)
105-169.

28. Nadal, *Fracaso*, Tables 1 and 2, pp. 137 and 142,
including a 15 per cent mark-up for the higher quality
of English coal, see Chapter III in *Thesis*, pp. 166-7.

29. Nadal, *Fracaso*, p. 183.

30. The 'consumption cost' of protection is cancelled out
given that the demand for rails is held constant.

31. Asturias enjoyed a locational advantage for the development of a modern iron industry through the abundance of
coal.

6 Britain

GARY HAWKE and JIM HIGGINS

1. THE CONCEPT OF 'SOCIAL OVERHEAD CAPITAL'

'Social Overhead Capital' is as much a term of everyday speech
as it is a technical concept in economics. It arose in
development economics and is useful for purposes such as
describing the characteristics of poor countries rather than
in the work of economic theorists. It refers to large and
bulky items of capital like transport systems but it is not
easy to define in a rigorous way. An early definition in
Hirschman is still one of the most acceptable (1). SOC is
defined in terms of four characteristics: it is capital
formation in an area which is somehow 'basic' to a range of
economic activities; it is usually carried out by public
authorities or is regulated by government agencies; it is
non-importable; and it is associated with technical
indivisibilities and high capital output ratios. Hirschman
suggests that a wide notion of SOC is defined by only the
first three characteristics and that the addition of the
fourth gives a 'narrow' concept, focusing attention on
transport facilities and power generation and away from
expenditures on things like health and education.

Hirschman was naturally enough concerned with the developing
countries of the 1950s. In carrying the concept into historical
studies, the requirement that SOC should be formed or at least
closely regulated by government agencies is much too restric-
tive. Such a requirement would make it a nice question whether
there was any significant amount of SOC in England between
1780 and 1860 and it is more convenient to drop that element
of the definition and frame a question as to why England did
obtain SOC without much government involvement (2). In the
particular case of Britain between 1780 and 1860, also, the
possibility of relying on imports rather than on domestic
production is not of great interest. The important notions in
SOC for our purpose are therefore that it is capital formation
of a kind that is important to a number of growing economic
activities, and that it is characterised by technically-
imposed 'lumpiness', long gestation periods and economies of
scale. This is very close to the conclusion reached by Youngson

that 'overhead capital' is a set of properties rather than of
things and that the important properties are the extent to
which an asset is a source of external economies and the
extent to which it has to be provided in large units ahead of
demand (3).

If such definitions seem to have an ad hoc nature, they
reflect the development of the concept in the literature (4).
The general notions of capital used by society at large rather
than particular enterprises and of government involvement are
clear enough, but most writers rely eventually on examples to
convey the definition of SOC. Even Hirschman does so in
detailing the difference between his wide and narrow concepts.
A theoretical approach would be to link SOC to variables other
than those which determine investment in other forms of
capital, but this is not easy to do (5). The concept lives on,
and has been taken into the literature of economic history,
not because of its analytical attractions but because
empirical measurements have suggested that the assets generally
understood as belonging within SOC form substantial fractions
of total capital formation as countries industrialise. 'It is
population growth and urbanisation, social overhead capital
and the transport system, which generate the really big demands
for capital, and it is necessary to view the relatively modest
demands of industrialization proper against this perspective (6).
Was this true in Britain from the mid-eighteenth to the mid-
nineteenth century?

2. THE FORMS OF SOC BETWEEN 1780 AND 1860

Estimates of capital formation in Britain between 1780 and 1860
are available in Floud and McCloskey and Feinstein (7). They
make it abundantly clear that the major components of capital
formation in the period were indeed various forms of buildings
and transport systems. Within buildings, the share of the
farming sector declined, and although industrial and commercial
building increased relative to the total, it was not until the
1840s that it overtook dwellings. While dwellings have an
obvious 'social' component, they were mostly built in small
units and entirely by private enterprise. The precise level of
spending on education is in doubt, but it too was achieved in
small units of private activity. Concern with SOC is therefore focused on the development of transport systems, although
Gould's linking of urbanisation and SOC as the big claimants
on investment resources is fully compatible with British
experience between 1780 and 1860.

Something closer to the contemporary view of expenditures on
transport systems than to the modern category of capital

formation is shown in Table 6.1. It is more than usually
difficult to separate repairs and maintenance from net capital
formation in the case of roads and canals and neither
eighteenth-century conceptual thinking nor accounting
techniques gave much attention to such a distinction. Both
activities were included under a heading such as 'improvements',
and the table follows that practice. It is compiled from the
accounting records of bodies such as parish authorities, turnpike trusts and canal companies using a simple 'grossing up'
procedure to account for gaps in the accounting material.
These gaps are large, but not as large as has usually been
assumed, and the figures are more reliable than most economic
data of the period. (Their major deficiency is probably the
exclusion of road improvements made in the course of
enclosures.)

The main features of the table are the relatively high level
of expenditure on parish roads, the fast growth of spending on
turnpikes, the eighteenth-century 'booms' in canals and the
continued high level of expenditures on 'improvements' in the
nineteenth century. Also clearly apparent is the very rapid
growth of railways to even higher levels of expenditures from
about 1830. It must be remembered that the table shows
expenditures in current prices and that fluctuations in price
levels affect the time pattern shown; but while adjustment
for prices would probably show that the resources devoted to
transport improvements in the early nineteenth century were
less relative to the period as a whole than is suggested by
the table, it is unlikely to alter the chief features described
above.

3. THE GROWTH OF TRANSPORT SYSTEMS

Expenditure on maintaining and improving roads was not a new
activity in the mid-eighteenth century. Table 6.1 shows
expenditures on parish roads to be substantial in 1750 and to
be maintained rather than markedly increased in the succeeding
century. The notion of the 'King's Highway' and the need to
maintain travel possibilities go back at least to mediaeval
times. Nevertheless, it is at least possible that between 1750
and 1850 there was an increase in the proportion of road
'improvements' which would be capital formation in modern
terms rather than resources devoted only to countering the
ravages of winter rains and harvest traffic. And both the total
of the expenditure on parish roads and the obvious importance
of such roads for local traffic and for feeding other transport
systems suggest strongly that the oldest instruments of
transport improvements should not be neglected.

Table 6.1: *Expenditure on creating, improving and maintaining canals, roads, etc., 1750-1850 (current prices £'000)*

	Turnpikes	Parish roads	Bridges	Canals	Railways
1750-1	66	870	8	16	
1751-2	81	887	8	27	
1752-3	96	879	9	43	
1753-4	110	877	15	23	
1754-5	108	869	15	25	
1755-6	115	878	8	22	
1756-7	121	885	12	46	
1757-8	114	886	26	16	
1758-9	125	884	30	76	
1759-60	135	877	25	148	
1760-1	135	880	57	134	
1761-2	133	871	43	87	
1762-3	153	884	29	83	
1763-4	299	895	44	100	
1764-5	145	890	39	138	
1765-6	179	890	50	53	
1766-7	190	902	61	83	
1767-8	174	907	61	105	
1768-9	178	924	34	190	
1769-70	178	910	65	348	
1770-1	202	880	55	344	
1771-2	205	877	76	228	
1772-3	215	888	50	342	
1773-4	224	882	67	323	
1774-5	222	923	76	300	
1775-6	190	911	82	281	
1776-7	218	884	84	342	
1777-8	260	890	71	321	
1778-9	249	882	78	236	
1779-80	265	888	21	165	
1780-1	272	904	56	201	
1781-2	290	879	13	135	
1782-3	302	931	45	140	
1783-4	285	886	27	121	
1784-5	317	870	45	125	
1785-6	332	882	67	148	
1786-7	350	882	50	166	
1787-8	429	931	38	176	
1788-9	367	944	30	191	
1789-90	404	1 008	32	195	*Continued*

Table 6.1: *Continued*

	Turnpikes	Parish roads	Bridges	Canals	Railways
1790–1	406	1 022	37	189	
1791–2	405	966	35	322	
1792–3	409	1 041	35	328	
1793–4	415	1 045	43	814	
1794–5	446	1 044	34	720	
1795–6	445	1 102	45	746	
1796–7	445	1 088	52	533	
1797–8	494	1 063	46	599	
1798–9	492	1 055	42	771	
1799–1800	562	1 101	44	875	
1800–01	591	1 176	-48	760	
1801–2	591	854	54	541	
1802–3	630	893	49	658	
1803–4	658	872	43	608	
1804–5	687	924	42	653	
1805–6	721	951	60	760	
1806–7	742	937	50	550	
1807–8	789	976	48	678	
1808–9	789	977	63	719	
1809–10	813	988	91	818	
1810–11	864	1 019	95	785	
1811–12	938	1 016	150	731	
1812–13	946	1 242	168	722	
1813–14	913	1 304	312	795	
1814–15	947	1 342	452	730	
1815–16	1 019	1 276	474	778	
1816–17	1 009	1 141	436	824	
1817–18	1 053	1 179	367	682	
1818–19	1 049	1 245	228	849	
1819–20	1 126	1 155	222	825	
1820–1	1 121	1 166	90	663	
1821–2	1 108	1 155	65	524	
1822–3	1 249	1 151	74	761	
1823–4	1 385	1 159	66	736	
1824–5	1 784	1 180	239	794	
1825–6	1 521	1 219	277	811	30
1826–7	1 484	1 272	222	1 025	110
1827–8	1 434	1 037	213	1 127	380
1828–9	1 455	1 109	215	1 234	300
1829–30	1 439	1 107	207	1 146	300
1830–1	1 399	1 089	212	1 101	300
1831–2	1 411	1 089	164	886	520

Continued

Table 6.1: *Continued*

	Turnpikes	Parish roads	Bridges	Canals	Railways
1832–3	1 420	1 089	168	795	540
1833–4	1 445	1 107	110	688	610
1834–5	1 490	1 114	128	751	620
1835–6	1 538	1 152	89	814	1 050
1836–7	1 591	1 217	75	876	2 989
1837–8	1 478	1 029	71	861	4 180
1838–9	1 470	1 264	73	'927	6 270
1839–40	1 470	1 310	89	1 013	8 180
1840–1	1 342	1 368	84	1 032	8 230
1841–2	1 326	1 366	74	1 101	6 290
1842–3	1 216	1 371	102	844	4 890
1843–4	1 153	1 372	69	734	3 490
1844–5	1 131	1 374	66	852	3 699
1845–6	1 130	1 771	60	777	7 210
1846–7	1 118	1 846	60	804	16 740
1847–8	1 053	1 848	62	630	24 750
1848–9	996	1 858	70	757	20 350
1849–50	864	1 726	59	567	15 130

Sources: The immediate source for all data but railways is
J. P. Higgins, 'An Interim Paper on the Rate of
Capital Formation in Britain, 1750-1850' (1971,
unpublished). The estimates result from the
Sheffield-SSRC project into capital formation and
are discussed in J. P. P. Higgins and S. Pollard
(eds), *Aspects of Capital Investment in Great
Britain* (London, 1971).
See also: C. Feinstein, 'Capital Formation in Great
Britain', in P. Mathias and M. Postan (eds) *The
Cambridge Economic History of Europe,* vol. VII,
part 1 (Cambridge, 1978); R. C. Floud and D. N.
McCloskey (eds), *The Economic History of Britain
since 1700* (Cambridge, 1981) Ch. 7 and J. E. Ginuarlis,
*Capital Formation in Transport in the Industrial
Revolution* (Ph.D. thesis Sheffield, 1970).
The railway data are from G. R. Hawke, *Railways and
Economic Growth in England and Wales, 1840-70*
(Oxford, 1970) t. VIII.

Nevertheless, the more significant development of the road system in the eighteenth century was the turnpike trust. The inequity of using parish rate assessments and forced labour by residents of a parish to 'improve' roads for the benefit of other people was overcome by forming a trust charged with maintaining a specified section of road and financing its activity by tolls levied on those who used the facilities provided. More precisely, road improvements could be financed by loans secured on future tolls and the loans serviced by those tolls. This did not solve all issues of equity; some residents of a locality objected to the loss of customary rights to use a particular road without charge but the greater inequity was that through traffic subsidised local traffic on turnpikes. Nevertheless, there can be little doubt that the net effect of the development of the turnpike was a more equitable as well as a more efficient allocation of the cost of road-building.

The 'turnpiking' of a particular section of road depended on the private initiative of people concerned with it. There was no central planning of a 'turnpike' system. But the most used roads were obviously those where the turnpike trust had most to offer both local residents and people engaged in long-distance travel, and a mapping of turnpiking suggests more the growth of a road system radiating from London and linking centres of population and economic activity than a random selection of roads (8). There were certainly gaps in the system, frequently causing marked inconvenience to travellers and transporters of goods, but then bottlenecks of various kinds are a familiar feature on the centrally-planned motorway systems of the present day.

It was the turnpike trusts which were mainly although not entirely responsible for introducing the technical improvements in road-making associated with names such as Metcalfe, Telford and McAdam. The improvement of road beds to enable the surface to sustain heavier traffic flows whether measured by vehicle numbers or load weights, and the formation of drainage systems to protect roads from water, were the main ways in which land transport was facilitated. It was the legislative promise of future toll income that enabled the turnpike trusts to employ engineers to introduce such innovations. The effect is seen most clearly in personal travel; by the 1820s England could be said to have a network of coaching services permitting vastly faster personal travel than had been available in the middle of the eighteenth century (9).

In the transport of goods, the effects of road improvements were outweighed by those of developments in water transport. Like the parish roads, human intervention with natural waterways to make them serviceable transport facilities predates the mid-eighteenth century. But from then a number of factors combined to give a new vigour to attempts to improve inland water transport, a vigour that resulted especially in the expenditures on canals shown in Table 6.1. These factors included: an increased demand for transport, especially for bulky items unsuited to pack-horses and even wagons on improved roads; greater competition for water supplies for industrial and agricultural uses as well as for transport; and an improved technical ability to retain water in a man-made channel and to build locks permitting transport over reasonable gradients (techniques at least in part borrowed from Holland); and after the 1750s, a demonstration that canal-building could be a profitable economic activity.

The essence of water transport is that greater weight does no damage to the transporting medium. The essence of a canal is that it provides a water medium more conveniently arranged for transport than is a river in that the water is confined into a channel supplied with a tow path, and free from obstructions such as rapids and the weirs of corn or cotton mills, and substantially free from uncontrolled water currents. The water must still, of course, be obtained from natural sources, and there may still be competition for those supplies, but their seasonality can be better controlled by reservoirs than is possible with a river system. The advantages can be obtained, however, only at the expense of the investment of resources in the canal bed and in facilities such as locks.

Provided it is realised that the line between a canal and a river improvement is far from clear, the first English canal can be recognised as that which linked the Duke of Bridgewater's Worsley coal mines to Manchester in 1761. Its importance is that it showed the profitability of investment in canals. In particular, it revealed the possibility of private profits from building a canal for the use of separate transporters. This was important because Parliament was still suspicious of 'monopolies' and while it was prepared to sanction the building of canals, it insisted on separating their ownership from the carriage of goods along them. The operators of the canal obtained their income from tolls, and with occasional exceptions such as Bridgewater himself, were not permitted to become carriers of goods.

The expectation of profit within this framework was sufficient to stimulate a network of canals. In the eighteenth century, canals linked the major rivers of England - the Trent, Mersey, Severn and Thames - and then added more direct links between major towns and London. From the toll income of early canals, and from new investment, branches were added, extended and 'improved'. It should be noted carefully that a substantial

fraction of all canal-building took place in the early nineteenth century rather than in the booms of the 1770s and 1790s
which receive disproportionate attention in much of the
literature.

Canals were almost entirely built by companies, incorporated
with the privilege of limited liability by Act of Parliament
along with restrictions imposed in the same way, such as the
prohibition of acting as carriers discussed earlier, and often
with limitations of permitted tolls or rates of dividend. It
is not immediately obvious why canals were organised as private
companies while road improvements were entrusted to turnpike
trusts, but the main reason was probably that the latter were
responsible for part of the 'King's Highway' - public property
while the former were to construct their own thoroughfares more
or less ab initio. Furthermore, the turnpike trusts evolved
from 'justice trusts', essentially the devolution of a local
taxing power on the parish apparatus for maintaining roads, and
the line from parish to trust to company was one of successive
experimentation rather than of logic.

Canal companies were organised in much the same way as modern
companies although the unit of investment was larger than is
now common and the facilities for exchanging shares very much
less developed. Investors in canals were widely spread among
the socio-occupational classes, as shown in Table 6.2. The
distribution is not markedly different from that implied by
contemporary estimates for the distribution of income among the
same groups. The main difference between the two chronological
periods is in the share of peers and that is attributable more
to the Duke of Bridgewater individually than to any change in
the activities of the peerage as a whole. The main investors
were the landed gentry, merchants and tradesmen, the first of
these being especially prominent in canals with rural hinter-
lands, the second in other canals, while the tradesmen,
consistent with their spread among both larger and smaller
urban areas were about equally prominent in both kinds.
Manufacturers were, if anything, less prominent than might be
expected, but since their share of investment was much the same
as their share of total income, this probably reflects the
mistaken nature of our conventional ideas about the size of
manufacturing in the eighteenth-century economy. Investors in
canals were generally local, except that London investors were
to be found in many canals and in the boom or 'stock market
mania' of the 1790s investments were more widely spread. It is
likely that those who made loans to turnpike trusts were even
more localised than was the case with canals and that the
landed gentry were more prominent than they are in Table 6.2.

Not all the profit expectations of investors in canals were
realised. Large profits were made by some of the earlier canals

(Percentages of nominal capital invested)

	Canals 1755–1815 (1)	Railways 1820–44 (2)	Canals 1755–80 (3)	Railways 'early years' (4)	Canals 1780–1815 (5)	Railways 'later years' (6)
1. Peers, gentry, 'gentlemen' etc.	22	28	41	22	22	37
2. Land; farmers; graziers, etc.	2	–	1	–	2	–
3. Commerce; merchants, traders, tradesmen, etc.	39	45	27	52	40	38
4. Manufacturers	15	11	8	15	15	7
5. Professions, incl. clergymen	16	9	16	8	16	10
6. Women	6	5	8	2	6	8
	100	100	100	100	100	100

Notes and Sources: The data is from J. R. Ward, *The Finance of Canal Building in Eighteenth Century England* (London, 1974) pp. 74–5 and M. C. Reed, *Investment in Railways in Britain, 1820–44* (London, 1975) pp. 124, 132, 137, 144, 151, 157, 161, 166, 176, 191.

Continued

Table 6.4: *Continued*

Row (1): Ward's classes I and II; Reed's class VII.
Row (2): Ward's class II; Reed's class VI.
Row (3): Ward's classes IV and VI; Reed's classes I, III and V.
Row (4): Ward's class V; Reed's class II.
Row (5): Ward's classes VII and VIII; Reed's class IV.
Row (6): Ward's class IV; Reed's class IX.

Reed's class VIII, unspecified, is redistributed proportionately among his other classes. Note that Reed's listing of his classes for individual railway companies differs in order from his description on p. 109.

All data are derived from samples. The canal figures use Ward's own summary. The railway figures are derived from Reed's data for 10 companies, weighted by the nominal capital involved in each case. Col (2) employs all the data cited by Reed. Col (4) uses the earliest year for which Reed has data for each of the 10 companies. Col (6) employs the data for the latest year. In the case of the Nth Midland Railway, the 'latest year' data is estimated from data on the occupational distribution of share-holders (rather than shareholdings) by assuming that the linear relationship between these concepts in 1836 applies also for 1842. The figures would be little affected if the Nth Midland were excluded altogether.

---

but others received more moderate returns and in the early nineteenth century a substantial fraction of total canal investments was returning no private dividends at all. We cannot determine the average return within a wide margin, but it seems that canal investment was carried to at least the margin of returns available elsewhere in the economy.

The social returns were spread more widely than dividends. Canals cheapened the cost of transporting many commodities, especially those with a high weight:value ratio. All the inputs and outputs of the growing industries of the eighteenth century as well as agricultural products were represented in the freights of canals, but it is likely that coal was by far the largest freight. Bridgewater's reported comment that 'A navigation must have coals at the heels of it' was much more than a comment on his own endeavours; coal was the commodity most in demand in the industrial north, and coal for domestic use and in agriculture was the largest item in the freight of the canals of southern England. This can be inferred from Hadfield and from some surviving canal records such as those of the Leeds and Liverpool Canal (10). The limited evidence available suggests that the greatest social gain from canal-building was a reduction in

the cost of transporting coal, probably by about 50 per
cent (11).

We have portrayed the growth of both the road and canal
systems between 1750 and c. 1830 as responses to the
opportunities for profit created by demand for cheaper transport. In the one case, a semi-public body, the turnpike trust,
left the profit to those who benefited from the cheaper
transport and those who lent to the trust; in the other,
canal companies took some for themselves while making it
easier for carriers to earn an income and leaving some of the
social gains for consumers of transported goods, especially
coal. In neither case is much 'building ahead of demand'
apparent; the turnpikes responded to the inadequacies of
existing roads and the canals emphasised existing traffic in
appealing to investors although their existence may well have
stimulated additional traffic. Nor is there much sign that
the transport developments were greatly limited by
unavailability of investment finance. Although canals and
turnpikes obviously depended on the availability of resources
for investment, their timing cannot be closely related to
national year to year changes in interest rates (12). Rather
each turnpike and canal, in the eighteenth century, was seen
mostly as a regional undertaking, not making an excessive
demand on regional sources of investment resources. The
eighteenth-century transport developments were in an economy,
or set of economies, in which incomes were not near
subsistence.

Narratives of the development of railways are readily
available, and only the briefest summary will be given
here (13). Railways were essentially a combination of
innovations, especially in the successful manufacture of
iron rails and in the construction of mobile steam engines,
which permitted a marked reduction in the cost of transport.
The period of experimentation can be traced back into the
eighteenth century (or even earlier in the case of rails
alone) and was not completed before the first quarter of the
nineteenth century. When the Stockton and Darlington railway
was planned in the 1820s, it was not completely fatuous to
argue, as some people did, that horse-drawn carts on iron
rails were preferable to trains drawn by steam engines.

But that argument was not tenable by the end of the decade.
The success of railways like the Stockton and Darlington,
and even more of the Liverpool and Manchester railway, the
first to be planned and operated as a transport service for
people as well as goods, proved that railways offered an
improvement over rival transport systems, such that the
building of railways was a profitable investment opportunity.
The profits that could reasonably be anticipated (even though

less than were often in fact anticipated) were large enough
to outweigh other economic considerations such as the rate
of interest available on government stocks, and the pace of
railway building in the 1830s was influenced more by the
availability of people like surveyors and by technical considerations of parliamentary procedures than the variables
which are usually prominent in investment decisions. In the
course of the 1830s and 1840s most of the trunk lines of the
English railway system were built, the exceptions being the
Great Northern built in the 1850s and the Great Central built
much later in the nineteenth century. In the 1850s and 1860s,
the trunk system was supplemented by secondary routes, often
built by existing railway companies or by contractors
intending to sell to an existing company. The British railway
system gradually came to resemble a web connecting all
significant centres of population.

British railways were built by essentially private companies, although the need for an Act of Parliament to give a
company the power to compulsorily acquire land and to
provide limited liability meant that the state had a role to
play. Railways usually began with local committees, formed
by people who saw an opportunity for private profits and who
were prepared to accept the initial expenses of surveying and
obtaining the necessary statutory powers. Once an Act was
obtained, the company became a legal entity very much like
modern business corporations, and it was in the interval
between original formation and statutory incorporation that
most of the gambling for which railways became renowned took
place. That is, the gambling was in the 'scrip' of
unincorporated units rather than in shares, the capital gains
coming from selecting those committees which would obtain
parliamentary sanction for their plans.

While railways were often initiated by local interests,
companies which had received parliamentary sanction offered
the prospect of good and reliable dividends (although
naturally some companies proved to be better than others).
Incorporated companies were therefore able to attract investment funds from throughout Britain and most railway
companies soon came to have a shareholders' register which
was widely distributed geographically. The contemporary view
that Liverpool was especially prominent in providing funds
for railways has been confirmed by modern research and is
presumably to be attributed to the early experience of
Lancashire with railways and to the availability of investment funds from the various economic activities especially
prominent in Liverpool. But the railways were soon drawing
on something close to a national market for capital.

Similarly, the occupational distribution of shareholders

in railways was widely varied. Contemporary sources emphasise
the difficulties which some 'hapless widows' and misguided
clergymen experienced, but as shown in Table 6.2 there can
now be no doubt that the most prominent groups among railway
shareholders were people whose incomes were derived from
trade and commerce. Such people were, of course, those in the
best position to judge the likely success of railway schemes.
They were even more prominent in the earlier railway schemes;
unlike canals, railways needed no aristocratic pioneers.

Most companies were formed to build railways between
precisely nominated points, and most began with limited
objectives. Some companies then extended their field of
operation, but more prominent in the 1840s was the amalgamation of distinct companies which had some obvious community
of interest. Thus the London & Birmingham Grand Junction,
and Liverpool and Manchester Railways came together into the
London and North Western Railway in 1846. Even more spectacu-
lar was George Hudson's formation of the Midland Railway from
a number of railway companies in central England and its
gradual evolution into one of the major trunks linking London
to the industrial north. Hudson's reputation was later
tarnished when he was shown to be engaged in at least near-
fraudulent business activities but he was only one of the
first of such business tycoons.

The amalgamation movement was not the only way in which the
independent companies were formed into something like a
railway 'system' by the middle of the nineteenth century.
Perhaps as important was the organisation of the Railway
Clearing House whereby passengers (from 1842) and goods (from
1848) could be consigned over the railways of two or more
companies in one transaction, the railway companies
themselves arranging the appropriate distribution of the
receipts. But even more important was the simple geographical
extension of railway lines so that there was at least one
link between almost any conceivable pair of places.

The role of the state was essentially subsidiary. An Act of
Parliament was necessary, and this gave a privileged position
to those people represented in the House of Commons or the
House of Lords since they were in a position to obstruct any
particular route for a railway line. Agreement was usually
reached (although not always) but the need for a parliamentary
granting of the power of compulsory acquisition gave a power-
ful bargaining weapon to such groups as the owners of land.
Furthermore, Parliament quickly accepted a responsibility to
ensure public safety on railways and so the state became
involved in the investigation of accidents and in the
certification as safe of new lines. And from the days of
canals, Parliament inherited an interest in the maximum charges

which could be imposed by railways, although regulations were
usually phrased in a manner that proved to make them largely
ineffective. Parliament did consider extending the
traditional concern with 'monopolies' and in 1844 it fore-
shadowed the possibility that all railways sanctioned after
that date might be compulsorily acquired by the state after
21 years. (A Royal Commission in 1865-7 recommended that such
an action was unnecessary and its advice was accepted.)
Parliament usually had to sanction amalgamations of railway
companies (since a railway company was strictly limited to
those powers conferred by its original private Act, and an
amending Act was required to extend them). By the 1850s
Parliament was taking a sceptical look at many proposed
amalgamations and refused some including the proposals of
the largest of railways companies. Laissez faire in England
never meant uninhibited freedom for businessmen; rather it
meant freedom to act within certain constraints, one of
which was the unacceptability of monopolies - 'monopolies'
in its everyday meaning rather than in the strict sense of
elementary economics.

Thus railways were built in Britain primarily by private
enterprise seeking private profit, drawing on a geographically and occupationally varied capital market and gradually
evolving a national railway system. The role of the state
was secondary but certainly not absent.

4. THE CONCEPT OF 'SOCIAL SAVING'

So far we have been concerned with various aspects of the ways
in which England acquired its SOC between 1750 and 1860. We
turn now to seek more precision to notions about the effects
which SOC had on the economy. For this purpose we employ the
concept of the 'social saving' associated with an innovation.

The social saving is measured as the difference between the
actual cost of the transportation services of a given year
provided by the railways and the hypothetical cost of those
same services in the absence of the railways using the best
available alternative source of transport services. If the
prices used accurately reflect resource use, this also
measures the difference in national income with and without
the railways, given that the economy is not allowed to adjust
to the absence of railways (by, for example, relocating
economic activity so that less transport is required for a
given level of total output).

The difference in the cost of specified transport by railways and by an alternative system involves more than a
direct comparison of rates charged on various goods.

Allowance has to be made for such things as differences in
the reliability of each system for transporting goods safely,
for differences in seasonal unavailability because of weather
conditions, for differences in speed, for differences in the
cost of transshipments and of supplementary haulage by
another transport means such as horse-drawn wagons if the two
systems differ in the amount of such services required, and
perhaps for other things as well. Furthermore, the difference
in transport costs cannot be equated with the difference in
national income if the improved transport system induces
external economies in other parts of the economy.

Equally, it is important not to double count the gain to
an economy from an innovation in transport. What might appear
to be distinct gains may well be different manifestations of
the cheapening of transport services. For example, the
formation of a railway can be expected to increase the rental
value of land close to it. The change in rents is an
alternative route to the measurement of the extent by which
transport costs were reduced but it is not a benefit
additional to a comparison of transport costs with and without
the railway; to add the two would be to double count by
including both a direct measure of the change in the income
stream and the change in the valuation of assets resulting
from the change in the income stream.

As expounded so far, the notion of social saving is really
simple. It is an ex post analogue to the ex ante notions
underlying any appraisal of a projected innovation or investment project and so widely used in many areas of applied
economics. Indeed, it is formally no more than a particular
application of the fundamental economic concept of
'opportunity cost', that the cost of anything is ultimately
what must be given up to attain it. But such simplicity
disappears as subtleties of interpretation are attached to
estimates of a social saving. The most significant complexi-
ties are readily apparent from the definition of the concept:
the use of the actual transport services in a given year, the
need for 'appropriate' prices, and the need to consider
external economies separately.

If a large innovation or investment project is not undertaken then the pattern of output of a particular economy is
unlikely to be the same as if it were undertaken. For
example, in the absence of railways, the British economy
might well have arranged production to require less transport so that although total production would have been lower
than the level achieved with railways the difference would
not be as great as the 'social saving'. This point has been
christened the problem of 'terminal weighting'. Its
significance depends on the precise question being asked. If

one is concerned with the impact on growth of a particular innovation, one can define the social saving (as a measure of that impact), as the difference between the resources which the economy has to devote to some activity such as transport so as to reach a certain production pattern with and without the innovation. No bias through 'terminal weighting' is involved. But it is still open to anybody to complain that other measurements would be more in line with normal notions and to seek modifications of the social saving (usually using an estimate of the elasticity of demand for transport services to try to evaluate the extent to which less transport would be required in the absence of the innovation). A second line of approach is to accept the bias imposed by terminal weighting and seek to use it in the argument being constructed. Since no adjustment which an economy is likely to make to the absence of railways would increase the gap between the level of income achieved and that which could be achieved by making no adjustment at all to the absence of railways, the 'social saving' can be interpreted as an upper bound on the effect of an innovation on income or as an upper bound to the social returns to an investment project. If one wishes merely to argue that the effects of railways were not as great as sometimes thought, then an upper bound may be sufficient. But it is unlikely that such an argument will be sufficient for all purposes; as soon as one is engaged in international comparisons one will want to go further. One then has to abandon any hope of simple solutions.

The prices which are conceptually appropriate for a social saving calculation are clear enough. In the case of railways they are the resource costs of certain transport services provided by the railways, and the resource costs of those same services by the best alternative transport means. For the railways, one needs to be concerned only about possible imperfections in the average price charged by the railway system. But for the alternative, one cannot have a direct observation. Any canals which survive railway competition can hardly be typical of a canal system required to undertake the transport services provided by the railways. (It is obvious enough that if two transport services coexist within one market in a perfectly competitive economy, then the social saving of replacing one with the other must be zero.) On the other hand, the *charges* made by canals in an earlier era may well be far from the resource cost of canal transport in later years. One needs to have some notion of the cost function of canal transport. Only then can we form some idea of at what cost the economy could have obtained the transport services of a later year without the use of railways.

Like 'social saving' and 'social overhead capital', the concept of 'external economy' soon proves to be less simple than it first appears. Again the general idea is clear. A particular innovation such as the railways may have more impact on national income than it does on transport costs because it enables a saving in resources elsewhere in the economy than the transport sector. If the railways are directly responsible for some secondary innovation in the iron industry, cheapening iron for all uses, then the effect of the railways will be greater than the social saving. In assessing the returns to investment in railways, it is not so clear that all external economies flowing from the investment in railways - whether they originate in the particular innovation or in the cheapening of transport however that is achieved - should not be added to the social saving.

In either case, it is important not to confuse an external economy with the direct effects of the cheaper transport made available by railways which are measured by the social saving itself. Cheaper transport makes resources available for other purposes but that is what the social saving is designed to measure. It is any secondary innovation which may require an addition to the social saving in assessing the effects of the railways. The difficulty with such external economies is simply that they must be identified and measured.

It may still be surprising to some readers, especially those with a background in orthodox historical methodology as distinct from historical practice, that we should take seriously the use of counterfactual methods such as imagining a British transport system without railways. For a long time, orthodoxy recommended study of what happened, not speculation about what might have happened. But such a dictum was not, and could not be followed. Statements of what happened inevitably imply statements about what did not happen; the proposal of causal connections immediately carries counter-factual implications which might be the most convenient means for subjecting the proposed connection to a demanding empirical test.

It must be remembered that concern with a counterfactual situation is an analytical tool for describing and analysing historical events. A counterfactual is obviously untrue in the sense that it does not directly describe reality (and some people have been concerned about whether a 'true' argument can be based on an obviously 'untrue' proposition) but counterfactuals are used in arguments not directly but as measures of effects or causal connections which are not themselves untrue. (As, indeed, they have long been in various

mathematical and logical arguments.) That 'railways did not
exist in England in 1865' is obviously untrue but that does
not imply the falsity of a proposition such as 'Maintenance
of 1865 levels of production without the use of railways
would require a diversion to transport of 10 per cent of the
1865 national income.'

More particularly, statements about the effects of an
innovation and investment project such as the railways always
have counterfactual implications and it is an obvious path
to greater precision of knowledge to seek to specify those
counterfactual implications more closely. It is, of course,
true that one can never hope to make definitive statements
about counterfactual situations, but then finality is as
much an illusion in historical writing as it was in Lord
John Russell's speeches about parliamentary reform.

Specifying the appropriate counterfactual for assessing any
proposition is often a tricky task. In our discussion of the
concept of social saving, we noted the different counterfactuals required for only slightly varying aspects of the
introduction of railways into the English economy. Each of
these has to be separately scrutinised and assessed. But
the essential defence of the use of explicit counterfactuals
is that the technique has advanced our knowledge in a number
of fields of economic history in the last ten to fifteen
years – not by as much as the most enthusiastic proponents
would claim but by enough to justify the technique itself.

The modern concern with counterfactuals should be clearly
seen as a concern about the *precision* of the specification
of the counterfactual situation. It is generalisations
about the 'importance' or 'significance' of the railways
which carry most counterfactual implications. Studies which
have given most explicit attention to the counterfactual
have been clearly limited in the area of their interest; the
economic effect of railways, and still more the effects of
railways on economic growth, constitute a much narrower
field of study than their importance or significance. Those
who wish to assess the effects of railways on the location
of industry, or on the distribution of income (and still
more on welfare) or on other aspects of history have to
construct different counterfactuals, or have to rely on more
traditional methods recognising that they cannot give such
precise results.

5. THE SOCIAL SAVING OF ENGLISH RAILWAYS IN 1865

Because there has been more study of railways than of earlier
innovations, and because information on railways is more

readily available, we turn first to the social saving of the
later innovation.

By 1865, the railways of England and Wales were providing
approximately 2.2 thousand million passenger miles of transport services to the economy, about half of those being in
third-class travel. That represents about a six-fold
increase in personal travel from the time when railways first
became available (14). By 1865, the railways of England and
Wales provided a comprehensive range of services and the
number of companies and alternative routes ensured that railway prices allowed for very little surplus over the resource
cost involved.

If the 1865 level of personal travel were to be sustained
in the absence of railways, some travel would have been
diverted to shipping (and some to canal boats), but if only
because of the inland nature of most travel, most would have
had to be accommodated on coaches. The cost of coach travel
fell between 1820 and 1840, partly because of competition
within the coaching industry and partly because the fear or
fact of railways eliminated monopoly rents, and it is probable
that coach fares approached long-run resource costs in that
period. Fares of 4d per passenger mile inside coaches and
2/d per passenger mile for outside travel were described as
'slightly over the mark' by a parliamentary committee in the
1840s but they were accepted as accurate by a Royal Commission
in the 1860s. In a six-fold increase in scale without
technical change the most likely movement of the long-run
cost curve is upwards as such items as road maintenance become
more burdensome, but those figures are taken as the
appropriate costs here.

More difficulty arises in assessing the relative comfort of
coach and rail travel. In the 1840s, it was not uncommon to
compare first-class rail travel with inside coach travel and
other classes with the outside seats of coaches. But in the
1860s, the Royal Commission compared first-class rail travel
with posting (i.e. the running of an individual coach
between any two points, changing horses at prearranged
'posts' on the route) at 24d per passenger mile. And in all
respects but the complete freedom from timetable constraints
in posting (and that is not a marked advantage over the
extremely frequent train services of the 1860s), the
comparison of the Royal Commission cannot be said to be unduly
favourable to the railways of 1865.

If we adopt the comparison of the Royal Commission, then
to maintain the 1865 level of personal travel by coach transport, the economy would have had to divert resources of about
£48 millions to the transport sector, or about 5.8 per cent
of the UK national income. If we adopt the comparison used

in the 1840s, the amount involved is about £13 millions, or about 1.6 per cent of the UK national income. We may combine these by saying that the 1865 levels would have required a diversion to transport of about 6 per cent of the UK national income, but that three-quarters of that diversion could be avoided by accepting a marked retrogression in the comfort enjoyed in travelling. (Even though there was a six-fold increase in personal travel from the 1840s to 1865, it is perhaps the change in the comfort of travel which most justifies thinking of the railways as introducing the new commodity of personal travel pleasure into the economy.) We would, of course, like to know more about the demand for travel in 1865 so that we could add further conclusions to the study of social saving. But the study of choices among the various classes of rail travel offered by individual railway companies makes it clear that the valuation of the difference between, for example, first- and second-class travel varied markedly among them. We have no firm basis for estimating what people in 1865 would have done about the comfort of travel had it markedly increased in price.

We do know that the average length of passenger journey in 1865 was very short – not much more than ten miles. This reflects the density of the rail network in 1865, and the success of the railways in attracting people for even short journeys. It also implies that there is no need for any significant addition to the social saving to reflect the greater speed of rail traffic.

In 1865, English railways provided approximately 3000 million ton-miles of freight transport services (15). The freights involved were obviously much less homogeneous than was the case with passenger services, as almost every conceivable type of commodity produced or consumed in England was represented in the freight of railways. But about two-thirds of the freight carried on railways, measured by either tons or ton-miles, consisted of minerals, mostly coal.

To maintain the 1865 level of transport services without railways would have required mostly an increased use of canals. Some traffic would have been diverted to coastal shipping and the livestock traffic of the railways could be diverted to droving (and the calculations reported here make some allowance for these alternatives) but most of the traffic must be considered as diverted to canals. In particular, railways permitted the development of *inland* coal-fields when they were competitive with coastal fields and the transport from those fields could not be provided to any significant extent by coastal shipping.

Much the weakest point in any attempt to measure the social

saving of railways is our knowledge of the costs involved in
such an alternative transport network. But the very limited
information available does suggest that canal costs were
roughly constant over increasing volume (although costs are
not, of course, observable up to the volume of 1865 transport
services). The costs of canals were however a much smaller
fraction of the cost of shipping by canal than much of the
literature would suggest. And the evidence on costs other
than those associated with the maintenance of the canal bed
itself - those connected with organisations running canal
boats - is least satisfactory although a priori expectations
of constant costs in an industry of small units are not
inconsistent with the scattered data which exist. (Much the
same is true of the droving alternative to the railways'
livestock traffic.) These data are used to make the first
calculation of the social saving on freight traffic shown in
Table 6.3.

Table 6.3: *The social saving on freight in 1865*

	£ million	UK national income
Freight traffic		
Aggregate	14.0	1.7
Livestock and meat supplies (additional saving)	0.35-2.54	0.04-0.31
Supplementary wagon haulage		
Minerals	7.1	0.9
Other	3.5	0.4
Inventory adjustments	0-1.0	0-0.1
Total	25.0-28.1	3.0-3.4

Source: Hawke, *Railways and Economic Growth* (1970) p. 188.

The additional saving shown for meat supplies is an explicit
recognition of the need for speedy transport for some freight
items. In 1865, the main such item was what contemporaries
referred to as 'dead meat' but which the modern tendency to

euphemism would label 'fresh meat'. Even this trade was in its infancy in 1865, being mostly concerned with meat supplies to London and being markedly promoted in the mid-1860s by various animal diseases which interrupted the livestock trade. Other trades in perishable commodities, such as milk and fresh vegetables, were developed mostly after 1865 and are not separately accounted for. A trade in fish was not new but the extra saving is not large enough to be significant.

Conceptually, the dead meat trade resembles the comfort of first-class passenger traffic. In the absence of railways, it would probably have been replaced by a larger livestock trade rather than by an alternative fast transport service. But that replacement could not be complete. The dead meat trade permitted the removal of abattoirs from city centres and eventually enabled salesmen to take advantage of divergent price trends in different markets for particular cuts of meat. It represented a genuine addition to the services available in the economy. If one wants to eliminate that consideration from the social saving attributable to the innovation of railways one has only to deduct between 0.1 and 0.7 million pounds from the total shown in the table.

The estimated cost of the non-rail canal-dominated alternative transport system used in the table allows for the approximately 20 per cent greater distance between two points by canal than by rail. But in addition to that, a canal system required a greater amount of supplementary wagon haulage between place of production and the transport system, or between the latter and place of consumption, and this is shown separately in the table. So is an allowance for the greater speed of rail transport through its effect on inventory costs. This cannot be other than small. The average distance for which freight was transported in 1865 was only between 30 and 35 miles and although this is obviously the average of both longer and shorter distances, the difference in stock requirements because of the difference in speed of goods trains and water transport cannot be large. The limited direct observations of stock levels lead to the same conclusion. Furthermore, for some commodities, especially agricultural products, stock levels are determined by seasonal production patterns, and speedier transport, while it can redistribute the holding of stock among producers, wholesalers, retailers and consumers, cannot affect the total level. And while the English climate is execrable, it did not make canal transport unavailable for large parts of the year as happened in some other countries. Floods and ice in winter and shortages of water in summer did occur but not usually for long periods and there is no need for a substantial adjustment for the greater reliability of rail transport.

   The table shows that the maintenance of 1865 freight transport services in the absence of English railways would have
required a diversion of 3 to 3 1/2 per cent of the UK national
income, which is equivalent to about 4 per cent of the
national income of England and Wales. That can probably be
extended to Britain or to the United Kingdom without
significant change.
   It is much easier to recognise that the social saving will
underestimate the effect on national income of railways if
they induced external economies than it is to identify means
by which the railways made an effective addition to the
resources of the economy other than by the provision of
cheaper transport services (16). The railways did use a
substantial fraction of total investment or the total labour
force in certain years, but this is the cost of the railways,
the means by which the social saving was achieved, rather than
any gain to the economy over and above the social saving.
   The item of investment which attracts most attention is the
iron content of rails and there have been numerous suggestions
that the demand for rails was a significant influence in the
growth of the iron industry (17). It is perfectly true that
rails were a substantial fraction of the output of both blast
furnaces and rolling mills, and indeed, the traditional case
is strengthened when it is noted that the demand for iron
for railways was more than proportionately directed to the
iron industry of South Wales and that rails used by railways
in England and Wales probably accounted for 10 to 15 per cent
of the output of the region's blast furnaces over the peak
years 1844-51. That percentage is much less than some accounts
would suggest but it is still substantial. But the industry
consisted of many plants, and if mere size of output was
sufficient to cheapen iron for uses other than railways – for
an external economy to be exploited – then simple amalgamation
of some individual plants would have sufficed to replace the
innovation of railways. It is not easy to trace any connection
between the specific demands of rail-making and technical
change in the industry. For example, among Welsh furnaces there
is no obvious connection between those which were prominent
suppliers of rails and those which were the early users of the
hot blast technique. And at least in the case of the Bessemer
industry before 1870, a similar conclusion must be reached
about the relationship between rails and the development of
the steel industry. Hesitancy and high standards of proof
that steel rails were superior to iron on the part of railway
companies meant that steel rails were not a large part of the
output of the steel industry in the 1860s. Nor were early
steel masters usually in firms that had supplied a large
quantity of iron rails; the switch from iron to steel rails

usually involved a switch to a new supplier.

Once this conclusion has been reached for the most likely sources of external economies, it is not surprising that it is difficult to find any in other parts of the economy. In particular, railways in England and Wales were built between existing centres of economic activity so that it is unlikely that economies arose from the relocation of industry over and above the cheaper transport available from sites close to a railway. The productivity record of railways was impressive but does not indicate that there were significant improvements in management techniques made available to other sectors; the productivity gains came mainly from improvements in the performance of assets peculiar to the railway industry. Direct scrutiny of the railways' use of management techniques in accountancy and marketing results in a similar conclusion. Changes in company law followed the logic of legal and political argument rather than simple experience with railways, and while railways had a substantial impact on such institutions as the stock exchange, no significant gain not otherwise available to other sectors of the economy can be detected.

The study of railway problems did lead directly to the theory of imperfect competition but the long-term gain from that is problematical and it certainly had no impact on the economy in the nineteenth century! But the particular pricing policy adopted by English railways, a rather sophisticated form of discrimination among commodities and among regions, may well have had the effect of bringing into the economy certain resources which would otherwise have remained unused. The railways seem genuinely to have accepted a public policy type of role which could have had the effect of some net gain to the economy. But overall, the incidence of external economies of the necessary kind is unlikely to alter the order of magnitude of the social saving as previously calculated.

It should be emphasised that this conclusion is in no way inconsistent with the more familiar proposition that railways markedly altered the English economy in such aspects as the location of industry, the total volume of iron output, the volume of business on stock exchanges, the relative fortunes of individual business units, and the creation of railway towns such as Crewe, Swindon and Wolverton. What this conclusion says is that such changes were the means by which the social saving was achieved, not additional gains to national income over and above social saving. In many ways, the nature of the railway towns is symbolic; what is significant is that they did not develop industries unrelated to railways, signifying gains to the non-railway sectors of the economy distinct from the provision of cheaper transport.

The social saving calculation summarised for 1865 can be repeated – with a greater degree of approximation – for each of the years 1840-70. The resulting estimates can then be combined with data on railway investments, and on the private profits of the railway companies, to determine the social rate of return on investment in English railways (18). The internal social rate of return on English railways between 1830 and 1870 is found to be of the order of 15 to 20 per cent, and it is unlikely that any alternative use of the resources involved could have earned a greater return.

We can be confident that the calculation underestimates the true social returns to investment in railways. Any technical external economies which should be added to the social saving to obtain a measure of the effects of the railways as an innovation should also be taken into account in assessing the returns to investment in railways. But one should also consider those ways in which the railways facilitated growth in other sectors whether or not the railways were technically necessary for the change in the other sectors. The test is simply gains elsewhere facilitated by investment in railways, rather than gains elsewhere dependent on the innovation of railways. It is not important whether the cheapening of iron from a greater scale of blast furnaces depended on the existence of railways, but only whether the railway demand for iron helped ironmasters to exploit the gains from increased scale of production. Similarly, even if the efficiency of the stock exchange was not dependent on the existence of railways, if the business associated with railway shares and debentures facilitated the improvement of exchange operations for other sectors, then the social returns to railway investment should take account of those effects. There are therefore reasons for believing the calculated social rate of return to be too low.

There are however biases in the other direction too. We have already mentioned the problem of 'terminal weighting' in the context of investment returns. (But removing the gains through comfort in passenger traffic as discussed above still leaves an impressive social rate of return.) There were also negative external economies, not of a technological kind but where the investment in railways imposed costs on other sectors in the economy. The costs imposed on residents of cheaper housing areas in some cities can exemplify this, although enforced slum clearance is perhaps best thought of as a redistribution of income within the society rather than as a net loss of income (19).

Evaluation of the net effect of unquantified elements in the social returns to railway investment must be impressionistic,

but the judgement can surely be made with confidence that
the social returns to investment in railways were greater
than the social returns available to any other use of the
investment resources. This is, of course, a judgement on
the investment as a whole; it is consistent with some
misallocation of resources in that certain parts of the
railway investment would have been better reallocated
either within the railway system or to entirely different
uses. Furthermore, the calculations reported here refer to
the railway system as developed up to 1865. The social gains
were not obtained by one flash of inspiration in which
railways were conceived but in a series of developments
before and after the introduction of railways (20).

6.   THE GAIN FROM EARLIER TRANSPORT IMPROVEMENTS

There is no study of the social saving of canals comparable
with that for railways. But it is likely that its order of
magnitude for freight traffic would be not dissimilar. The
basis of this assertion is shown in Table 6.4.

The manipulations of the table concern coal alone, the
largest but by no means the sole freight carried by canals.
The key missing information is the average distance for
which coal was carried by canal, the average being
calculated over the whole output of coal (that is, including
the coal for which the 'lead' was zero). We exclude the coal
exported from north-east England, even though some of it was
probably carried by canals inland from ports in southern
England after being carried there by sea. The reduction in
cost attributed to canals is the difference between the costs
of shipping by canal (not tolls alone) and of land transport
used in the study of railways drawn on in the preceding
section. It is therefore an estimate of the difference in
the cost of both the developed canal system and the improved
road system of the early nineteenth century.

We can do no more than guess at the lead on canals at the
beginning of the nineteenth century. But it is more likely
to be near the lower than the higher figures of the table.
It has to include all coal other than exports from the north-
east, and coal freight on canals was probably at least as
concentrated in the north of England as was coal carried on
railways in the early 1850s. This would suggest that the
social saving on canals in 1800 was a smaller proportion of
national income than was that of the railways in 1865. On
the other hand, it may be that the contribution of coal was
a smaller proportion of the total in the former case, and

Table 6.4: *Hypothetical social saving of canals, 1800*

(1)	Coal output	11m tons
(2)	North-east exports	2.2m tons
(3)	Output ton-miles	
	(a) av. lead 20 miles	177m ton-miles
	(b) av. lead 50 miles	442m ton-miles
	(c) av. lead 100 miles	883m ton-miles
(4)	Reduction in cost	2 6d per ton-mile
(5)	'Social saving'	
	(a) av. lead 20 miles	£1.91m
	(b) av. lead 50 miles	£4.8m
	(c) av. lead 100 miles	£9.6m
(6)	Percentage of GNP	
	(a) av. lead 20 miles	1.4
	(b) av. lead 50 miles	3.4
	(c) av. lead 100 miles	6.9

Notes and Sources:

(1) P. Deane and W. A. Cole, *British Economic Growth, 1688–1959* (2nd edn. Cambridge, 1969) p. 216.

(2) B. R. Mitchell and P. Deane, *Abstract of British Historical Statistics* (Cambridge, 1962) p. 110 (817 000 chaldron of 53 cwt).

(3) $[(1) - (2)]$ x specified average distance.

(4) Hawke, *Railways and Economic Growth* (1970).

(5) (3) x (4)

(6) 1801 GNP. GDP £140m in 1851–60 prices. Feinstein, 'Capital Formation in Great Britain', p. 84.

especially that the inventory effects were then greater
(although equally there would be no saving on 'supplementary
wagon haulage').

The whole exercise is conjectural, non-factual rather than
'counterfactual' in the sense of Section 4, but it does
establish that the social saving of canals was probably of
the same order of magnitude as that of railways in that it
was almost certainly neither a tenth as small, nor ten times
as large relative to national income.

We have to remain even less knowledgeable about the returns
to investment in canals. The volume of resources devoted to
such investment was certainly less than that embodied in
railways and the social saving might therefore be thought to
guarantee a substantial social rate of return to the investment. But the social saving incorporates guesses as to the
resource cost of canal and land transport. Some part of it
was appropriated by the canal companies, if the contemporary
allegations of monopoly pricing by canals have any substance
at all. (And the reductions of tolls in response to planned
railways indicates that they had some substance although not
as much as often thought.) Some part of the social return to
canals was therefore incorporated in the dividend payouts of
canals, and, as we have already noted, for the canal system
as a whole this was by no means remarkable.

Similarly, we have to admit to ignorance about the economic
benefits of the road improvements of the eighteenth and
nineteenth centuries. The cost reductions were probably
proportionately smaller than those associated with canals and
the volume of freight less. But it is probably best to think
of the road improvements as more analogous to the passenger
traffic of railways, involved most in making personal travel
possible.

7. SOCIAL OVERHEAD CAPITAL AND ECONOMIC DEVELOPMENT

Britain's experience with transport between 1750 and 1860
raises several interesting questions. Perhaps the two most
interesting are the way in which a gap between social and
private returns to investment in transport were overcome,
and the way in which the SOC in the form of transport was
achieved with so little government intervention. Other
people might, of course, find more interest in the origins
of the innovations whose exploitation had been the key
feature of our analysis of transport developments.

There can be little doubt that in all the major transport
improvements of the period the private returns to investors
did not exhaust the social gains. There were probably

differences among the various improvements with the gap being
larger in the cases of railways and turnpikes than of canals,
but in no case did the gap prevent the investment from being
undertaken. There were, it is true, various devices by which
some of the social gains from the investment were internalised.
Much the most important was the regional nature of transport
investment until railways were well established. Those who
were the beneficiaries of the uncaptured social gains were
the residents of the geographical area served by a particular
canal or railway, and the same group constituted the main
investors and so recipients of private returns. The
coincidence could not, of course, be exact, but it was
substantial enough for the social/private gap not to be a
major impediment to the investment.

The same point explains why privileged positions for
particular interests were relatively unimportant. There were
certainly cases of privileges which in modern poor countries
would probably be taken as signs of corruption. Freights on
agricultural commodities and inputs, or on building
materials for parish authorities, were sometimes held
especially low. Manufacturers and others were sometimes given
special consideration in the allocation of shares but
generally they were content with equal treatment with other
shareholders paying equal tolls and receiving equal dividends
rather than offsetting these. Special tolls were more common
on turnpikes than on canals. The general eighteenth-century
progression towards the impersonality of property can be
applied to transport investment (21).

Probably even more important was the simple matter that the
private return was sufficient to make transport investment an
attractive proposition. Essentially, this was an implication
of the wealth of even eighteenth-century Britain relative to
many contemporary poor countries so that investment funds
were not guaranteed a high price because of their scarcity.
It is likely that the private returns were greater in the
fast growing industries of Britain - the high levels of
retained profits in many industries would certainly suggest
so even when it is recognised that many canal extensions were
also financed internally - but the opportunities for investment in family concerns were limited. The implication of this
is not so much that investment in SOC was facilitated by
imperfections in the capital market as that the available
pool of investment resources was much more than could flow
into industry, especially given the imperfect channels to
the latter.

The limited role of government is explicable in a way
clearly related to the foregoing analysis. Transport
investment between 1750 and 1860 simply called for little

central direction. A localised organisation was sufficient.
That organisation might be a traditional parish authority or
municipal corporation, a trust, or a company. In all of these
cases, a 'public' component might be identified within it, and
even canal and railway companies were expected or required to
pay some heed to the interests of the public as well as of
their shareholders if in no other way than observing maximum
charges. But because the activity was regional rather than
national, the central government need not be involved after
setting such basic rules. (Satisfaction with this arrangement
might well owe something to the contemporary practice of near-
identification of the interests of the public with those of
property-owners.)

That Britain could build its SOC by means of regional
activities was fundamentally a result of the slowness of its
economic growth relative to that demanded and expected in
contemporary poor countries. It is the modern goal of economic
growth much faster than that achieved in eighteenth- and
nineteenth-century Britain, together perhaps with a greater
modern concern about regional equity, which provides the
pressure for centralised planning of SOC (although much else is
involved in making centralised direction of the economy
possible). And it is the modern rate of population growth which
has brought housing into the usual classification of SOC while
Britain could leave it to private investment.

The slowness of British economic change also highlights the
significance of a distinction between development and growth.
None of the transport developments discussed here can be
regarded as indispensable (although any one of them might be,
as can readily be seen by a rough assessment of the social
saving of nineteenth-century railways with unimproved roads of
1750 as the only alternative system). And the institutional
changes historically associated with the transport changes were
probably not dependent on them. The gradual evolution of trusts,
geographically-based companies, to a national capital market
could have taken place under some other stimulus but was
historically associated with roads, canals and railways. The
learning process was not a functional relationship between
output and technology, but a gradual acceptance of new ways of
doing things or thinking about them. In the case of England, no
major sudden changes were required; there were opportunities
for small steps at a time. The turnpike trust could be grafted
on to the ancient system of maintaining roads; the limited
liability company could be grafted on to trusts and municipal
corporations. New sources of investment funds could be tapped
gradually. Adaptability is much enhanced when change comes in
nearly unnoticeable steps. And economic development in this
sense is facilitated by the first project drawing attention to

the institutional change required. In Britain between 1750 and 1860, those projects were often concerned with transport.

8. CONCLUSION

Between 1750 and 1860, the British economy exploited a sequence of innovations which made transport markedly cheaper. While no single innovation can be counted as indispensable, those innovations were of such significance that the economy would have required a substantial grant of free resources from elsewhere to compensate for their absence.

The building of improved inland transport systems was the nearest activity in Britain between 1750 and 1860 to the modern category of social overhead capital. But because England was a rich country, and because the economic growth of the period was not rapid by modern standards and there was no influential aspiration towards such rapid growth, the investment could be implemented on a regional basis by organisations with very little participation by the central government.

NOTES AND REFERENCES

1. A. O. Hirschman, *The Strategy of Economic Development* (New Haven, 1958) pp. 83-4.
2. P. H. Cootner, 'Social Overhead Capital and Economic Growth', in W. W. Rostow (ed), *The Economics of Take-off into Sustained Growth* (London, 1963) p. 262.
3. A. J. Youngson, *Overhead Capital: A Study of Development Economics* (Edinburgh, 1967) p. 68.
4. S. Enke, *Economics for Development* (London, 1964) pp. 263-4; B. Higgins, *Economic Development* (London, 1959) p. 204; R. Nurkse, *Problems of Capital Formation in Underdeveloped Countries* (Oxford, 1960) p. 152.
5. A. J. Youngson, *Possibilities of Economic Progress* (Cambridge, 1959) Ch. V; P. H. Cootner, 'Social Overhead Capital', pp. 261-84.
6. J. D. Gould, *Economic Growth in History* (London, 1972) p. 152.
7. C. H. Feinstein, 'Capital Formation in Great Britain', in P. Mathias and M. M. Postan (eds), *The Cambridge Economic History of Europe*, vol. VII, part 1 (Cambridge, 1978) and R. C. Floud and D. N. McCloskey (eds), *The Economic History of Britain since 1760* (Cambridge, 1981) ch. 7.
8. W. Albert, *The Turnpike Road System in England, 1663-1840* (Cambridge, 1972); E. Pawson, *Transport and Economy: The Turnpike Roads of Eighteenth Century Britain* (London and

8. (continued)

New York, 1977) and E. Pawson, 'The Turnpike Trusts of the
Eighteenth Century: A Study of Innovation and Diffusion',
Oxford School of Geography Research Paper 14 (1975).

9. H. W. Hart, 'Some Notes on Coach Travel, 1750–1848',
Journal of Transport History, IV (1959–60) pp. 146–50 and
E. Pawson, *Transport and Economy*, pp. 288–91.

10. C. Hadfield, *The Canals of Southern England* (London, 1955).
On canals see H. Hanson, *The Canal Boatmen, 1760–1914*
(Manchester 1975).

11. W. T. Jackman, *The Development of Transportation in Modern
England*, 2nd edn (London, 1962).

12. T. S. Ashton, *Economic Fluctuations in England, 1700–1800*
(Oxford, 1959).

13. H. Pollins, *Britain's Railways: An Industrial History*
(Newton Abbot, 1971); M. C. Reed, *Investment in Railways
in Britain, 1820–1844* (London, 1975).

14. G. R. Hawke, *Railways and Economic Growth in England and
Wales, 1840–1870* (Oxford, 1970); G. R. Hawke, 'Railway
Passenger Traffic in 1865', in D. N. McCloskey (ed),
Essays on a Mature Economy: Britain after 1840 (London,
1971).

15. For freight see Hawke, *Railways and Economic Growth*,
chs. III–VII.

16. On external economies, see Hawke, *Railways and Economic
Growth*, chs. VIII–XV. On the social savings methodology see
T. R. Gourvish, *Railways and the British Economy* (London,
1980) and P. K. O'Brien, *The New Economic History of the
Railways* (London, 1977).

17. E. J. Hobsbawm, *Industry and Empire* (London, 1968) pp. 70–1
and 114–16.

18. See Hawke, *Railways and Economic Growth*, pp. 405–8.

19. J. R. Kellett, *The Impact of Railways on Victorian Cities*
(London, 1969).

20. Hawke, *Railways and Economic Growth*, pp. 49 and 89.

21. E. P. Thompson, *Whigs and Hunters* (London, 1975); D. Hay
et al., *Albion's Fatal Tree* (London, 1975).

7 Belgium

MICHEL LAFFUT

1. INTRODUCTION (1)

Railways were born and diffused at a propitious time in
Belgium history which coincided with the progress of the
industrial revolution, the political revolution of 1830 and
the consolidation of Belgium independence. Industrialisation
revealed the inadequacies of existing communications,
awakened Belgium's businessmen to English experience and
provided finance of the construction of the new transport
network (2). At the same time, the achievement of national
independence cut the important link of communication from
Anvers to Prussia via the mouth of the Rhine and presented
the need for a quick and national solution to the transport
problems of the new state.

Belgium railways, in contrast to the systems of other
countries, were conceived in international terms. The network
was designed as a system to link the newly independent economy
to the rest of Europe (3). From their inception Belgium lines
were thought of in commercial terms as complementary to the
lines of neighbouring countries. As such they formed the
subject of negotiations between states and that is why,
despite some lively opposition, the tendency towards
nationalisation of the trunk lines triumphed at an early
stage of railroad construction when a division was established
between major lines, defined as part of a national and international network, and secondary lines which could be left to
private initiative.

The law which established the Belgium railway system was
passed by Parliament in May 1834 and it provided for a network
in the form of a cross intersecting at Malines with cardinal
points set towards Prussia, France, England and the sea at
Anvers. (Not until much later was an extension towards Holland
planned.) The law placed responsibility for construction under
the Treasury and provided for finance through the sale of
government bonds. Tolls and tariffs were regulated to cover
the cost of maintenance, wages, administration and the
amortization of the debt to the government. Profits were
earned by the state and losses would fall on Belgium taxpayers.

The historiography of Belgium railways, which is interesting
to trace, begins as early as 1835 with the writings of
officials concerned to demonstrate that their young country
should construct a railway network (4). It moves quickly to
discussions of whether the system should be operated under
private or public enterprise (5). A few years later, there
appeared handbooks by Loisel and others of great interest to
historians but written for those actively involved in the
promotion of and investment in railways (6). But the writings
of most historians such as Pauly and including the economist
De Laveleye are basically designed to describe the relationship between railways and the state (7). In addition there
are technical histories published in large part by railway
enthusiasts. But an analysis of railways to clarify their
economic and social significance has yet to be written (8).

Although railways operate across space the economics and
geography of railways are rarely combined, partly because
these disciplines are compartmentalised but mainly because
geographers normally work within regional frameworks and
economists on a national scale. But Belgium, a country of
only 30 000 square kilometres, offers us a unique possibility of studying the history of a complete and integrated
national system of trade and transport. In Lebrun's famous
phase, from 1830 to 1913 Belgium was a Unité Expérimentale.
The term implies that the country was politically unified,
was not disrupted by wars and revolutions and during the
nineteenth century there were no profound changes in its
political or monetary systems (9). Finally, the emphasis
accorded by Belgium's political leaders to the unification
of their young country led. to a remarkable effort to acquire
statistical and cartographical information about all aspects
of the nation's people, economy and transport. Thus historians
of Belgium railways are fortunate in having at their disposal
lengthy and valuable annual reports on the working of the
railways from 1836-1913, completed by fifteen Railway Year-
books published by Loisel after 1865. Thus my chapter can
meaningfully analyse the relationship between railways and
the evolution of the Belgium economy as a whole without
derogating or simplifying regional variations which are an
essential feature of the histories of France and Germany. I
have dealt with problems concerning the finance of railways
elsewhere (10).

2. THE ORGANISATION OF RAILWAYS

Railway policy marks the emergence of state enterprise in
Belgium as a definite departure from its limited involvement

with canals and roads (11). It was the Belgium state which
endowed the economy with a system of modern transportation,
and private enterprise was only gradually admitted and invited
to participate after lengthy debates in Parliament (12).

The network was laid down in three stages (13). During the
first phase from 1835-43 only the state built the lines.
Although the government had settled in 1832 on a scale of tolls
for private concessions, private initiative remained dormant.
The first private concession was awarded to Deridder in 1843,
an official from the administration of state railways, but that
was a narrow gauge line and disconnected from the main trunk
system. Before 1845 Belgium entrepreneurs apparently found
state railways adequate for the needs of industry and commerce
and apparently saw little scope for private profit in
extensions to that system.

The second phase, one of private initiative, was really
inaugurated by English promoters and investors and Belgium
capitalists were then stimulated to bid for similar concessions.
Finance was raised through the sale of shares and bonds by
limited liability companies (société anonyme) (14). In response
to the financial difficulties experienced by many companies a
movement towards concentration promoted by large banks appeared
from 1860-6. That movement was led by the Compagnie des
Bassins Houillers du Hainaut supported by the Banque de
Belgique and the Grand Central Belge backed by the Société
Générale de Belgique. Foreign companies (particularly French)
were also active and in 1857/8 the government intervened to
limit the ambitions of the Compagnie du Nord Francais which
remained, however, an important company in Belgium (15).
Between 1843 and 1870 some fifty private companies laid down
about 2500 kilometres of track. In this phase the state
expanded its network basically by operating lines constructed
by private enterprise.

The third phase witnessed the re-emergence of the state in
building new lines and repurchasing private concessions in
order to rationalise the system and to save unprofitable lines
from closure (16). When La Société Nationale des Chemins de
Fer Belges was formed in 1926, to effect a separation of the
finances of the railways from the budget of the state,
Belgium possessed a network of 4600 kilometres of which 4100 km
were operated by the government.

3. THE GEOGRAPHY OF RAILWAY CONSTRUCTION

The geography of railway construction can be demarcated into
extensive and intensive phases. The primary objective in the
initial phase (1835-43) promoted and directed by the state, was

to establish international lines of communication across the
borders of Belgium. The route to England was secured when a
line to the North Sea was completed in 1838, the route to
France was in place by 1842 and to Prussia a year later.
Projects for international lines continued to emerge after
1843 and although they were only partially realised, they
were characteristic of an expansionist mentality and which
left its mark on the Belgium network. For example, the
ambitious English idea to connect London to Trieste as the
first part of an overland route to India was designed to
cross Belgium from Ostend to Brussels and received
government sanction in 1846 (17). Another interesting example
is the Brussels-Lille-Calais line which was initially a
Belgium line integrated into the European system (18). The
maps (Figures 7.1, 7.2) compare the main lines of 1843 with
the network of 1913. The building of feeders followed no plan.
Rather it evolved as a series of projects great and small
including service lines, regional branch lines, industrial
networks and sections of international lines, managed by a
multiplicity of public and private administrations.

The evolution of railways which can be comprehended through
coefficients of penetration (the length of line constructed
per 000 kms of territory) and its obverse, the coefficient of
couverture (the area served by km of track), has been set out
in Table 7.1.

It appears from column 1 that until 1880 growth was
exponential and fell off thereafter. While the saturation
point for railways emerged at around 150 km of line per 1000
square kilometres of course the track was not distributed
equally across all parts of Belgium. Certain regions such as
the province of Luxembourg were less well served with lines
in relation to area than heavily industrialised regions like
Borinage (Mons), La Louvière and the Charleroi Basin.

Our coefficients of penetration and *couverture* become more
illuminating if they are conjoined with data on access to
railways, because lines are accessible for freight and
passengers only at specified points - stations, halts, stops,
etc. Table 7.2 provides statistical information on the number
of access points in the system from 1835 to 1914 and reveals
the gradual decline in the distances between access points
over the same period (19).

This picture is not seriously modified by the exclusion of
'stops' from the data and demonstrates how access to the
system improved markedly over time. By 1908 more than 80 per
cent of a random sample of 757 communes were located less
than 5 kilometres from an access point to a railway line and
the average distance for the sample (calculated from the
centre of each commune) was only 2.4 km. We can conclude that

Figure 7.1: *Development of the Belgian railway network, 1843*

Figure 7.2: *Development of the Belgian railway network, 1913*

Table 7.1: *Development of the Belgian railways system, 1825-1913*

	(1)	(2)	(3)
	Length of the lines	Coefficient of penetration	Coefficient of couverture
	km	km	km^2
1835	20	0.679	1 472.75
1840	385	13.071	76.51
1845	634	21.524	46.46
1850	916	31.098	32.16
1855	1 433	48.650	20.56
1860	1 818	61.721	16.20
1865	2 365	80.292	12.46
1870	3 128	106.196	9.42
1875	3 454	117.264	8.53
1880	4 044	137.294	7.28
1885	4 361	148.056	6.75
1890	4 468	151.689	6.59
1895	4 499	152.741	6.55
1900	4 503	152.877	6.54
1905	4 491	152.470	6.56
1910	4 634	157.325	6.36
1913	4 629	157.155	6.36

Source: M. Laffut, *Les Chemins de fer Belges,* pp. 174-6.

the obstacles constraining access to railway lines disappear over time and that the network became free of access.

4. ORDERS TO INDUSTRY

The construction and operation of railways exercised feedback effects on Belgium industry which was prepared to meet new demands even before the railway law of 1834 had passed through Parliament. At the very beginning railway demand was met by imports from England but Belgium entrepreneurs were very quickly on the scene. For example, the first five locomotives were supplied by Robert Stephenson but the sixth came from Cockerill's workshop and was put into service just eight months after the opening of the first line. By the end of 1839, 123 locomotives were in operation: 42 emanated from

Table 7.2: *Access points to the railway system, 1835–1914, and average distance between two points of access*

	Number in the state system	Number in the entire system	Distances between access points (state system) km	Distances between access points (entire system) km
1835	2	2	10.00	10.00
1840	50	50	6.66	6.66
1850	111	–	5.05	–
1860	150	–	4.01	–
1870	221	–	2.84	–
1880	582	898	4.26	4.50
1890	891	1 247	3.29	3.58
1900	1 266	1 457	2.98	3.09
1910	1 407	1 552	2.89	2.99
1913	1 439	1 573	2.85	2.94

Source: M. Laffut, *Les Chemins de fer Belges*, pp. 239–44.

Table 7.3: *Distribution of the distances to the railways in 1908 (for 757 Belgian communes)*

Distances in km	No. of communes	%	Cumulative %
0	357	47.16	47.16
0.5	5	0.66	47.82
1	11	1.45	49.27
1.5	20	2.64	51.92
2	32	4.23	56.14
2.5	43	5.68	61.82
3	41	5.42	67.24
3.5	37	4.89	72.13
4	40	5.28	77.41
4.5	21	2.77	80.18
5	24	3.17	83.36
5.5	28	3.70	87.05
6	20	2.64	89.70
6.5	13	1.72	91.41
7	11	1.45	92.87
7.5	5	0.66	93.53
8	8	1.06	94.58
8.5	9	1.19	95.77
9	3	0.40	96.17
9.5	2	0.26	96.43
10	7	0.92	97.36
10.5	6	0.79	98.15
12	3	0.40	98.55
12.5	3	0.40	98.94
13	3	0.40	99.34
14	1	0.13	99.47
16	2	0.26	99.74
16.5	1	0.13	99.87
23	1	0.13	100.00

Source: Dictionnaire des Distances Légales Rendu Applicable aux Frais de Justice (en Belgique), (Brussels, 1908).

England (Stephenson, Longridge, Fenton, Sharp), 81 were made in Belgium (68 from Cockerill and 10 from the Société Renard of Brussels and three from the Société Saint Léonard of

Liège) (20).

The rate of import substitution is even more remarkable for rails. First orders by Belgium railways were despatched to Gordons of Cardiff for 200 tons of rails - sufficient to lay 5 km of permanent way. Several days later a contract for 2000 tons was signed by Cockerill of Seraing and a further contract for 2000 tons by Dupont du Fayt (21). Subsequently rail supplies came entirely from Belgium firms and in 1840 the total quantity of rails and other items of iron equipment delivered under contracts worth 17 million francs amounted to 48 000 tons (22). A similar process of import substitution can be traced in the purchases of carriages and goods wagons (23).

A rough estimate of the magnitude of orders from railways for the Belgium iron industry can now be constructed (24). In 1913 the network operated by the state included 21 000 km of rails. At 41.2 kilogrammes of iron and steel per metre, the weight of entire system was about 850 000 tons of iron and steel (25). The 700 kilometres of concessionary lines added an extra 25 000 tons. To this total of 875 000 tons we must add estimates for the replacement and renewal of rails. Assuming that iron rails were renewed every 13 years and steel rails every 50 years, the number of renewals before 1913 would be four and if we apply this coefficient to, say, half the 1913 network, we obtain a total consumption estimate of 1.7 million tons (26). My estimates take no account of iron or steel supplied as fastenings, fitments and other accessories. Nor does it include replacements due to breakages.

Given the information that from 1860-1913 consumption of rails by state railways amounted to 1.6 million tons (an average rate of 30 000 tons a year) it may not be rash to claim that the construction and operation of railways within Belgium generated orders for 2 million to 3 million tons of iron and steel. Furthermore, the knowledge and experience which the iron and steel industry acquired enabled it to become a major exporter of railway equipment (27). In 1890 rails and sleepers represented more than 60 per cent of finished steel made in Belgium but in 1913 that proportion fell to 20 per cent (28).

Railways also required large quantities of coal. Fuel accounted for a high percentage of operating costs and there was a continuous search for economy. From 1835-53 locomotives burned coke - some of it produced by the government's own furnaces - but as costs of production rose the railways shifted from coke to coal briquettes (29). By 1865 the changeover was complete. Further economies in fuel consumption emerged with the introduction of small coal in 1861 - a year when coke cost 20.6 francs per ton, briquettes 15.7 francs and small coal only 9 francs (30). Substitution of small coal was rendered possible

by a Belgium invention: the Belpaire flat bottomed furnace
designed specifically to burn low quality coal (31).

Table 7.4 offers estimates of fuel consumed by locomotives
on Belgium railways from 1840-1913. Those estimates are based
on coal consumption per kilometre travelled by locomotives
running on the state network and the relevant coefficient was
applied to the private lines.

Table 7.4: *Fuel consumption on Belgian railways (1840-1913)*

	State ('000 tons)	Companies ('000 tons)	Total ('000 tons)	As a % of total Belgian consumption
1840	23	–	23	0.78
1845	32	–	32	1.04
1850	49	–	–	1.41
1855	71	–	–	1.43
1860	75	–	–	1.33
1865	130	147	277	4.01
1870	133	193	326	3.59
1875	396	179	575	5.84
1880	550	175	725	6.56
1885	610	178	788	6.50
1890	751	192	943	6.44
1895	800	207	1 007	6.73
1900	1 268	129	1 397	7.58
1905	1 583	148	1 731	8.25
1910	1 875	132	2 007	8.88
1913	2 284	150	2 434	9 98

*Source: Comptes Rendus des opérations des Chemins de Fer de
l'état,* F. Loisel, *Annuaire Spécial des Chemins de
Fer,* for the years quoted.

Even though railways were an important customer for the coal
industry, their consumption at the end of our period accounted
for less than 10 per cent of a total coal output of some
2 million tons. The growth of the coal industry cannot be
explained by the development of railways. Although railway
consumption grew more rapidly than national consumption as a
whole. Nevertheless the diffusion of the network contributed
to the growth in the demand for coal by widening the market
and providing access to and cheap transport for a fuel which
was too heavy and bulky for other modes of transport to carry

cheaply (32).

5. THE OUTPUT OF RAILWAYS

Railway output consists of ton-kilometres of freight and passenger-kilometre. For Belgium such statistics are difficult to find and my new series, which refers to the entire network, are presented in Tables 7.5 and 7.6. The estimates have been built up from data related to gross receipts, heavy goods tonnage and average distances travelled by passengers and freight (33).

Table 7.5: *Output of Belgian railways, 1835-1913 (passenger services)*

	Gross receipts (francs millions)	No. of travellers ('000s)	Passenger-kilometres (millions)	Distance travelled per passenger (kilometres)
1835	269	421	8	18.939
1840	5 335	2 199	81	36.534
1845	12 491	3 576	123	34.409
1850	16 970	4 869	149	30.547
1855	31 899	7 487	200	26.829
1860	48 435	12 575	314	24.927
1865	71 998	20 029	455	22.720
1870	92 396	26 925	613	22.766
1875	127 530	48 953	1 062	21.693
1880	152 513	56 306	1 266	22.498
1885	156 851	65 522	1 453	22.182
1890	182 158	82 389	1 715	20.814
1895	196 568	99 600	2 057	20.651
1900	237 226	139 138	3 060	21.988
1905	277 992	163 422	3 629	22.202
1910	340 518	193 070	4 619	23.926
1913	377 543	224 250	6 698	29.871

Source: Compte Rendu des Opérations des Chemins de Fer de l'état; Exposés de la Situation du Royaume; Annuaire Statistique; F. Loisel, Annuaire Special des Chemins de Fer.

Both series for freight and passengers rise exponentially at 6 per cent and 7 per cent per annum respectively. Passenger traffic grew as the use of trains became widespread but average distances travelled tended to remain short. Goods moved over twice the distances travelled by passengers and the average load for freight evolved from long journeys at the beginning of the period to far shorter journeys by 1870 and back again to longer journeys again just before the First World War.

Table 7.6: *Output of Belgian railways, 1835-1913 (heavy goods traffic)*

	('000 tons)	Ton-kilometre (millions)	Average load (kilometres)
1835	–	–	–
1840	97	7	72.108
1845	650	40	61.851
1850	1 607	86	52.299
1855	4 330	156	35.159
1860	8 362	296	34.141
1865	15 691	606	37.424
1870	26 457	674	24.473
1875	26 292	1 442	53.661
1880	32 799	1 844	55.355
1885	33 615	1 982	58.047
1890	43 019	2 556	58.606
1895	46 700	2 798	59.037
1900	55 121	3 647	65.562
1905	64 454	4 470	68.780
1910	76 180	4 936	64.388
1913	87 430	6 385	72.515

Source: See Table 7.5

Until the early years of the twentieth century, movements in passenger output were influenced far more by the numbers of people carried on trains than by distance travelled, while in goods there is a distinction between pre- and post-1870. Before 1870, output rises basically in response to increases in the tonnage carried; after that volume grew less rapidly but longer distances maintained the growth of ton kilometres. Table 7.7 presents decennial growth rates for passenger and freight outputs, 1840-1914.

To conclude this section we should mention fares and freight rates. Government policy favoured low rates and private companies complied. From 1845 to 1913 passenger fares declined from 5.25 centimes a kilometre to 1.80 centimes. Over the same

era freight rates fell from 10.3 centimes a ton kilometre to
3.6 centimes. These reductions came about through the introduction from 1860 of tariffs for goods which decreased with
distances travelled (34), and also through the proliferation
(particularly after 1868) of special tariffs for different
categories of transport service (35). Low fares for passengers
were accepted as early as 1842 and the principle was
exemplified by the introduction of season tickets for
different categories of user in 1868, 1870 and 1871 (36).

Table 7.7: *Annual average growth rates*

| | Passengers | | Goods | |
	Numbers %	Passenger kilometres %	Volumes %	Ton-kilometres %
1840–50	8.27	6.28	32.41	28.50
1850–60	9.95	7.74	17.93	13.16
1860–70	7.91	6.92	12.21	8.58
1870–80	7.66	7.52	2.17	10.59
1880–90	3.88	3.08	2.75	3.32
1890–1900	5.38	5.96	2.51	3.62
1900–10	3.33	4.20	3.29	3.07
1910–13	5.12	13.19	4.70	4.40
1845–1913	6.27	6.05		
1850–1913			6.55	7.10

Sources: See Tables 7.5 and 7.6.

6. COMPETITION IN THE TRANSPORT SECTOR

Before 1835 considerable improvements had been made to
internal navigation (37). New canals had been built (including
Maastricht-Bois-le-Duc in 1826, Gand-Terneuzen 1827 and
Charleroi-Brussels in 1832); rivers were canalised and efforts
made to widen and deepen the canals from Bruge to Ostend and
Brussels to Rupel. Navigable waterways had great advantage
over roads. They were cheaper, and loading capacities were
higher, especially for heavy or bulky industrial products.
But traffic flows were slow and could be interrupted in the
dry season. Not all regions possessed navigable waterways and
although projects for canals surfaced constantly they were
realised all too infrequently.

The construction of railways, which offered a regular, safe and speedy mode of transportation, did not arise from a demand to displace navigable waterways but rather from a wish to remedy the deficiencies of transport by water. Thus railways were complementary to waterways and the statistics show that traffic on canals tended to increase after the advent of railways (38).

Even where the two modes of transport offered a competitive service (such as the Brussels to Anvers rail line and the Willebroeck Canal), canals managed to hold their own often by cutting prices and demand was sufficiently elastic to maintain both forms of transport (39). Nevertheless the output of Belgium's navigable waterways rose more slowly than the output of railways. The former increased from 320 million ton-kilometres in 1846 to 1607 million ton-kilometres by 1912 – an annual average rate of growth of 2.48 per cent compared to 7.74 per cent for the railways (40). But we should point out that the construction of navigable waterways declined with the diffusion of railways and if we measure and compare traffic flows per kilometre of line and waterway in operation the performance of the latter is enhanced (Table 7.8).

Road transport was more seriously affected by competition from railways (41), particularly in the sphere of passenger traffic. In analysing competition between road and rail, historians should distinguish between the large commercial axes (parallel to lines) and local or regional roads (perpendicular to lines). The former are managed by the state and the latter are part of provincial and private networks. The former competed with railways for the carriage of passengers and freight while provincial and private roads complemented railways (42).

Although no statistics on road traffic are available before 1879, we do have data on tolls collected on trunk and secondary roads between 1835 and 1866. On trunk roads tolls declined from 2.2 million francs to 1.5 million francs but on provincial roads revenues increased from 179 000 francs to 380 000 francs over the same period (43).

Data on tolls can be used (following the method suggested by Belpaire in 1845, see Table 7.9) to calculate ton-kilometres of freight carried on both provincial and state roads from 1835 to 1865 (44). In 1879 and 1908 the Department of Bridges and Roadways conducted a census of the movement of freight along roads which links up with less reliable data for the earlier period (45).

Statisticians have often used figures of the average daily tonnage of freight passing an observation point to measure variations in the output of road transport over time. This figure dropped from 200 tons in 1834 to 54 tons in 1879 and

Table 7.8: *Comparisons between navigable waterways and railways*

---

1. Length of the system (km)	Navigable waterways	Railways
in 1845–46	1312	634
in 1912–13	1646	4629
Growth 1845–1913	25.5%	630%

2. Goods trade (in millions of ton-kilometres)		
in 1845–46	320	40
in 1912–13	1607	6385
Growth 1845–1913	2.48%	7.74%

3. Density of goods traffic (in thousands of tons per operational kilometre)		
in 1845–46	244	63
in 1912–13	976	1379
Growth 1845–1913	2.12%	4.64%

Sources: Statistics of the Situation in the Kingdom, 1841-50,
        (IV) pp. 246, et seq.; *Annuaire Statistique de la*
        Belgique, 1914, pp. 522-3, include figures for
        waterways deemed officially to be navigable. My
        figures exclude navigable waterways which were not
        used for navigation purposes.

then up again to 179 tons by 1908 (46). Although these
figures are correct they do not properly reflect the
competition from railways and from the emergence of the motor
car in the first decade of the twentieth century because they
do not take account of the evolution of the road network as
displayed in Table 7.10.

Table 7.10 shows that the Belgium network of roads trebled
from 1830-1913. Most of this increase emanated from widening
paving and improving existing roadways and tracks rather than
from the construction of completely new roads, while waterborne traffic densities went up markedly, largely because
traffic intensified along a static or slowly changing length
of navigable waterways. By contrast roads ramified in all
directions and traffic densities decreased. From 1835-79 total

Table 7.9: *Road traffic in millions of ton-kilometres*

	State roads	Provincial roads	Total
1835	155	15	170
1840	161	22	183
1845	145	28	173
1850	131	30	161
1855	133	33	166
1860	127	32	159
1865	125	33	158
1879	123	(30?)	(153?)
1908	235	(30?)	(265?)

Sources: Our calculations are based on the figures in the
*Exposés de la Situation du Royaume pour 1841-1850,
1851-1860, 1861-1876,* and the *Annuaire Statistique
de la Belgique* for 1914.

Table 7.10: *Development of Belgium roads (in kilometres)*

	State roads	Provincial roads	Concessionary roads	Total
1830	2 593	514	134	3 241
1840	3 096	806	275	4 177
1850	4 080	1 486	670	6 236
1860	4 548	1 507	621	6 676
1870	5 338	1 439	612	7 389
1880	6 731	1 444	351	8 526
1890	7 307	1 497	233	9 037
1900	7 664	1 597	103	9 364
1910	8 115	1 579	64	9 758
1913	8 327	1 554	32	9 913

*Sources: Album du Développement Progressif du Réseau des
Routes* (Bruxelles, 1880); *Annuaire Statistique de la
Belgique, Année 1914,* p. 514.

traffic along roads did not undergo significant changes. Railways at one and the same time both restrained and promoted the
increase of transportation by road. Roads were, however,
capable of rendering unique services. For example, they
obviated the need for intermediate transshipments and the
increase in traffic by road after 1908 marks not only the

emergence of motor transport but an increase in demand which could not be satisfied by waterborne carriers or railways.

But before the new era of road traffic, which became visible in the twentieth century, two factors had assured the success of railways in competition with other modes of transport: speed and cost (47). There can be no doubt that goods could be carried far more rapidly by rail than by water but the superiority of railways came not simply from the kilometres per hour travelled by cargoes of freight as they moved along water and railed ways but also from time taken to load and reload boats and trains - turnabout time. For example, a barge took no less than 86 days to carry a load of coal from Mons to Paris and return to its mooring. Loading, unloading and customs clearance absorbed 15 days; the outward journey 32 days and the return trip 29 days. A further 10 days were allowed for delays (48). Along the roads vehicles travelled at an average speed of 10 or 11 kilometres per hour compared to a speed of 30-40 kilometres by rail. As early as the 1830s speed by rail increased steadily to attain 60 kilometres per hour for passenger trains.

The costs per ton mile by water and rail were much the same in the middle of the nineteenth century and for both services the cost was roughly half the cost of road transport (Table 7.11).

Table 7.11: *Costs of transport (in centimes) for one passenger and of one ton of goods over one kilometre about 1850*

	Passengers (average price) centimes	Goods (averages) centimes
Canals	10	3-8.4
Roads	23	9
Railways	10	5

Sources: L. du Vivier, *Aperçu Historique, Statistique, Economique, Financier et Commercial sur les Opérations du Chemin de Fer de l'état* (Brussels, 1850) pp. 161-5. E. Perrot, 'Les Chemins de fer Belges; in *Bulletin de la Commission Centrale de Statistique*, II, (1845) pp. 132-4.

My social savings estimates for Belgium railways for 1846 are almost complete and details will be published elsewhere (49). My social savings estimate accounts for 1 per cent of the Belgian GNP in 1846. We can provisionally set social savings at 2.5 per cent in 1865 more or less and 4.5 per cent in 1912.

Meanwhile, there is no need to exaggerate the importance of speed for the economy in the early phases of railway development. Producers in the 1840s could be satisfied by rather slight increases in speed and were equally concerned with safety and regularity of delivery. As time became more important to the economy, speed gradually assumed more and more significance in the competition between different forms of transport.

7. CONCLUSIONS

The data in Tables 7.12 and 7.13 will help to synthesise this discussion.

Table 7.12: *Expansion of freight traffic 1845/46-1908/13 (in millions of ton kilometres)*

	1845-6	1908-13
Railways	40	6 385
Navigable waterways	320	1 607
Roads	173	265
Total	533	8 257

Annual average growth rate of all traffic (%)	
from 1845 to 1913	4.10
from 1846 to 1908	4.24

Sources: See Tables 7.8 and 7.9

These tables indicate that transportation services for freight as a whole grew at an average annual rate of around 4 per cent from 1845-1913 and Jean Gadisseur's recent research on the growth of commodity output permits a comparison with industrial production (50). That comparison shows that the output of the transport sector grew faster than the industrial

Table 7.13: *Annual average growth rates of Belgian industrial production in the nineteenth century*

	Rate %		Rate %
1840–50	1.77	1880–90	1.89
1850–60	4.42	1890–1900	2.80
1860–70	4.15	1900–10	3.30
1870–80	1.62	1910–13	4.10
		1845–1913	3.02
		1850–1913	3.08

Source: Jean Gadisseur, 'Le Produit Physique de l'Economie Belge, 1831-1913', *Présentation Critique des Données Statistiques,* vol. IX, p. 235, Liège, 1980.

output basically because the growth of transport widened the market and stimulated commercial exchange. In the expansion of transportation, railways were clearly a leading sector and grew at a rate of over 7 per cent per annum, a rate far in excess of the growth of freight traffic by waterways and roads. Their relative contribution to the expansion of passenger services was far more significant.

Railways were at the same time a cause and a reflection of economic growth. They exercised a profound influence on political social, demographic, architectural and military history of Belgium: an influence which transcends the purely economic analysis which has been the focus of this essay which is merely an introduction to the history of Belgium railways.

NOTES AND REFERENCES

1. The main synthesis on Belgian railways can still be found in U. Lamalle, *Histoire des Chemins de Fer Belges,* 3rd edn (Brussels, 1953). However, one should add the following general works which I quote chronologically: E. Perrot, 'Les Chemins de Fer Belges', *Bulletin de la Commission Centrale de Statistique,* vol. II (1845) pp. 1-156; J. Malou, *Etudes sur les Chemins de Fer Belges* (Brussels, 1860); A. de Laveleye, *Histoire des Vingt-cinq Premières Anneés des Chemins de Fer Belges* (Brussels, 1862); E. Nicolai, *Les Chemins de Fer de l'Etat en Belgique (1834-1884). Etude Historique,*

1. *Continued*

Economique et Statistique (Brussels, 1885); G. de Leener, *Les Chemins de Fer en Belgique* (Brussels, 1923); L. Avakian, 'Le Rythme de Développement des Voies Férrées en Belgique de 1835 à 1935', *Bulletin de l'Institut des Sciences Economiques*, (1936) pp. 449–82. Also, the early findings of my own research, M. Laffut, *Les Chemins de Fer Belges (1835-1913), L'Etablissement du Réseau, Etude Descriptive et Instruments de Travail* (Liège, 1974) mimeo.

2. On the progress of the Belgian Industrial Revolution, see P. Lebrun, M. Bruwier, J. Dhondt, G. Hansotte, *Essai sur la Révolution Industrielle en Belgique, 1770-1847* (Brussels, 1979).

3. That is why the Belgian network is to be considered as the embryo of the European network.

4. See note 1.

5. See in particular the works by Nicolai (quoted in note 1) and L. du Vivier, *Aperçu Historique, Statistique, Economique, Financier et Comercial sur les Opérations du Chemin de Fer de l'Etat, depuis son Origine jusqu'à ce jour* (Brussels, 1850).

6. F. Loisel, *Annuaire Spécial des Chemins de Fer Belges,* 15 vols (Brussels, 1867-92).

7. It will give rise to the 'Question Financière' of Belgian railways, see L. de Litwinski, *La Question de la Situation Financière des Chemins de Fer de l'Etat Belge* (Brussels, 1911). J. Pauly, *Le Chemin de Fer Belge et le Parlement* (Brussels, 1935). None the less, Pauly also wrote economic works, see below note 35. Laveleye was a regular contributor to the *Moniteur des Intérêts Matériels*.

8. This research is the object of my doctoral dissertation, as part of the work undertaken by the Centre d'Histoire Quantitative at the University of Liege, under the direction of Professor P. Lebrun. My final research will be published in the eighth volume of *Histoire Quantitative et Développement de la Belgique au XIXème Siècle*.

9. P. Lebrun, 'Histoire Quantitative et Développement de la Belgique au XIXème Siècle' in *Festschrift für Hermann Kellenbenz*, vol. III (1978) p. 356.

10. See M. Laffut, 'Statistiques et Comptabilité. Deux approches de l'Histoire Financière des Chemins de Fer Belges au XIXème Siècle' and also P. Lebrun, J. Pirard, M. Laffut, 'Capitaux Privés et Capitaux Publics dans l'Industrialisation de la Belgique au XIXème Siècle'.

10. *Continued*

The financial aspects of railway expansion are dealt with
in the eighth volume of *Histoire Quantitative*. Volume VI,
devoted by J. Pirard to *L'Etat et les Finances Publiques
Belges (1830-1913)* is already in print.

11. See M. Laffut, 'La Maturation des Projets de Chemin de Fer
en Belgique au XIXème Siècle', to be published in the
proceedings of the conference on *Aspect de l'Administration Belge au XIXe Siècle* (1978).

12. *Bulletin du Ministère de l'Intérieur* (1845) vol. II, pp.
68-70, 71-2.

13. On the bibliography relating to the history of Belgian
railways, see note 1.

14. On the development of limited liability companies, see
A. Demeur, *Les Sociétés Anonymes de Belgique en 1857*
(Brussels, 1859) which was followed by a series of similar
works until 1873. Also, L. Frère, *Etudes Historiques des
Sociétés Anonymes Belges*, I, SLND.

15. See F. Caron, *Histoire de l'Exploitation d'un Grand Réseau.
La Compagnie du Chemin de Fer du Nord, 1846-1937* (Paris,
1973).

16. On the early stages of this purchasing policy, see in
particular G. Kurgan-Van Hentenrijk, 'Aspects Financiers
de la Réorganisation des Chemins de Fer Belges: La
Reprise du Réseau des Bassins Houillers du Hainaut per
l'Etat (1870-77)', *Revue de la Banque*, vol. VIII (1975)
pp. 796-817 and III (1976) pp. 197-218.

17. F. Loisel, *Annuaire Spécial*, vol. I, pp. 480-7.

18. Ibid, pp. 256-60; M. Laffut, *Les Chemins de Fer*, p. 43.

19. There were also private junctions and stations, see
M. Laffut, *Les Chemins de Fer*, pp. 204-24.

20. M. Laffut, 'Pour une description des Chemins de Fer
Belges, Exemples d'Application', *FNRS Groupe de Contact,
Croissance Economique et Révolution Industrielle en
Belgique* (Brussels, 1974) pp. 187-96.

21. *Chemin de Fer et Routes Ordinaires 1830-9* (Brussels, 1839)
Appendix VI; *Compte Rendu des Opérations des Chemins de
Fer de l'Etat* (1840) Appendix XVI.

22. *Chemin de Fer et Routes Ordinaires, 1830-9* (Brussels, 1839)
p. 17; *Compte Rendu des Opérations des Chemins de Fer de
l'Etat* (1840) Appendix XIII.

23. *Chemin de Fer et Routes Ordinaires, 1830-9* (Brussels, 1839)
p. 27; P. Scholler, 'La Transformation Economique de la
Belgique de 1832 a 1844', *Bulletin de l'Institut de
Science Economique* (1948) 581.

24. When in 1843, the construction of state lines ended,
wrought iron output was 287 tons. The year after, private

24. *Continued*

lines started to be laid down and wrought iron output
rose to 9394 tons, see *Exposé de la Situation du Royaume
de 1841 à 1850*, VIème partie, pp. 122-3.

25. *Compte Rendu des Opérations des Chemins de Fer de l'Etat,
1913*, pp. A14, A16, A119.

26. *Compte Rendu des Opérations, 1860*, p. 110; G. Humbert,
Traite Complet des Chemins de Fer, 2nd edn (Paris-Liège,
1908) vol. 2, p. 287.

27. On Belgian railroad iron exports, see U. Lamalle, 'Le
Role de la Belgique dans le Développement des Chemins de
Fer' in La Société Belge des Ingénieurs et des
Industriels (ed), *Memorial du Centenaire de
l'Indépendance de la Belgique*, vol. 2 (Brussels, 1930)
pp. 535-65.

28. *Annuaire Statistique de la Belgique, Année 1914*, p. 442.

29. *Compte Rendu des Opérations, 1854*, p. LVII.

30. *Compte Rendu des Opérations, 1861*, p. 116.

31. See G. Humbert, *Traité Complet*, vol. 3, p. 6.

32. See A. Wibail, 'L'Evolution de l'Industrie Charbonnière
Belge depuis 1831', *Bulletin de l'Institut de Sciences
Economiques* (1933) pp. 31-62.

33. See *Chemins de Fer de l'Etat. Transport des Merchandises.
Rapport Présente à M. le Ministre des Travaux Publics sur
les Résultats des Tarifs du 1er Septembre 1848*, Part I
(Brussels, 1850) p. VI.

34. *Exposé de la Situation du Royaume de 1861 à 1875*, vol. 2,
p. 952 and *Exposé ... de 1876 à 1900*, vol. 3, p. 498.

35. J. Pauly, *Etudes sur les Tarifs des Chemin de Fer -
Transport des Marchandises*, p. 43.

36. See references in note 34, and also E. Mahaim, *Les
Abonnements d'Ouvriers sur les Lignes de Chemin de Fer
Belge et leurs effects sociaux* (Brussels, 1910).

37. On internal waterways, see J. B. Vifquain, *Des Voies
Navigables en Belgique* (Brussels, 1842); *Album du
Développement Progressif du Réseau de Routes, Voies
Navigables et des Chemins de Fer de 1830 à 1880*
(Brussels, 1880); E. de Brabandere, 'Le Belgique au point
de vue des travaux publics' and J. Zone, 'Les Transfor-
mations des canaux Brabançons pendant la periode 1830-70',
Mémorial du Centenaire de l'Indépendance de la Belgique,
vol. 1 (Brussels, 1930) pp. 180-263 and pp. 309-54.

38. E. Perrot, 'Les Chemins de Fer Belges', *Bulletin de la
Commission Centrale de Statistique*, II (1845) pp. 140-1.

39. *Ibid*, p. 140.

40. My estimates on the traffic of internal waterways are

40. *Continued*

based upon the gross revenue of tolls, with a coverage
of 80 per cent of the network. For 1912, see *Annuaire
Statistique de la Belgique, année 1914*, pp. 524-5.

41. On road traffic, see *Chemins de Fer et Routes Ordinaires
1830-9* (Brussels, 1839); Also *Album du Développement
Progressif*, quoted in note 37 above; finally, G. Placq,
'Les Variations du Traffic Routier Belge de 1830 à 1940',
Bulletin de Sciences Economiques (1952) pp. 519-36.

42. E. Perrot, 'Les Chemins de Fer Belges', p. 141.

43. G. Placq, 'Les Variations du Traffic Routier Belge', pp.
532-3.

44. A. Belpaire, *Notice sur les Cartes du Mouvements des
Transports en Belgique* (Brussels, 1847).

45. In particular see *Les Exposés de la Situation du Royaume,
Les Statistiques de la Belgique,* and G. Placq, 'Les
Variations du Traffic Routier Belge'.

46. G. Placq, ibid, p. 536.

47. On this particular point see E. Perrot, 'Les Chemins de
Fer Belges', pp. 1-156 and L. du Vivier, *Aperçu
Historique*.

48. E. de Teisserenc, *Etudes sur les Voies de Communication
Perfectionées*, pp. 902-3.

49. 1846 coincides with the first population census. We also
have for that particular year a GNP estimate, see A.
Dubois, *Essai d'Evaluation du Produit National Belge en
1846* (stencilled dissertation, Liège, 1978) 2 vols.

50. J. Gadisseur, 'Le Produit Physique de l'Economie Belge,
1831-1913', *Présentation Critiques des Données
Statistiques, Thèse Polycopiée* (Liège, 1980) pp. 249-51.

8 Railways and Economic Growth in Mediterranean Countries: Some Methodological Remarks

GIANNI TONIOLO

The complaint that 'these Italian trains go at about the rate of an American funeral' must have been rather common in the 1870s and 1880s when comtemporaries often criticised the Italian railway network for widespread inefficiency combined with high rates both for passengers and freight (1). As late as the early 1900s it was apparently more convenient to deliver goods by wagon rather than by rail up to distances of about one hundred and twenty miles (2). Almost any town in central or southern Italy is within that distance from a good seaport. Even in the Po Valley, rivers and canals could offer a viable alternative to railways.

Such a situation seems to provide all the ingredients for a successful attempt - conducted on Fogelian lines - to show that 'social savings' of railways were rather small in the case of Italy. And 'if the crux of the transport revolution ... was the substitution of low cost water and railroad transportation for high cost transportation', a plausible hypothesis might be that no such revolution took place in Italy - not at least before 1900 (3). In the case of Spain, on the other hand, one should probably start off with the assumption that orography and geography were less favourable to alternative modes of transportation and that the 'social savings' from railways may very well have been substantial and certainly higher than in Italy.

But is the 'social savings-social rate of return' approach fruitful for the study of the contribution of railways to economic growth in such 'latecomers' as these two important Mediterranean economies? The aim of the present note is to show that the appropriate answer should be No!

Before discussing some of the methodological issues connected with measuring the impact of railways on backward economies like Italy and Spain in the second half of the nineteenth century, it is perhaps appropriate to say that I am sceptical about the merits of any 'social savings' exercise, independent of the context of its applications. To be sure, the reasons for my scepticism are grounded in economic theory rather than on broad questions about historical methodology.

Fogel's masterfully constructed 'Presidential Address' on

the subject provides rather unconvincing answers to the
criticisms put forward against him in recent years by
economic historians of the strictest neo-classical
persuasion (4). Among such criticism the most crucial seem to
be related to issues of (a) the probable association between
the movement in relative prices and a major change in the
productive function; (b) the difficulties connected with
assuming an equality between prices and marginal costs in
railway operating firms, and (c) the construction of a
meaningful long run supply curve. In addition, investments
related to such an 'epochal' innovation as railways, would
probably affect income distribution and thus the aggregate
saving and investment functions themselves. Finally, some
points - like McClelland's - about the specification of the
model seem to be particularly well made and one finds
answers to them in Fogel's most recent paper unconvincing
and too little weight is given to the crucial issue of
externalities (5).

Generally speaking, my scepticism about 'social savings'
and related approaches to railways, can be summarised in
Schumpeter's words:

> Static analysis is not only unable to predict the
> consequences of discontinuous changes in the way
> of doing things, it can neither explain the
> occurrence of such productive revolutions nor the
> phenomena which accompany them. It can only
> investigate the new equilibrium position after the
> changes have taken place   (6).

This latter accomplishment is the highest possible aim of
"social savings" exercises, until and when historians are
in a position to build and test comprehensive general
equilibrium models. Meanwhile, we should recognise that
partial equilibrium and simple Cobb-Douglas production
functions are just the tools of a 'bricolage'. A high-
class 'bricolage' one must add, from which the profession has
derived tremendous externalities but for which one must not
make more claims than it honestly deserves. Nevertheless, I
shall assume that the social savings approach to the history
of railways is sound enough for the study of relatively
advanced countries such as the United States and England and
I propose to confine my comments to some specific features
of the Mediterranean area during the second half of the
nineteenth century.

.The specific features of Mediterranean 'latecomers' such as
Italy and Spain considered here are related to the labour and
capital markets. Fenoaltea pointed out that 'in view of the

unemployment and mass migration of labour on the one hand and the unrestricted international flow of capital (and capitalists) on the other Italy appears essentially as an underemployed international interest taker' (7).

Unemployment and underemployment characterised Italy's labour market well into the present century. Recent careful computations suggest that as late as 1911 most of the Italian industrial labour force was employed only for a small fraction (perhaps 50 per cent) of the total working days in the year (8). Moreover, a very high percentage of the total labour force (over 60%) was retained in agriculture, and there is every reason to believe that its marginal productivity was nearly zero if not negative. Towards the end of the century overseas countries required increasing labour inputs from the Mediterranean and emigration took off at an incredible rate. This fact did not preclude a very substantial increase of gross output by agriculture from taking place over the same period. It seems safe to assume that disguised unemployment was extensive in the Italian countryside before the great emigration boom. Evidence from local history confirms and documents an excess of labour supply in agriculture, and shows how the equivalent of a subsistence wage could be shared in various ways among the community or among the extended family (9). Much the same story can be told about Spain. A rather poor agriculture supported 70 per cent of the total labour force in the 1870s and 66 per cent as late as 1910 (10). Again emigration was high in the first decade of the present century and seems to have been conditioned by the developing economic opportunities overseas rather than by demographic pressure on land which existed long before that time (11).

Turning to capital, suffice it to say that domestic savings could have been mobilised by more efficient financial institutions, or could have been induced to enter the capital market by the creation of sound investment opportunities. Furthermore, there were few constraints on the international mobility of investible funds: in fact, their supply elasticity for rather small countries such as Italy and Spain in the nineteenth century can be regarded for all practical purposes as very high.

In contrast to the United States or Britain, full employment of resources cannot be assumed to exist in Italy or in Spain at the time of their great railroad booms. Fenoaltea's point is that, in such contexts, 'supply side effects (of railways) were negligible'. My own position is that there is no way of measuring such effects, not even roughly. Substantial unemployment makes the whole 'social savings-social rates of return' machinery unfit for the task for which it was designed, since full employment is obviously one of the cornerstone assumptions underlying its production and allocation theory. And indeed one does not need to theorise profoundly to question the meaning of resource saving (at least in the reallocative context of social savings) if resources are plentiful. Moreover, in a situation where resources are kept idle, how can one be assured that workers saved or released by moving from an inferior to a superior production function will be reallocated to more productive uses. The social opportunity cost of railways could turn out to be negligible. In this case, the long standing debates about the time patterns of investment in railways and their relation to the process of industrialisation both in Italy and in Spain could seem irrelevant. For all practical purposes, we have no way of assessing the social opportunity cost of investments once we recognise unemployment of both labour and capital.

Unalleviated scepticism, admittedly, is not the best recipe for empirical research. The last part of this note is, therefore, devoted to discussing ways of dealing with the railway problem in conditions of open and/or disguised unemployment. Both, but especially the latter, mean that a certain amount of labour with marginal productivity very close to zero somehow manages to put together the equivalent of a subsistence wage. The extended family is the single most important institution which guarantees a means of support to all its members, regardless of productivity, and operated almost everywhere, as a means of providing a yearly minimum subsistence income to as many workers as possible and ensured social stability of a kind. In Italy and Spain underemployment was rife. Workers were all employed in turn for a limited number of days every year. Not even at harvest time was the entire working force simultaneously employed.

This is not without relevance to our problem since in such a situation the private (Z) and social (S) rates of return on capital will diverge. As a first approximation one can assume that the difference is equal to the wage bill paid by investors. Wages must, in fact, be taken into account when computing Z since they generated actual operating expenses met by railway companies. They can, on the other hand, be disregarded when estimating S since the society as a whole was already paying the equivalent of a subsistence wage to the unemployed labour force.

For a given year (following the simplest of Fogel's formulations) we thus have:

$$Z = \frac{GR-LW-NWOE-D}{Gl}$$

where:
GR = gross receipts

L = labour force employed in railways

$$S = \frac{GR - NWOE - D}{Gl}$$

W = wage rate

NWOE = non-wage operating expenses

D = depreciation

Gl = gross investment

Since LW is always fairly large, Z can never be taken as a proxy of S. As shown in the figure below the optimum quantity of capital to be invested in railways would be larger if the social rather than the private rate of return is taken into account. In the simple case of our figure, given

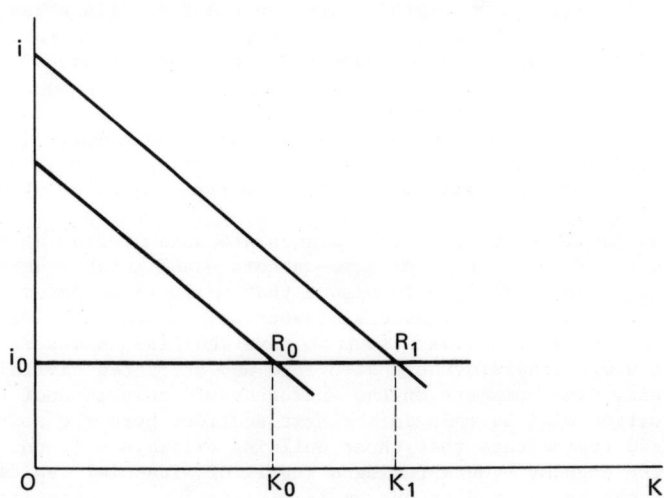

the rate of interest i_o, private firms will invest OK_o while the optimum investment for the society as a whole will be OK_1. This is not, of course, without relevance for the current debate on the pattern of investment in railways both in Italy and in Spain.

Under these assumptions, in order to compare the social rate of return of two transport projects with different production functions, one needs to know the amount of labour employed in each of them. Computations become more complicated when a wage above the subsistence level is being paid by one or both investors. But this is unfortunately just the beginning of the empirical complications. Labour is not homogeneous and an infinite elasticity of supply can only be assumed for unskilled workers. Realistically we should assume that some segments of the labour force (i.e. those with a certain type of skills, some kinds of agricultural workers, or those located in more developed areas, etc.) are fully employed. In that case, a precise assessment of 'social rates of returns' will require a knowledge of the occupational skills demanded for the various types of operations needed in the building and in the current working of a railway, both on the construction site and for the industrial sectors supplying material and equipment for the project and for its subsequent operation. And, of course, the supply elasticity of labour in all these occupational categories must be estimated. A formidable task indeed given what we know of the labour markets of nineteenth century Italy and Spain. The building of the counterfactual world is, of course, made more difficult by the fact that the construction of a railway is very likely to affect the relative wages of the various types of skilled labour.

The low level of domestic savings and accumulation as a percentage of GNP has led some authors - and notably Romeo (12) in the case of Italy - to assume that railways competed with industry for scarce financial resources. But this does not seem to be the case. Railways seem to have mobilised domestic savings that would otherwise have been idle and attracted capital from abroad. Some comments on the macroeconomic relevance of this situation will be made in the next section: here the point is raised to indicate that those building railways - if not the entire economy - were facing a supply of financial capital that can be assumed as extremely elastic for all practical purposes.

If one considers a single year, the situation just described means that financial capital for railways had a very low social opportunity cost and, thus, a very high social rate of return. But the difficulty is that foreign capital has an opportunity cost for the economy as a whole if we consider

long run implications. Repayments must be made sooner or
later. In this case, the initial-final year approach has to
be abandoned to be replaced by a flow analysis. Aside from
the empirical complications of the model, the standard index-
number problem emerges with all its disrupting force. In due
time, the borrowing country will have to pay back the foreign
loans, usually by selling goods and services abroad.
Meanwhile, world market conditions and relative prices will
be continuously changing. Moreover, the country's terms of
trade will be affected by the new investment and by changes
in the domestic production functions generated by the very
fact of railway building. The choice of any set of relative
prices is obviously an arbitrary one but it is very likely
to affect the resulting 'social savings-social rate of
return' measurement in a substantial way. Even were we able
to build and handle the model there would be, as we know, no
logical way out of the index number trap.

Nor could we disregard the fact that the necessity of paying
back foreign capital might oblige the country in question to
adopt monetary and fiscal policies that would be likely
(*ceteris paribus*) to slow down the rate of growth of GNP.
This may or may not be the case but a realistic assessment of
the social opportunity cost of borrowed capital must include
a close investigation of this kind.

Having so far indicated some rather obvious but apparently
not irrelevant theoretical points about dealing with idle
(unemployed) resources, let me now turn briefly to history.
François Caron (13) argues that, in France, railways were at
least partially responsible for the substantial improvements
that took place in the Paris Stock Exchange market, especially
in the 1850s and 1860s. And, if financial institutions are of
some relevance for the development of a capitalist economy,
here is another externality of railways that cannot easily be
measured but which must definitely be taken into account.

In Italy and Spain the contribution of railways to the
improvement of financial institutions was quite different in
kind but probably even more important. In those more backward
areas foreign investors not only brought capital with them but
also the technical knowledge of how to mobilise idle domestic
savings and to channel them to investment both in railways and
in industry. The Pereire Brothers established the Credito
Mobiliar Español in 1856 and the Credito Mobiliare of Turin in
1863. The Rothschilds were behind the Sociedad Española
Mercantil e Industrial of Madrid and the Caisse du Commerce et
de l'industrie of Turin both established in 1856. In the same
year Alfred Prost and other French financiers set up the
Compañia General de Credito en España. There is little doubt
that, at least at the beginning, railway construction was one

of the major concerns of these banks, especially in Spain. In other words, it can be argued very plausibly that railroads were responsible for the introduction into the two peninsulae of new and more aggressive types of bank that modernised and shaped the entire system of financial intermediation in both countries. Here again we observe a peculiarity of the backward Mediterranean economies that cannot be disregarded in a discussion of the railway problem. Both countries were characterised by the existence of specific feedbacks which enabled railways, once exogenously started, to create to some extent their own supply of investible funds via the establishment and operation of so-called 'industrial banks'. An economy with unemployed or underemployed has resources that can be mobilised and which can generate a standard multiplier effect by innovation in the system of financial intermediation.

Standard historical questions about Italian and Spanish railways in the nineteenth century are concerned with the time pattern of their construction, the optimum amount of investment in the transport innovation and with the relation between railways and economic growth. A rigorous new economic historian, of the strictest neo-classical observance, McClelland (15) drew what seems to him to be an inevitable conclusion: since such broad questions cannot be answered they should no longer be asked. The above observations about the difficulty - to say the least - of a social savings computation in conditions of unemployed resources should strengthen this conclusion. Econometric history is a tremendous step forward for the discipline provided that the tools fit the problems to be investigated. And the use of these tools is limited first of all by the theoretical assumptions on which they rest. This type of awareness alongside an overall self-consciousness does not entail the end of cliometrics as we know it, on the contrary it indicates its coming of age, and its growing ability to fructify by solving an incredible number of well defined and limited problems.

But can we really avoid asking those broad and most interesting questions about our past that have passionately interested generations of historians? Does the search for precision necessarily mean that research must be narrow and, finally, perhaps quite dull? The very fact that we continue to address ourselves to these questions means that we cannot escape from them. And it seems to me that between the ambition of quantifying the impact of an epochal innovation to the last decimal point and the mere ('old') description of some of its more visible effects, there lies a vast no man's land. It is the territory where econometrics finds it difficult to penetrate (at least for the time being) but in which the use of an appropriate economic theory (where

appropriate means that underlying hypotheses are consistent
with historical reality) may be of great help to the historian
who seeks: (a) to address himself to the relevant questions;
(b) to specify the interrelations of the phenomena under
investigation, and (c) to establish the direction of a given
movement and, perhaps, its broad order of magnitude. In other
words, the use of economic theory, of the kind most appropriate to the situation, is not limited by the fact that it
cannot lead to a testable model. The instance, quoted above,
of the connection between an innovation such as railways and
the creation (or the enlargement) of a financial market is
just one illustration of the point. We leave it to those keen
on labelling to see whether this kind of historical research
is of the 'old' or the 'new' variety. The answer might indeed
depend on how ecumenically the new Clio is defined.

What matters here is simply to stress that when the underlying historical conditions make it difficult or, perhaps,
impossible to use a technique (like the social savings
approach) that has proved its usefulness when different
circumstances can be assumed, it is certainly necessary to
change some major features of that technique or perhaps to
drop it altogether. This does not mean that Italian or
Spanish railways can be approached only in a traditional
descriptive way. Alternative routes may, and indeed have,
been followed: their relative merit can only be assessed
case-by-case, but it may perhaps be not totally inappropriate
to judge them also in the light of the relevant changes, to
say the least, that must be introduced into a social savings
model when unemployment of resources and a self-generating
elastic supply of investible funds must necessarily be
assumed.

NOTES AND REFERENCES

1. H. James, *The Portrait of a Lady* (London, 1978) p. 327.
2. G. Baglioni, 'Per la riforma ferroviaria', 'Critica
   Sociale', 1910.
3. R. Fogel, 'Notes on the Social Savings Controversy',
   Journal of Economic History, XXXIX 1979 , p. 50. In that
   year about 16,000 kilometres of rail in operation over
   the Peninsula seem to have been carrying, in ton-miles,
   the equivalent of about 10 per cent of the German
   traffic. Data from B. R. Mitchell, *European Historical
   Statistics,* Macmillan, London, 1957, p. 328.
4. R. Fogel, 'Notes on the Social Savings Controversy',
   Journal of Economic History, XXXIX 1979.
5. P. McClelland, 'Social Rates of Return on American Rail-

5. *Continued*
    roads in the Nineteenth Century', *Economic History Review*,
    XXX 1972, pp. 471–88.
6. J. A. Schumpeter, *The Theory of Economic Development*,
    (New York, 1961) p. 85.
7. S. Fenoaltea, 'Railroads and Italian Industrial Growth,
    1861–1913', *Explorations in Economic History*, vol. IX
    (Summer 1972) pp. 327–8. Consistent with this view of
    infinite factor supply elasticity, Fenoaltea considers
    'supply side effects (as) negligible' and carries on his
    analysis on lines other than 'social savings'.
8. The exercise can be conducted by comparing the population
    and the industrial censuses for the year 1911. For the
    first, see O. Vitali, *Aspetti della sviluppo economico
    italiano alla luce della ricostruzione della popolazione
    attiva* (Rome, 1970). For an analysis of the second and
    for general considerations about the labour market, see
    V. Zamagni, *Industrializzione e equilibri regionali in
    Italia* (Bologna, 1978).
9. For a survey of some of these studies and bibliography,
    see G. Giorgetti, *Contadini e proprietari vell' Italia
    moderna* (Turin, 1974).
10. Even taking into account all possible inaccuracies, the
    order of magnitude of the figures is such as to leave no
    doubt about the existence of disguised unemployment.
    J. Harrison, *An Economic History of Modern Spain*
    (Manchester, 1978) p. 69.
11. P. Voles Bou, *Historica de la Economica Española en los
    siglos XIX y XX* (Madrid, 1974) vol. I, pp. 91–2.
12. R. Romeo, *Risorgimento e Capitalismo* (Rome, 1958).
13. See, for instance, his contribution to the present volume.
14. P. McClelland, 'Social Rates of Return on American Rail-
    roads in the Nineteenth Century', *Economic History Review*,
    XXX 1972, pp. 471–88.

Index